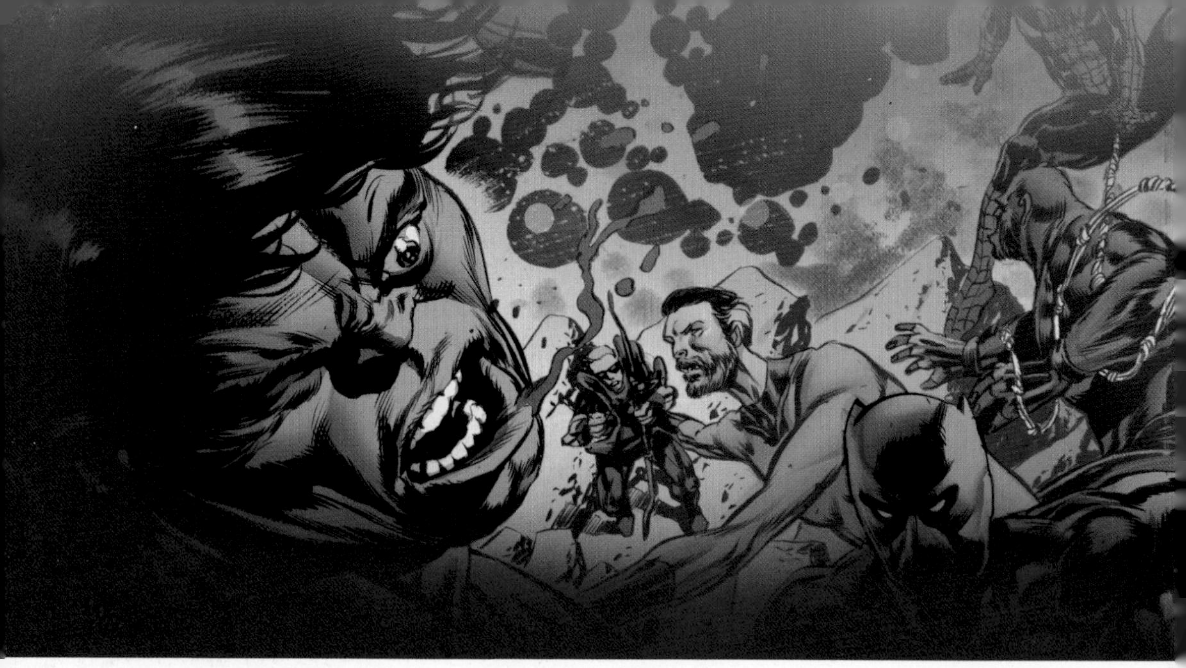

COLLECTION EDITOR: **JENNIFER GRÜNWALD**
ASSISTANT EDITOR: **SARAH BRUNSTAD**
ASSOCIATE MANAGING EDITOR: **ALEX STARBUCK**
EDITOR, SPECIAL PROJECTS: **MARK D. BEAZLEY**
SENIOR EDITOR, SPECIAL PROJECTS: **JEFF YOUNGQUIST**
SVP PRINT, SALES & MARKETING: **DAVID GABRIEL**

EDITOR IN CHIEF: **AXEL ALONSO**
CHIEF CREATIVE OFFICER: **JOE QUESADA**
PUBLISHER: **DAN BUCKLEY**
EXECUTIVE PRODUCER: **ALAN FINE**

AVENGERS: TIME RUNS OUT VOL. 2. Contains material originally published in magazine form as AVENGERS #38-39 and NEW AVENGERS #26-28. First printing 2015. ISBN# 978-0-7851-9373-9. Published by MARVE WORLDWIDE, INC., a subsidiary of MARVEL ENTERTAINMENT, LLC. OFFICE OF PUBLICATION: 135 West 50th Street, New York, NY 10020. **Printed in the U.S.A.** ALAN FINE, Presider Marvel Entertainment; DAN BUCKLEY, President, TV, Publishing and Brand Management; JOE QUESADA, Chief Creative Officer; TOM BREVOORT, SVP of Publishing; DAVID BOGART, SVP of Operations & Procuremer Publishing; C.B. CEBULSKI, VP of International Development & Brand Management; DAVID GABRIEL, SVP Print, Sales & Marketing; JIM O'KEEFE, VP of Operations & Logistics; DAN CARR, Executive Director of Publishir Technology; SUSAN CRESPI, Editorial Operations Manager; ALEX MORALES, Publishing Operations Manager; STAN LEE, Chairman Emeritus. For information regarding advertising in Marvel Comics or on Marvel.cor please contact Jonathan Rheingold, VP of Custom Solutions & Ad Sales, at jrheingold@marvel.com. For Marvel subscription inquiries, please call 800-217-9158. **Manufactured between 9/4/2015 and 10/12/2015 b R.R. DONNELLEY, INC., SALEM, VA, USA.**

10 9 8 7 6 5 4 3 2 1

AVENGERS

WRITER: **JONATHAN HICKMAN**

NEW AVENGERS #26
ARTIST: **KEV WALKER**
INK ASSIST: **SCOTT HANNA**
COLOR ARTISTS: **FRANK MARTIN & DONO SANCHEZ ALMARA**
LETTERER: **VC'S JOE CARAMAGNA**
COVER ART: **SALVADOR LARROCA & PAUL MOUNTS**

AVENGERS #38
ARTIST: **STEFANO CASELLI**
COLOR ARTIST: **FRANK MARTIN**
LETTERER: **VC'S CORY PETIT**
COVER ART: **SIMONE BIANCHI**

NEW AVENGERS #27
ARTIST: **SZYMON KUDRANSKI**
COLOR ARTIST: **DONO SANCHEZ ALMARA**
LETTERER: **VC'S JOE CARAMAGNA**
COVER ART: **SALVADOR LARROCA
& PAUL MOUNTS**

AVENGERS #39
ARTIST: **MIKE DEODATO**
COLOR ARTIST: **FRANK MARTIN**
LETTERER: **VC'S CORY PETIT**
COVER ART: **ALAN DAVIS, MARK FARMER
& BRAD ANDERSON**

NEW AVENGERS #28
ARTISTS: **MIKE DEODATO
& MIKE PERKINS**
COLOR ARTIST: **FRANK MARTIN**
LETTERER: **VC'S JOE CARAMAGNA**
COVER ART: **ALAN DAVIS, MARK FARMER
& BRAD ANDERSON**

ASSISTANT EDITOR: **JAKE THOMAS**
EDITORS: **TOM BREVOORT** WITH **WIL MOSS**
AVENGERS CREATED BY STAN LEE & JACK KIRBY

"CAGES"

THE ILLUMINATI

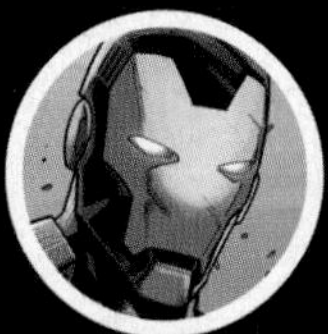

IRON MAN

THE CABAL

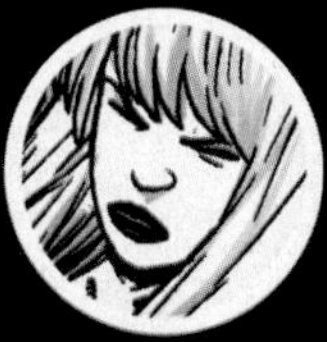

BLACK SWAN

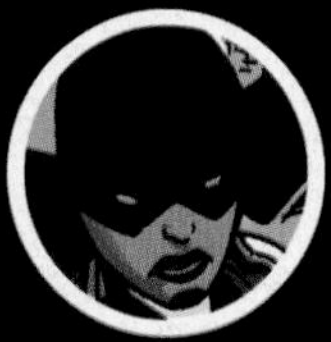

PROXIMA MIDNIGHT

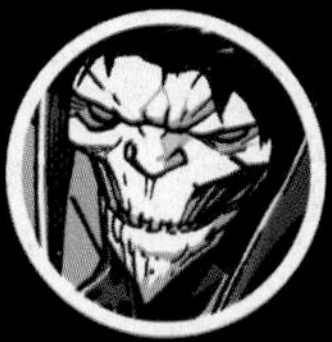

CORVUS GLAIVE

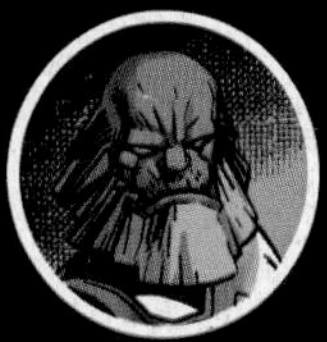

TERRAX

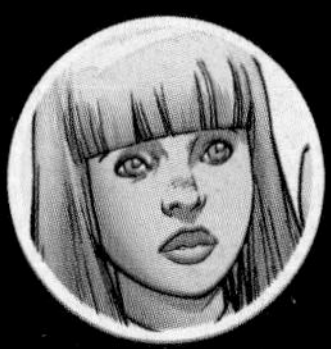

VALERIA RICHARDS

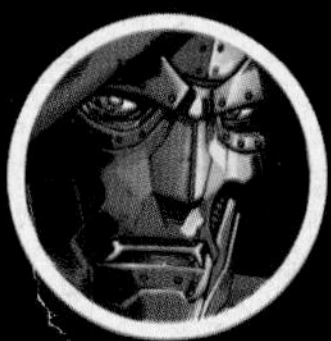

DOCTOR DOOM

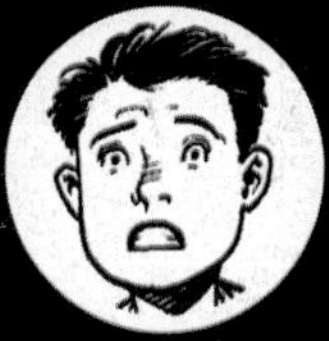

BENTLEY-23

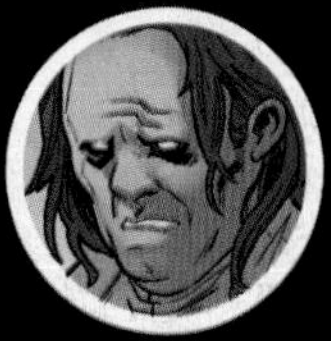

THE MAD THINKER

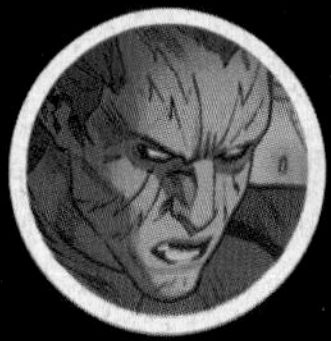

MOLECULE MAN

PREVIOUSLY IN NEW AVENGERS

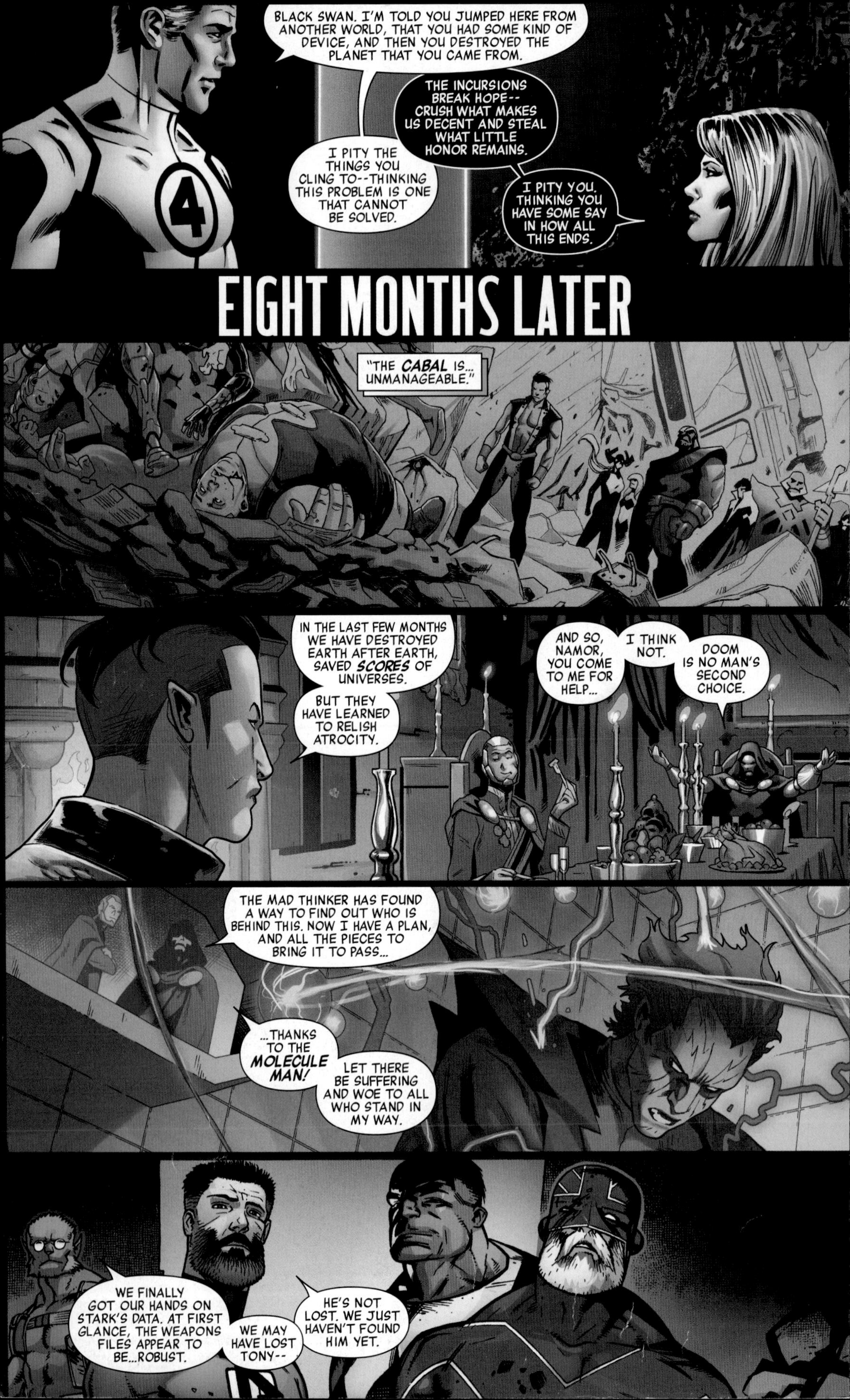

BLACK SWAN. I'M TOLD YOU JUMPED HERE FROM ANOTHER WORLD, THAT YOU HAD SOME KIND OF DEVICE, AND THEN YOU DESTROYED THE PLANET THAT YOU CAME FROM.
THE INCURSIONS BREAK HOPE--CRUSH WHAT MAKES US DECENT AND STEAL WHAT LITTLE HONOR REMAINS.
I PITY THE THINGS YOU CLING TO--THINKING THIS PROBLEM IS ONE THAT CANNOT BE SOLVED.
I PITY YOU. THINKING YOU HAVE SOME SAY IN HOW ALL THIS ENDS.
EIGHT MONTHS LATER
"THE CABAL IS... UNMANAGEABLE."
IN THE LAST FEW MONTHS WE HAVE DESTROYED EARTH AFTER EARTH, SAVED SCORES OF UNIVERSES.
BUT THEY HAVE LEARNED TO RELISH ATROCITY.
AND SO, NAMOR, YOU COME TO ME FOR HELP...
I THINK NOT.
DOOM IS NO MAN'S SECOND CHOICE.
THE MAD THINKER HAS FOUND A WAY TO FIND OUT WHO IS BEHIND THIS. NOW I HAVE A PLAN, AND ALL THE PIECES TO BRING IT TO PASS...
...THANKS TO THE MOLECULE MAN!
LET THERE BE SUFFERING AND WOE TO ALL WHO STAND IN MY WAY.
WE FINALLY GOT OUR HANDS ON STARK'S DATA. AT FIRST GLANCE, THE WEAPONS FILES APPEAR TO BE...ROBUST.
WE MAY HAVE LOST TONY--
HE'S NOT LOST. WE JUST HAVEN'T FOUND HIM YET.

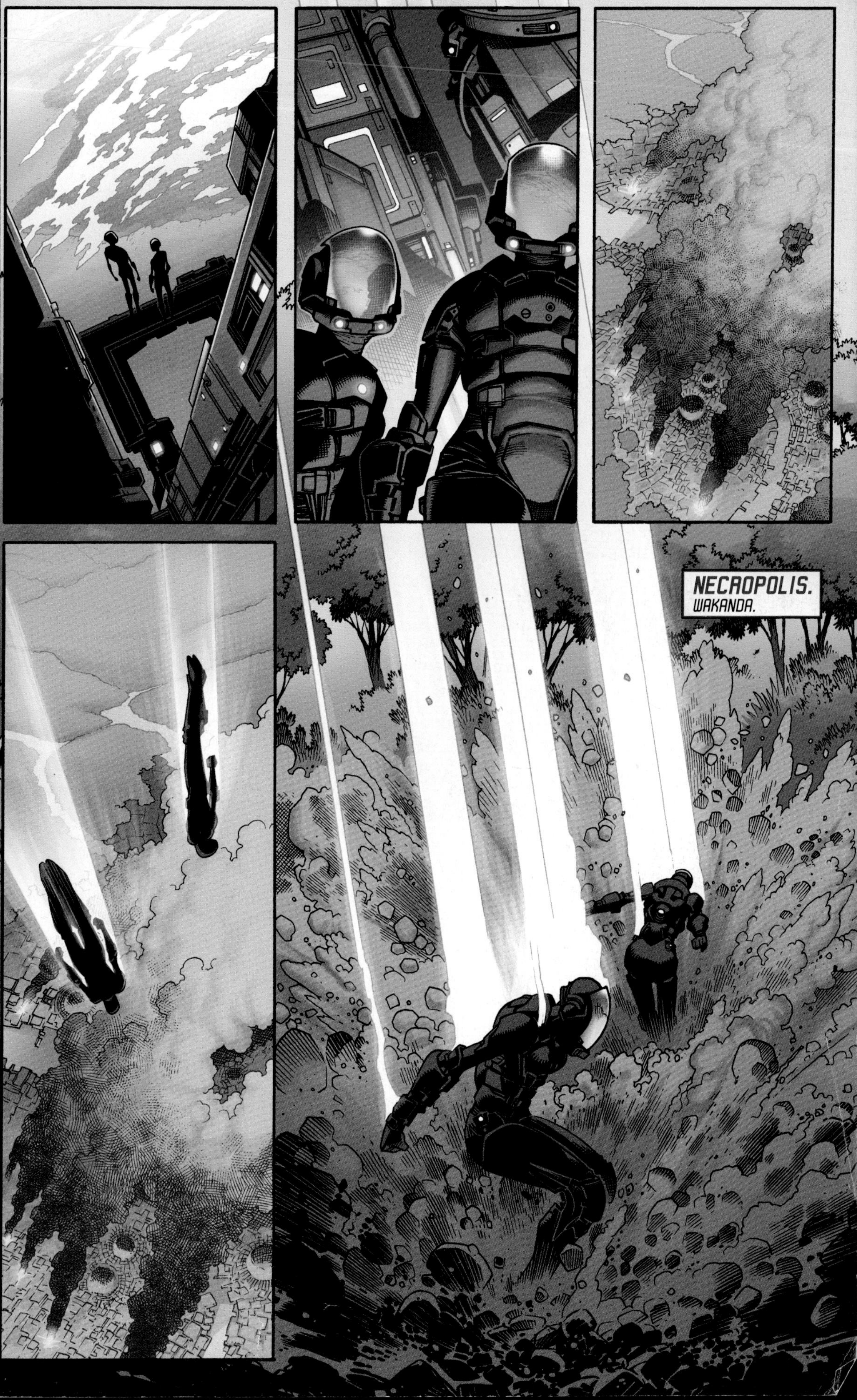
NECROPOLIS.
WAKANDA.

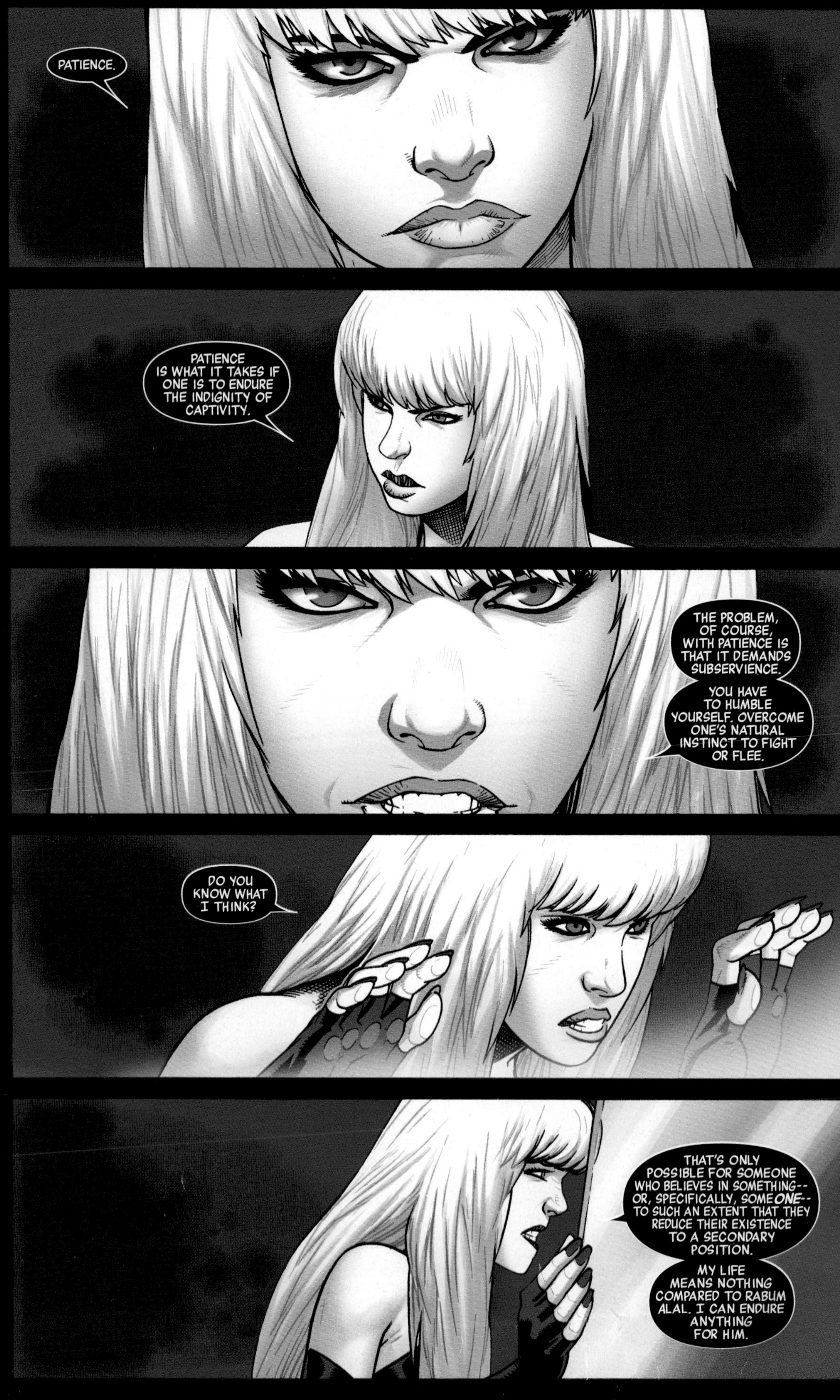
PATIENCE.
PATIENCE IS WHAT IT TAKES IF ONE IS TO ENDURE THE INDIGNITY OF CAPTIVITY.
THE PROBLEM, OF COURSE, WITH PATIENCE IS THAT IT DEMANDS SUBSERVIENCE.
YOU HAVE TO HUMBLE YOURSELF. OVERCOME ONE'S NATURAL INSTINCT TO FIGHT OR FLEE.
DO YOU KNOW WHAT I THINK?
THAT'S ONLY POSSIBLE FOR SOMEONE WHO BELIEVES IN SOMETHING-- OR, SPECIFICALLY, SOME*ONE*-- TO SUCH AN EXTENT THAT THEY REDUCE THEIR EXISTENCE TO A SECONDARY POSITION.
MY LIFE MEANS NOTHING COMPARED TO RABUM ALAL. I CAN ENDURE ANYTHING FOR HIM.

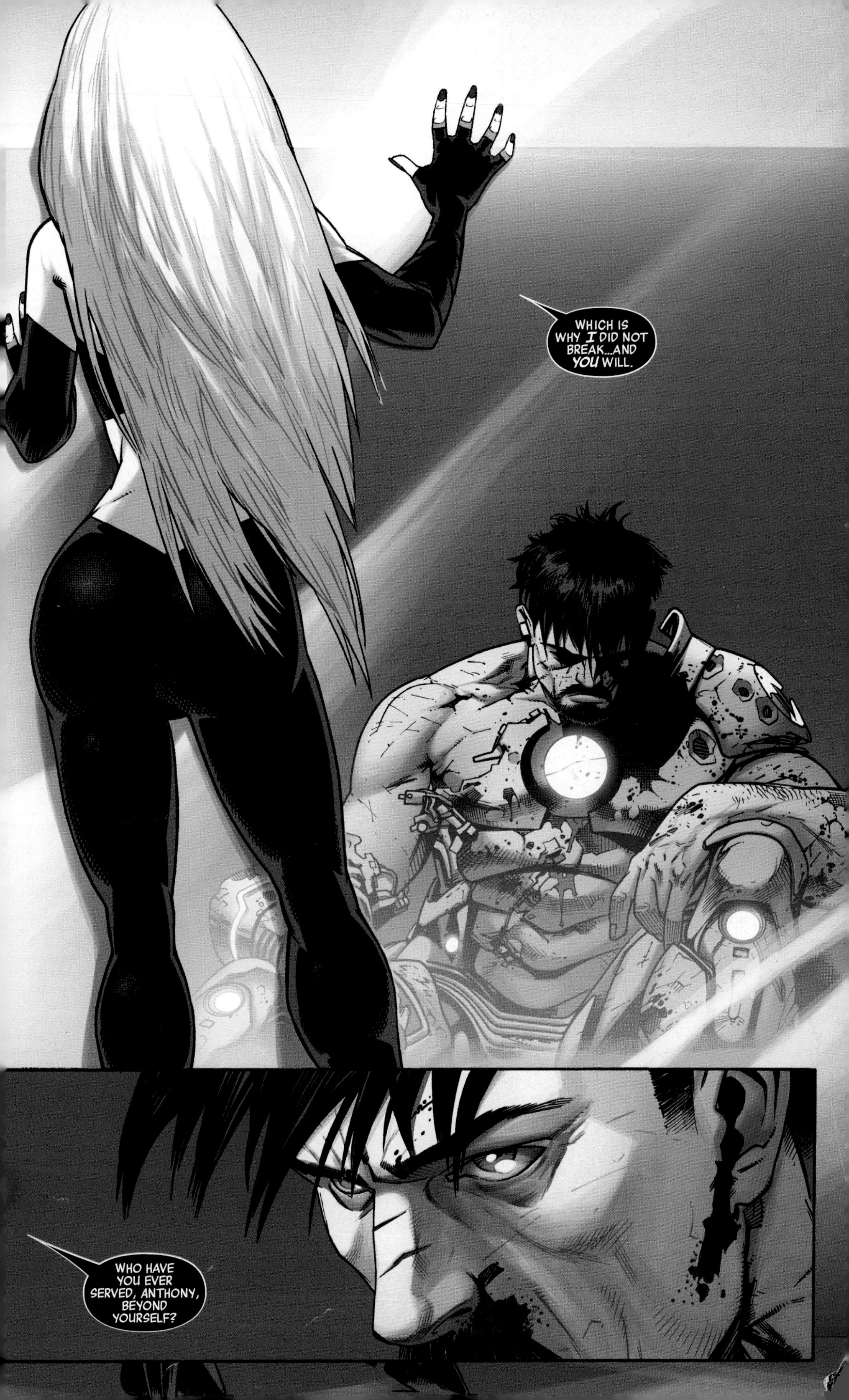
WHICH IS WHY I DID NOT BREAK...AND YOU WILL.
WHO HAVE YOU EVER SERVED, ANTHONY, BEYOND YOURSELF?

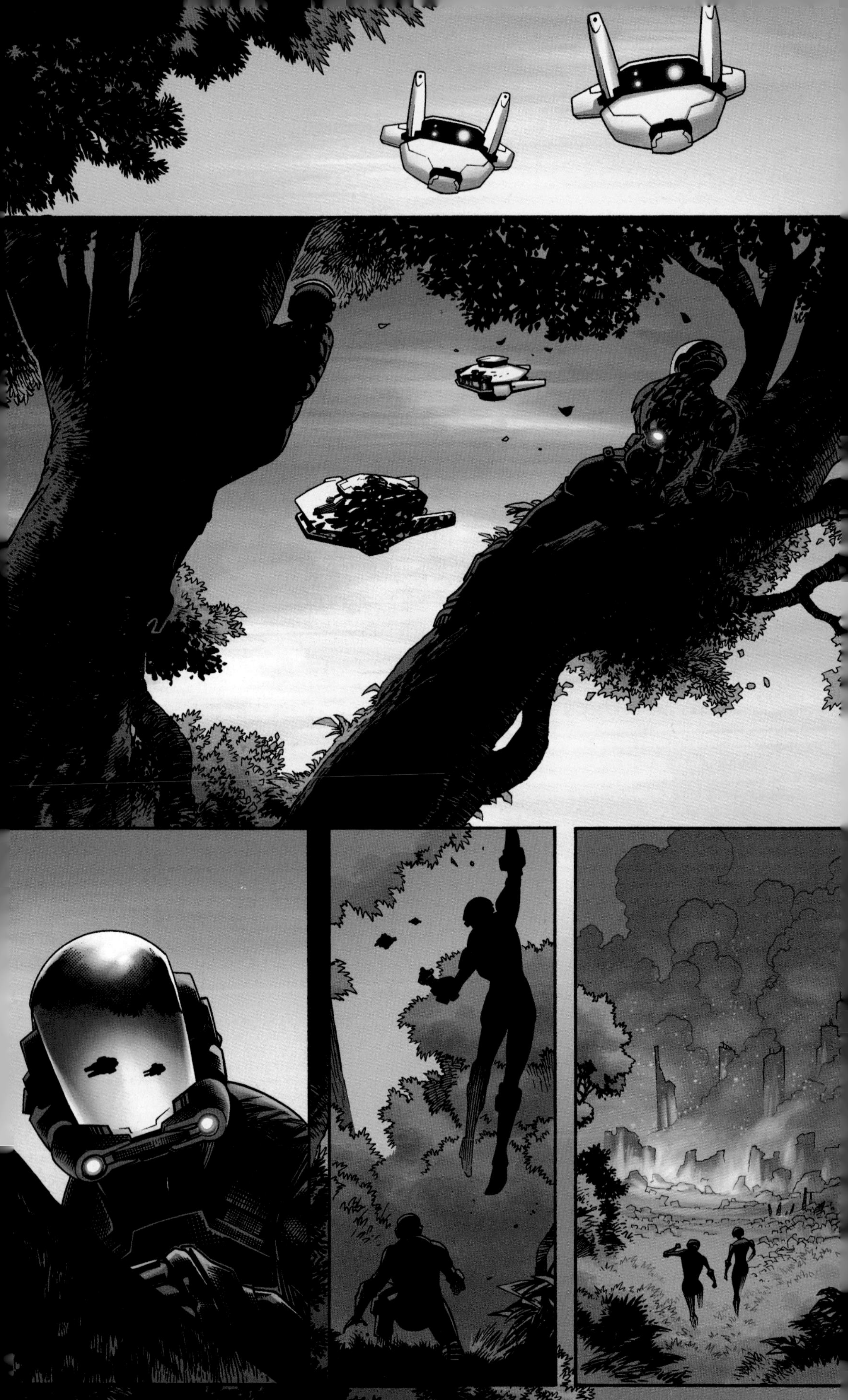

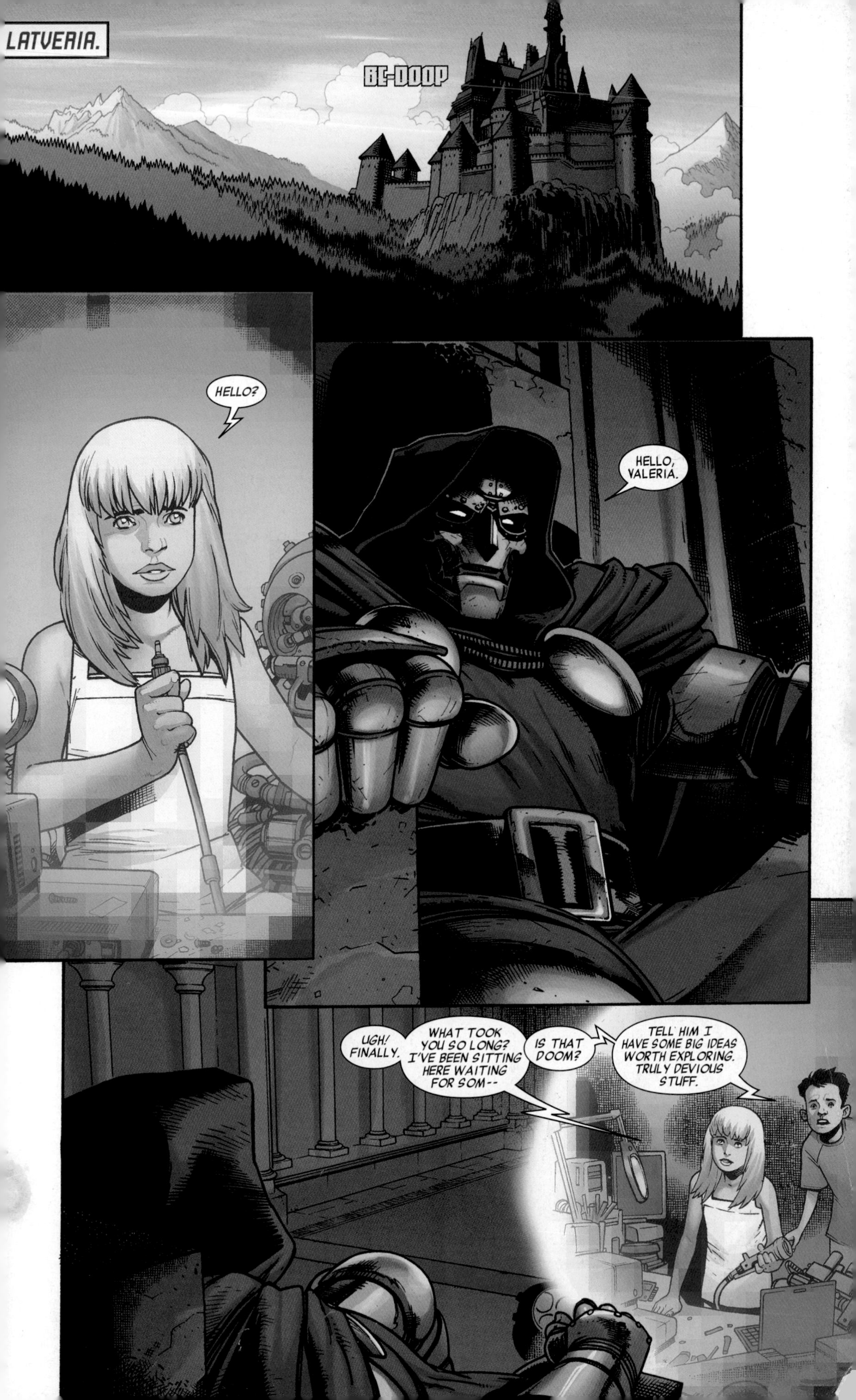
LATVERIA.
BE-DOOP
HELLO?
HELLO, VALERIA.
UGH! FINALLY.
WHAT TOOK YOU SO LONG? I'VE BEEN SITTING HERE WAITING FOR SOM--
IS THAT DOOM?
TELL HIM I HAVE SOME BIG IDEAS WORTH EXPLORING. TRULY DEVIOUS STUFF.

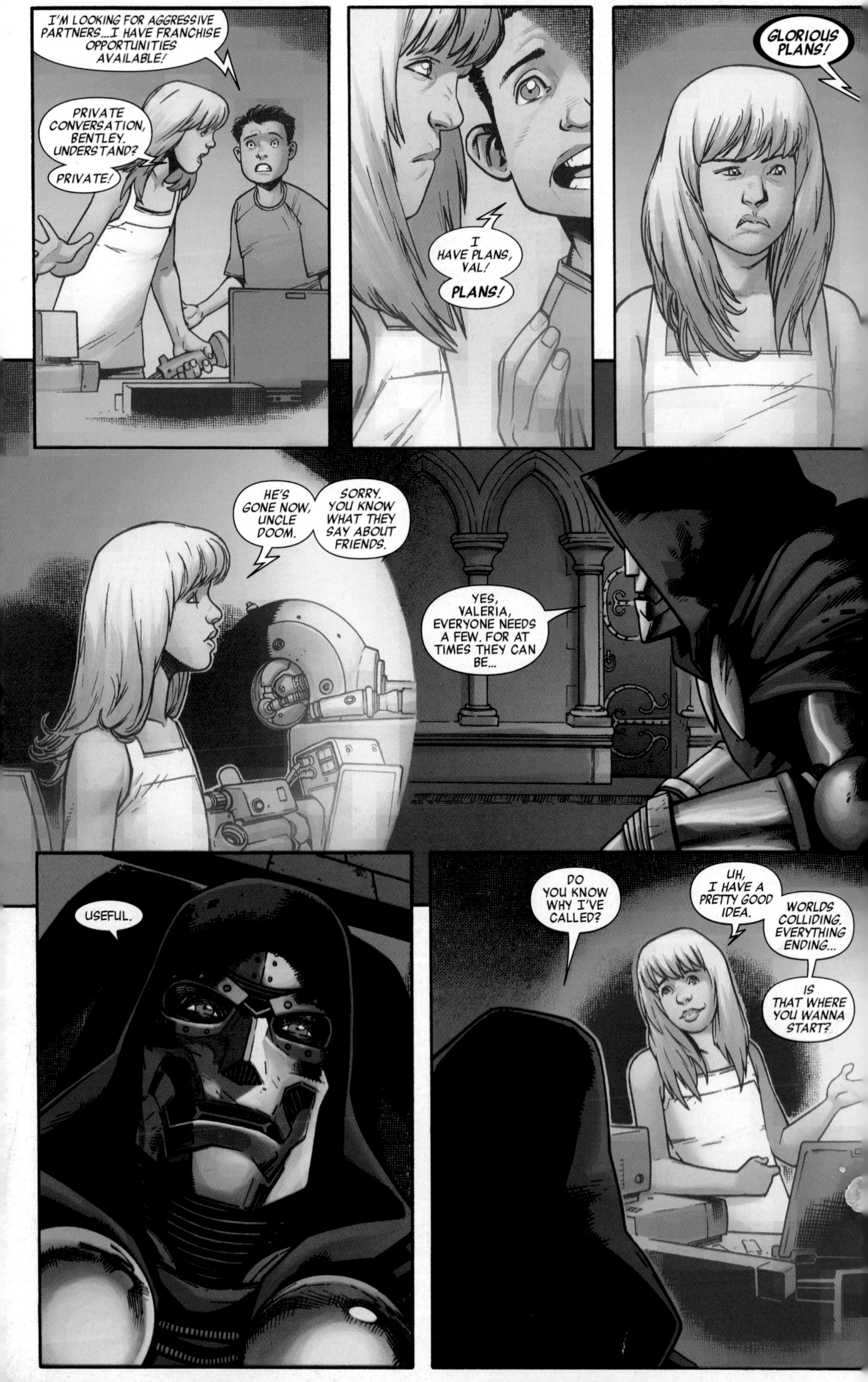

I'M LOOKING FOR AGGRESSIVE PARTNERS...I HAVE FRANCHISE OPPORTUNITIES AVAILABLE!
PRIVATE CONVERSATION, BENTLEY. UNDERSTAND?
PRIVATE!
I HAVE PLANS, VAL!
PLANS!
GLORIOUS PLANS!
HE'S GONE NOW, UNCLE DOOM.
SORRY. YOU KNOW WHAT THEY SAY ABOUT FRIENDS.
YES, VALERIA, EVERYONE NEEDS A FEW. FOR AT TIMES THEY CAN BE...
USEFUL.
DO YOU KNOW WHY I'VE CALLED?
UH, I HAVE A PRETTY GOOD IDEA.
WORLDS COLLIDING. EVERYTHING ENDING...
IS THAT WHERE YOU WANNA START?

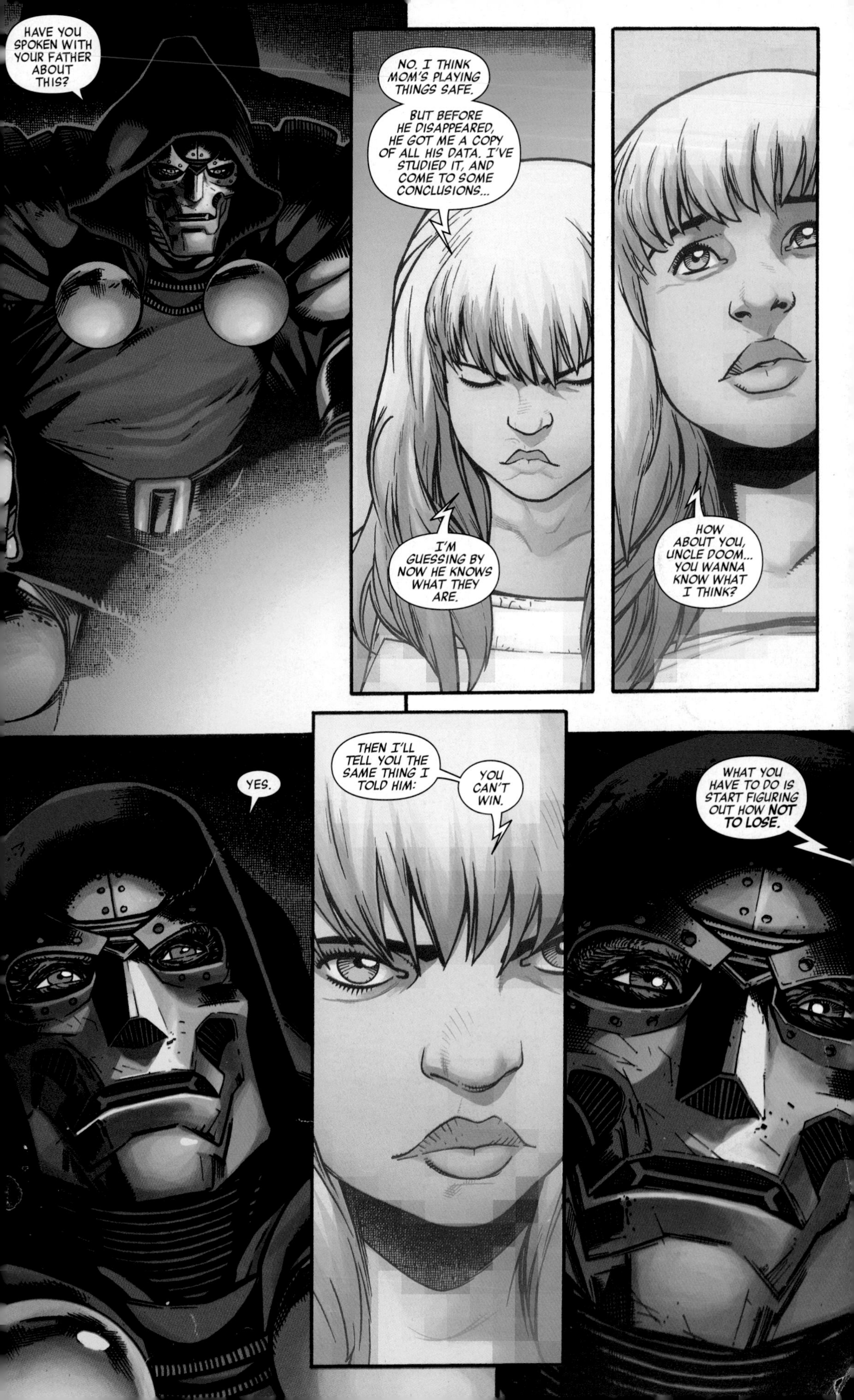
HAVE YOU SPOKEN WITH YOUR FATHER ABOUT THIS?
NO. I THINK MOM'S PLAYING THINGS SAFE.
BUT BEFORE HE DISAPPEARED, HE GOT ME A COPY OF ALL HIS DATA. I'VE STUDIED IT, AND COME TO SOME CONCLUSIONS...
I'M GUESSING BY NOW HE KNOWS WHAT THEY ARE.
HOW ABOUT YOU, UNCLE DOOM... YOU WANNA KNOW WHAT I THINK?
YES.
THEN I'LL TELL YOU THE SAME THING I TOLD HIM:
YOU CAN'T WIN.
WHAT YOU HAVE TO DO IS START FIGURING OUT HOW NOT TO LOSE.

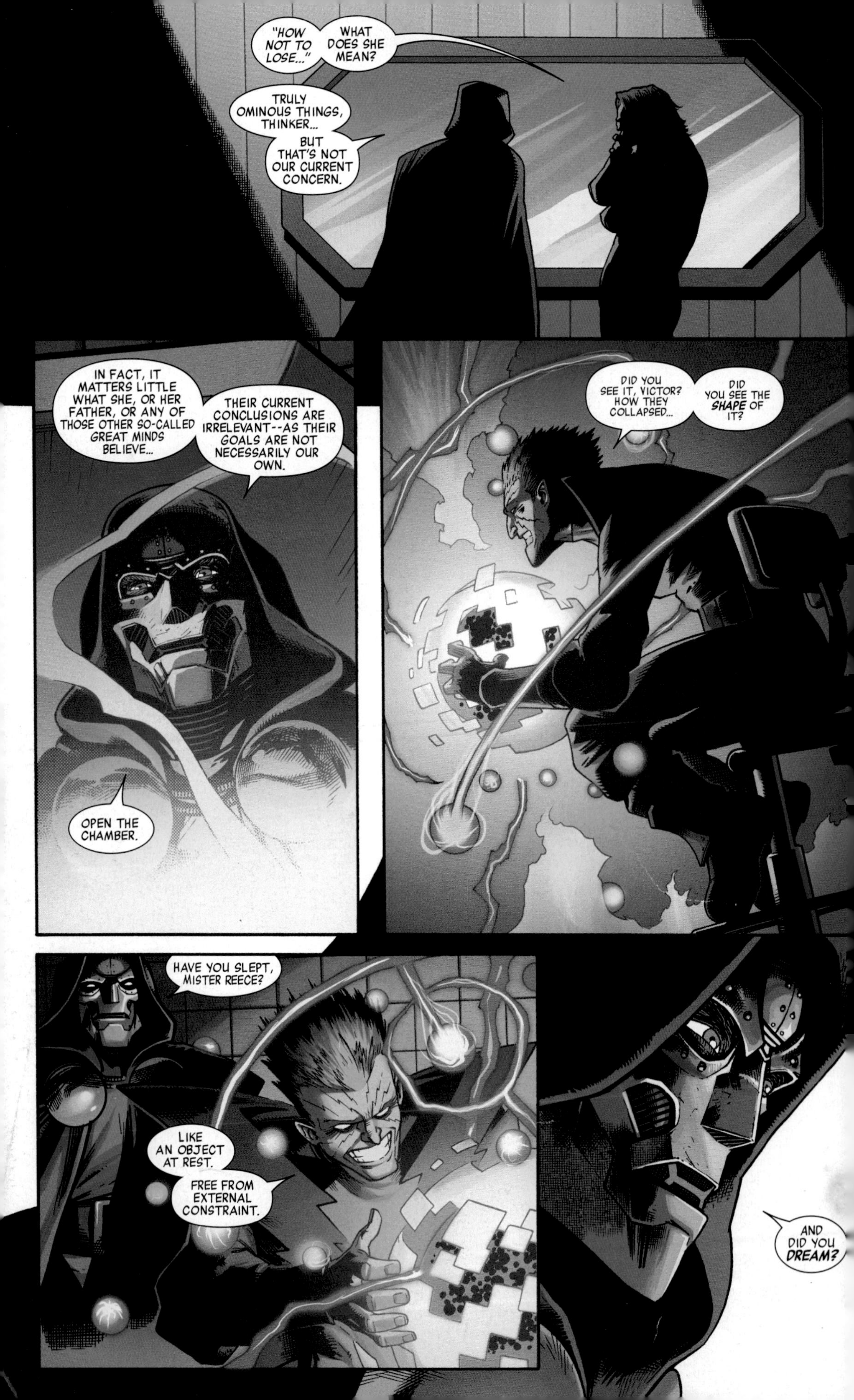
"HOW NOT TO LOSE..."
WHAT DOES SHE MEAN?
TRULY OMINOUS THINGS, THINKER...
BUT THAT'S NOT OUR CURRENT CONCERN.
IN FACT, IT MATTERS LITTLE WHAT SHE, OR HER FATHER, OR ANY OF THOSE OTHER SO-CALLED GREAT MINDS BELIEVE...
THEIR CURRENT CONCLUSIONS ARE IRRELEVANT--AS THEIR GOALS ARE NOT NECESSARILY OUR OWN.
OPEN THE CHAMBER.
DID YOU SEE IT, VICTOR? HOW THEY COLLAPSED...
DID YOU SEE THE SHAPE OF IT?
HAVE YOU SLEPT, MISTER REECE?
LIKE AN OBJECT AT REST.
FREE FROM EXTERNAL CONSTRAINT.
AND DID YOU DREAM?

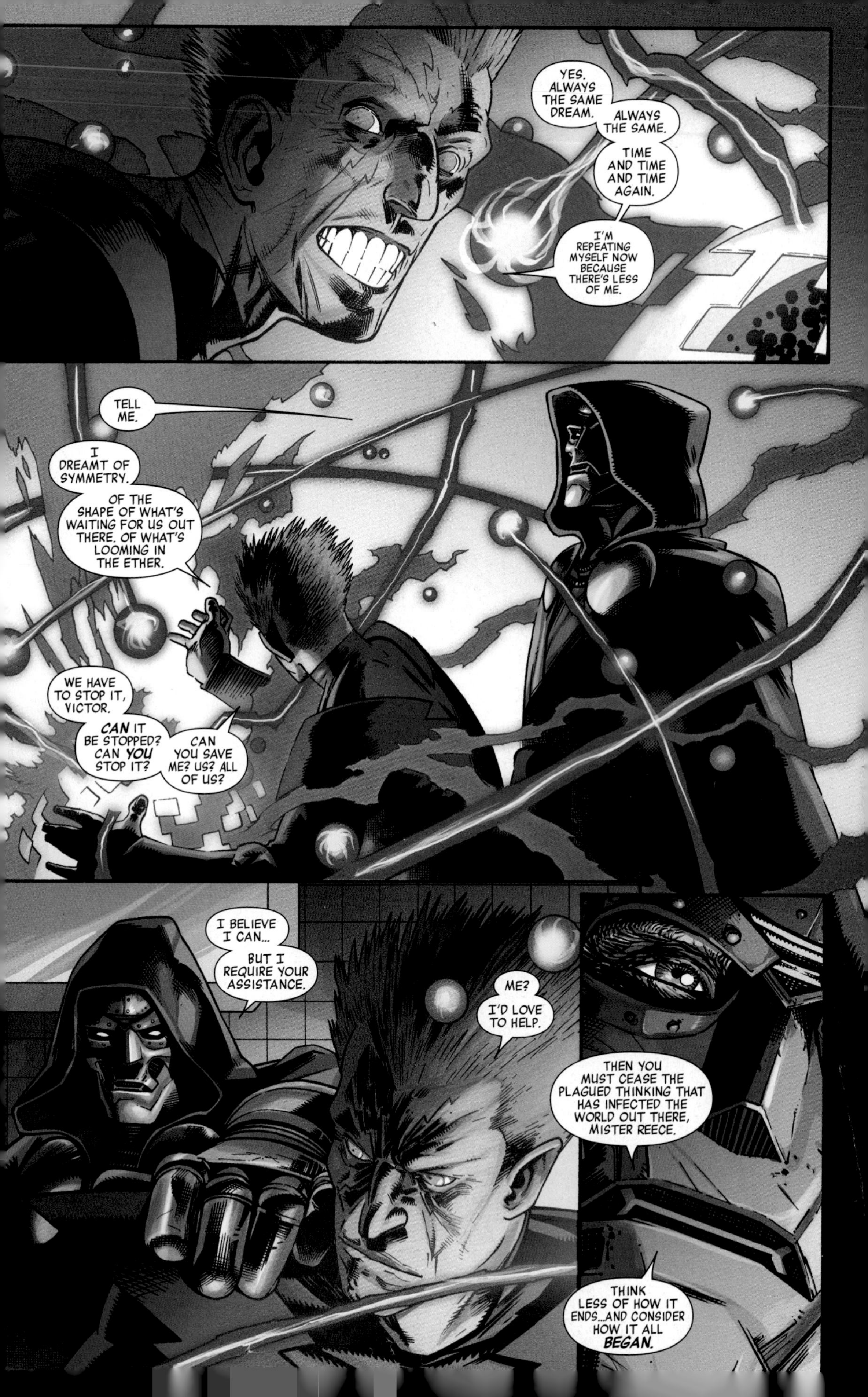
YES. ALWAYS THE SAME DREAM.
ALWAYS THE SAME.
TIME AND TIME AND TIME AGAIN.
I'M REPEATING MYSELF NOW BECAUSE THERE'S LESS OF ME.
TELL ME.
I DREAMT OF SYMMETRY.
OF THE SHAPE OF WHAT'S WAITING FOR US OUT THERE. OF WHAT'S LOOMING IN THE ETHER.
WE HAVE TO STOP IT, VICTOR.
CAN IT BE STOPPED? CAN YOU STOP IT?
CAN YOU SAVE ME? US? ALL OF US?
I BELIEVE I CAN...
BUT I REQUIRE YOUR ASSISTANCE.
ME?
I'D LOVE TO HELP.
THEN YOU MUST CEASE THE PLAGUED THINKING THAT HAS INFECTED THE WORLD OUT THERE, MISTER REECE.
THINK LESS OF HOW IT ENDS...AND CONSIDER HOW IT ALL BEGAN.

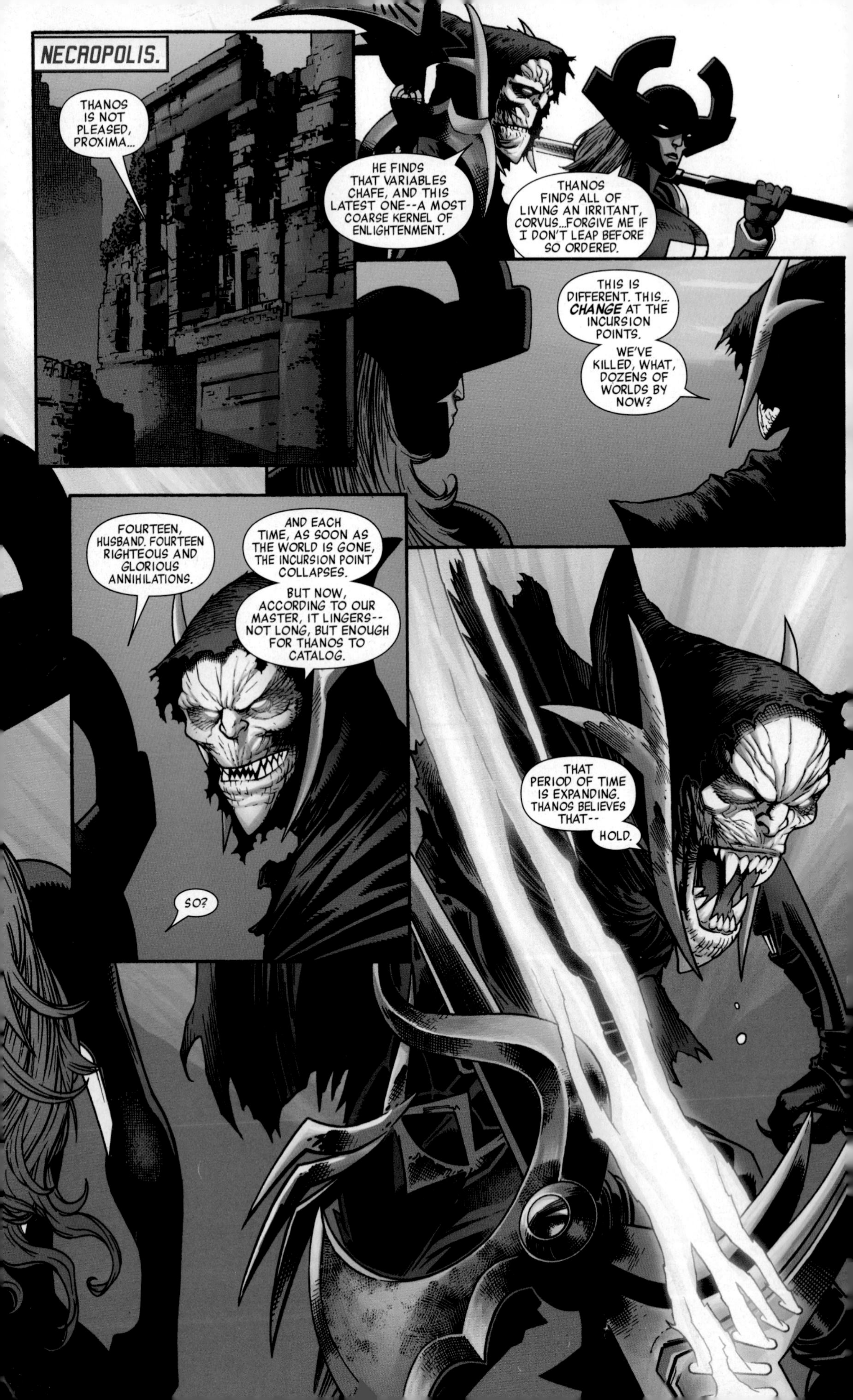
NECROPOLIS.
THANOS IS NOT PLEASED, PROXIMA...
HE FINDS THAT VARIABLES CHAFE, AND THIS LATEST ONE--A MOST COARSE KERNEL OF ENLIGHTENMENT.
THANOS FINDS ALL OF LIVING AN IRRITANT, CORVUS...FORGIVE ME IF I DON'T LEAP BEFORE SO ORDERED.
THIS IS DIFFERENT. THIS... CHANGE AT THE INCURSION POINTS.
WE'VE KILLED, WHAT, DOZENS OF WORLDS BY NOW?
FOURTEEN, HUSBAND. FOURTEEN RIGHTEOUS AND GLORIOUS ANNIHILATIONS.
AND EACH TIME, AS SOON AS THE WORLD IS GONE, THE INCURSION POINT COLLAPSES.
BUT NOW, ACCORDING TO OUR MASTER, IT LINGERS-- NOT LONG, BUT ENOUGH FOR THANOS TO CATALOG.
SO?
THAT PERIOD OF TIME IS EXPANDING. THANOS BELIEVES THAT--
HOLD.

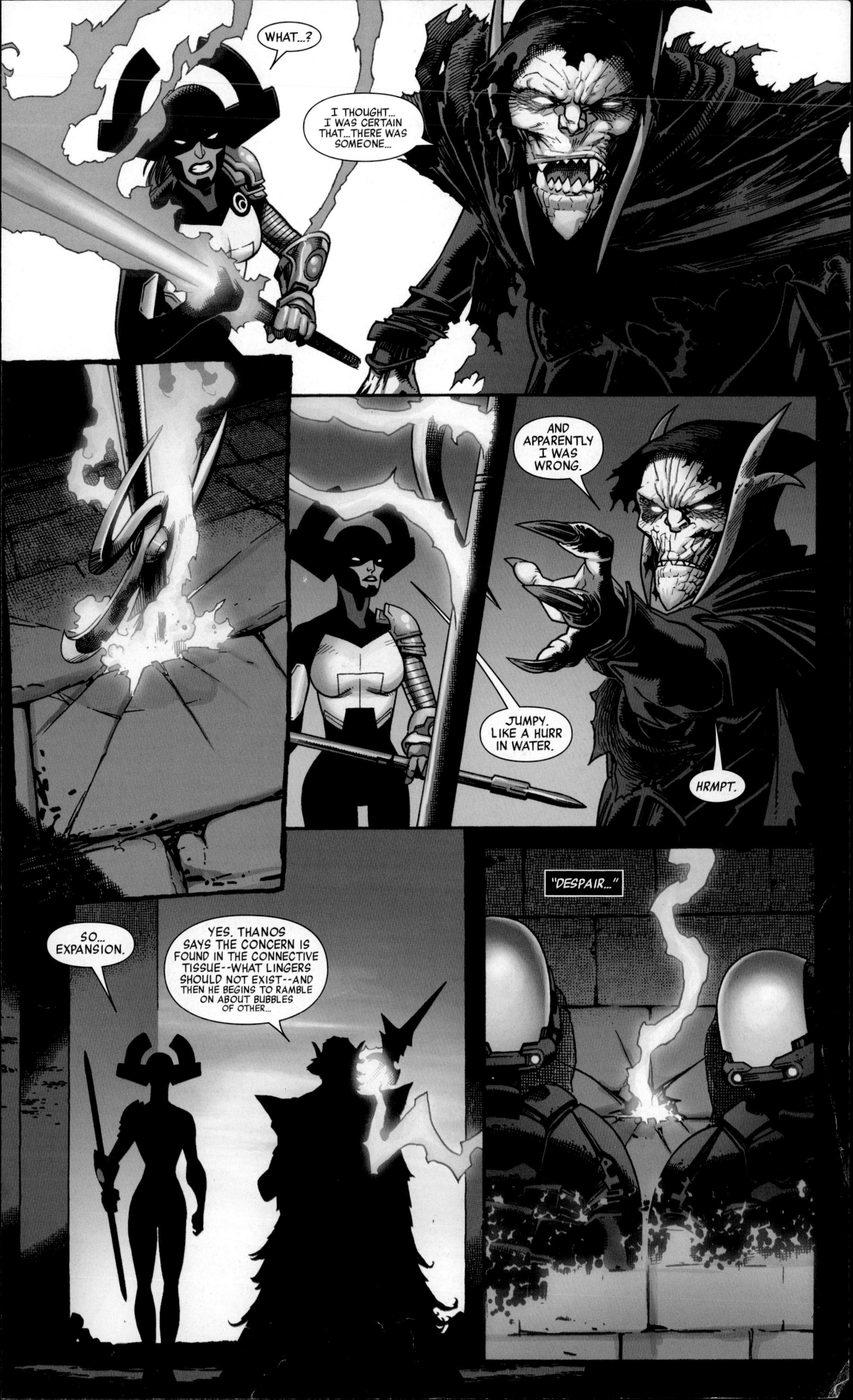

WHAT...?
I THOUGHT... I WAS CERTAIN THAT...THERE WAS SOMEONE...
AND APPARENTLY I WAS WRONG.
JUMPY. LIKE A HURR IN WATER.
HRMPT.
SO... EXPANSION.
YES. THANOS SAYS THE CONCERN IS FOUND IN THE CONNECTIVE TISSUE--WHAT LINGERS SHOULD NOT EXIST--AND THEN HE BEGINS TO RAMBLE ON ABOUT BUBBLES OF OTHER...
"DESPAIR..."

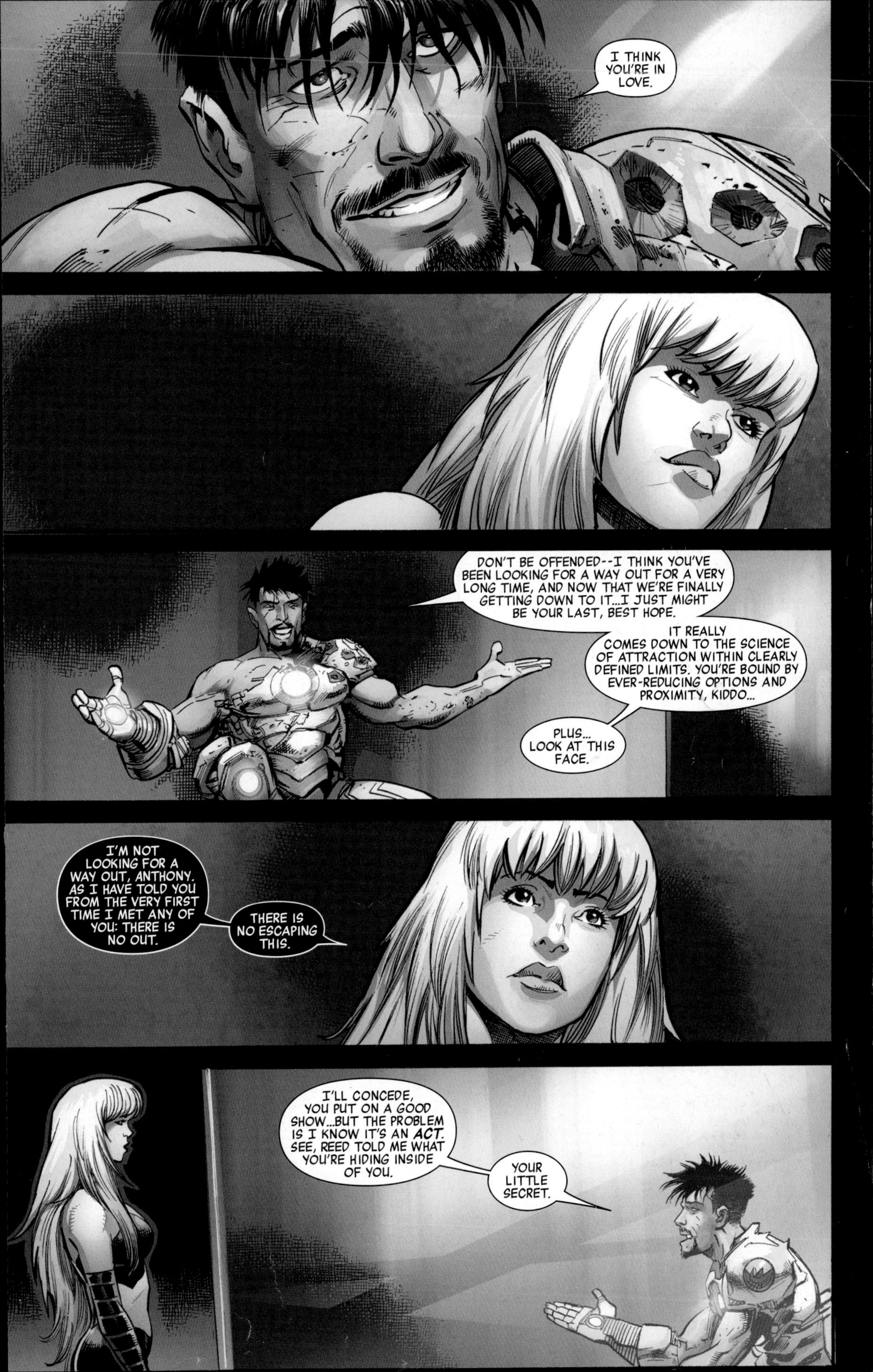
I THINK YOU'RE IN LOVE.
DON'T BE OFFENDED--I THINK YOU'VE BEEN LOOKING FOR A WAY OUT FOR A VERY LONG TIME, AND NOW THAT WE'RE FINALLY GETTING DOWN TO IT...I JUST MIGHT BE YOUR LAST, BEST HOPE.
IT REALLY COMES DOWN TO THE SCIENCE OF ATTRACTION WITHIN CLEARLY DEFINED LIMITS. YOU'RE BOUND BY EVER-REDUCING OPTIONS AND PROXIMITY, KIDDO...
PLUS... LOOK AT THIS FACE.
I'M NOT LOOKING FOR A WAY OUT, ANTHONY. AS I HAVE TOLD YOU FROM THE VERY FIRST TIME I MET ANY OF YOU: THERE IS NO OUT.
THERE IS NO ESCAPING THIS.
I'LL CONCEDE, YOU PUT ON A GOOD SHOW...BUT THE PROBLEM IS I KNOW IT'S AN ACT. SEE, REED TOLD ME WHAT YOU'RE HIDING INSIDE OF YOU.
YOUR LITTLE SECRET.

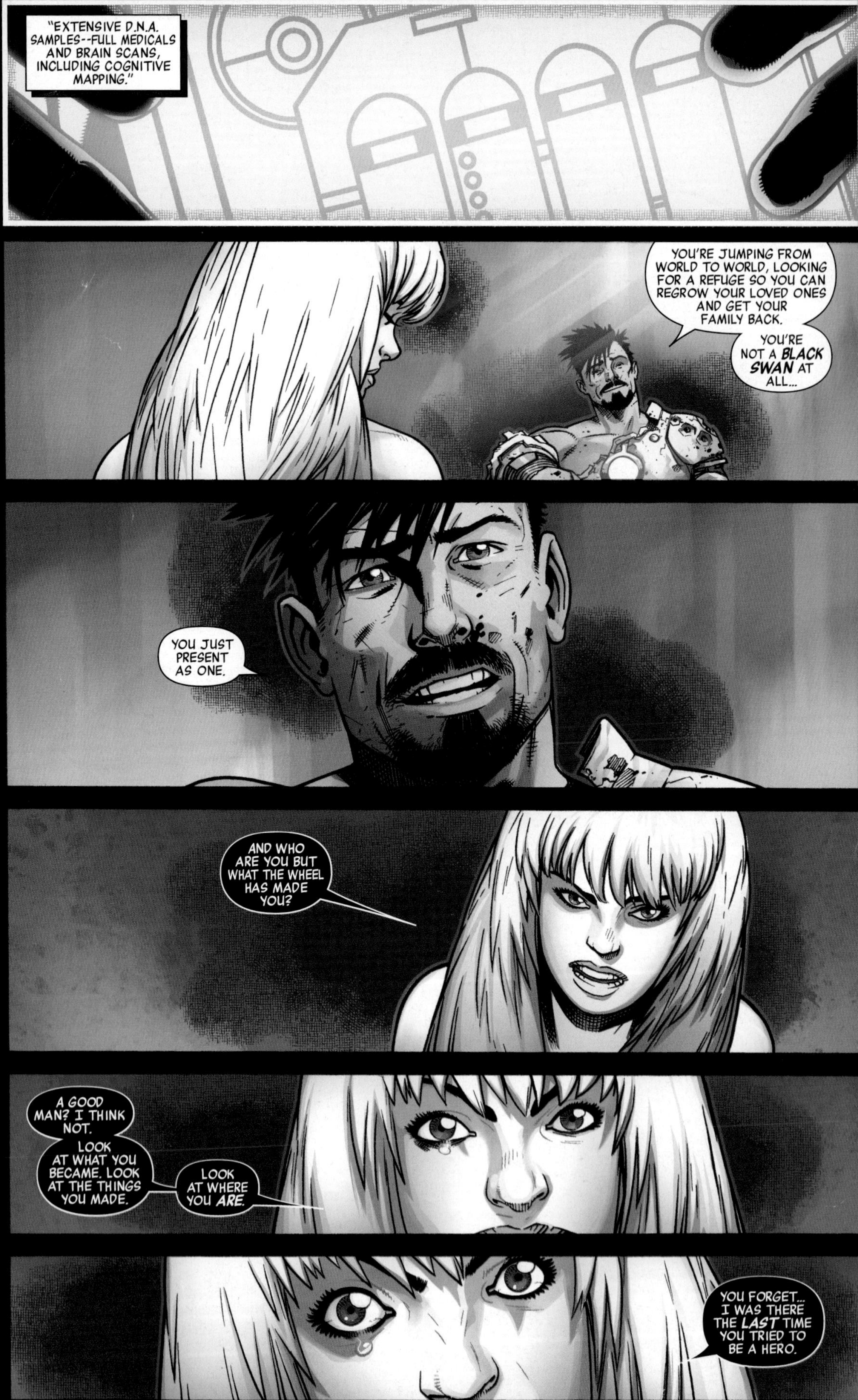
"EXTENSIVE D.N.A. SAMPLES--FULL MEDICALS AND BRAIN SCANS, INCLUDING COGNITIVE MAPPING."
YOU'RE JUMPING FROM WORLD TO WORLD, LOOKING FOR A REFUGE SO YOU CAN REGROW YOUR LOVED ONES AND GET YOUR FAMILY BACK.
YOU'RE NOT A BLACK SWAN AT ALL...
YOU JUST PRESENT AS ONE.
AND WHO ARE YOU BUT WHAT THE WHEEL HAS MADE YOU?
A GOOD MAN? I THINK NOT.
LOOK AT WHAT YOU BECAME. LOOK AT THE THINGS YOU MADE.
LOOK AT WHERE YOU ARE.
YOU FORGET... I WAS THERE THE LAST TIME YOU TRIED TO BE A HERO.

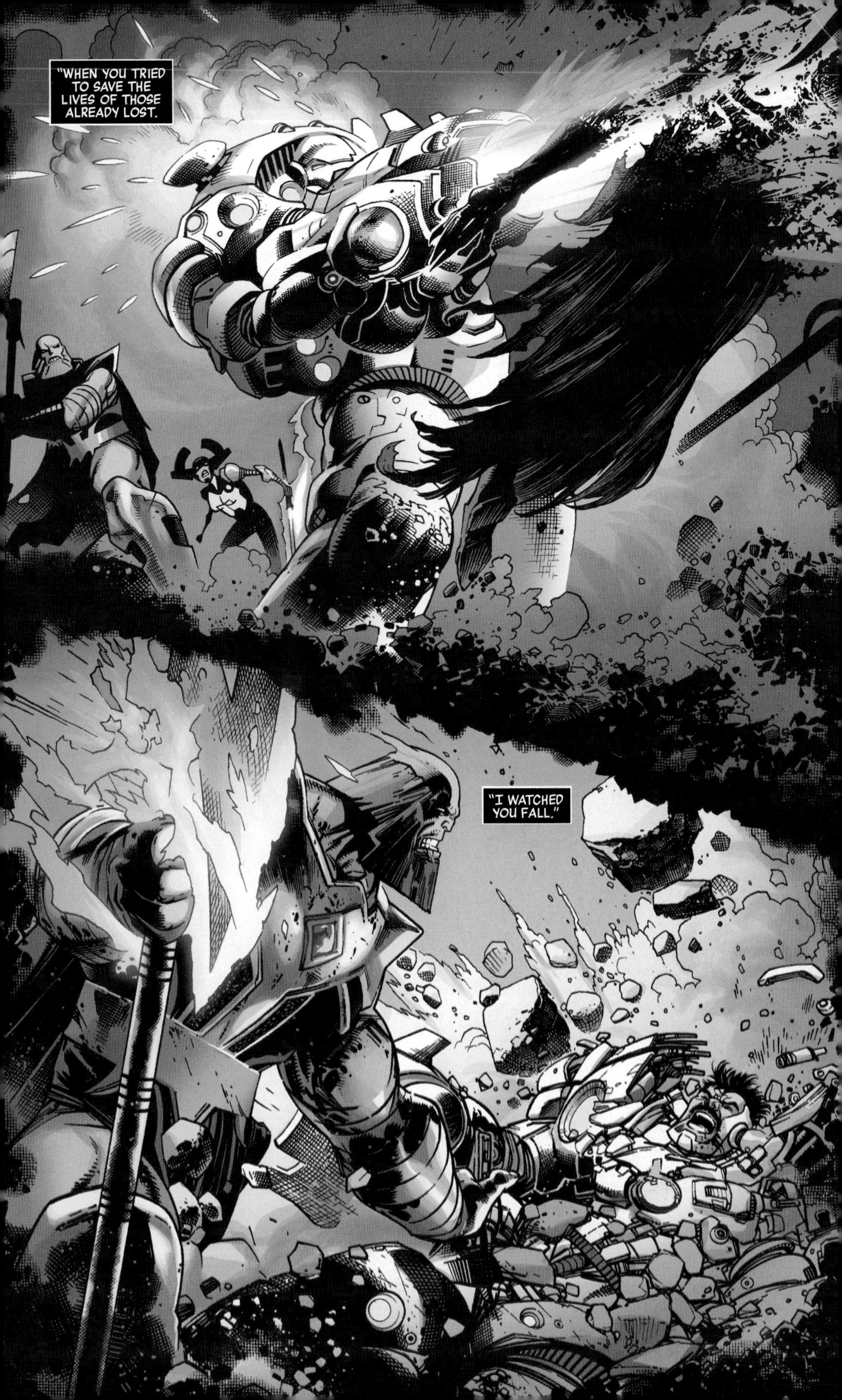
"WHEN YOU TRIED TO SAVE THE LIVES OF THOSE ALREADY LOST.
"I WATCHED YOU FALL."

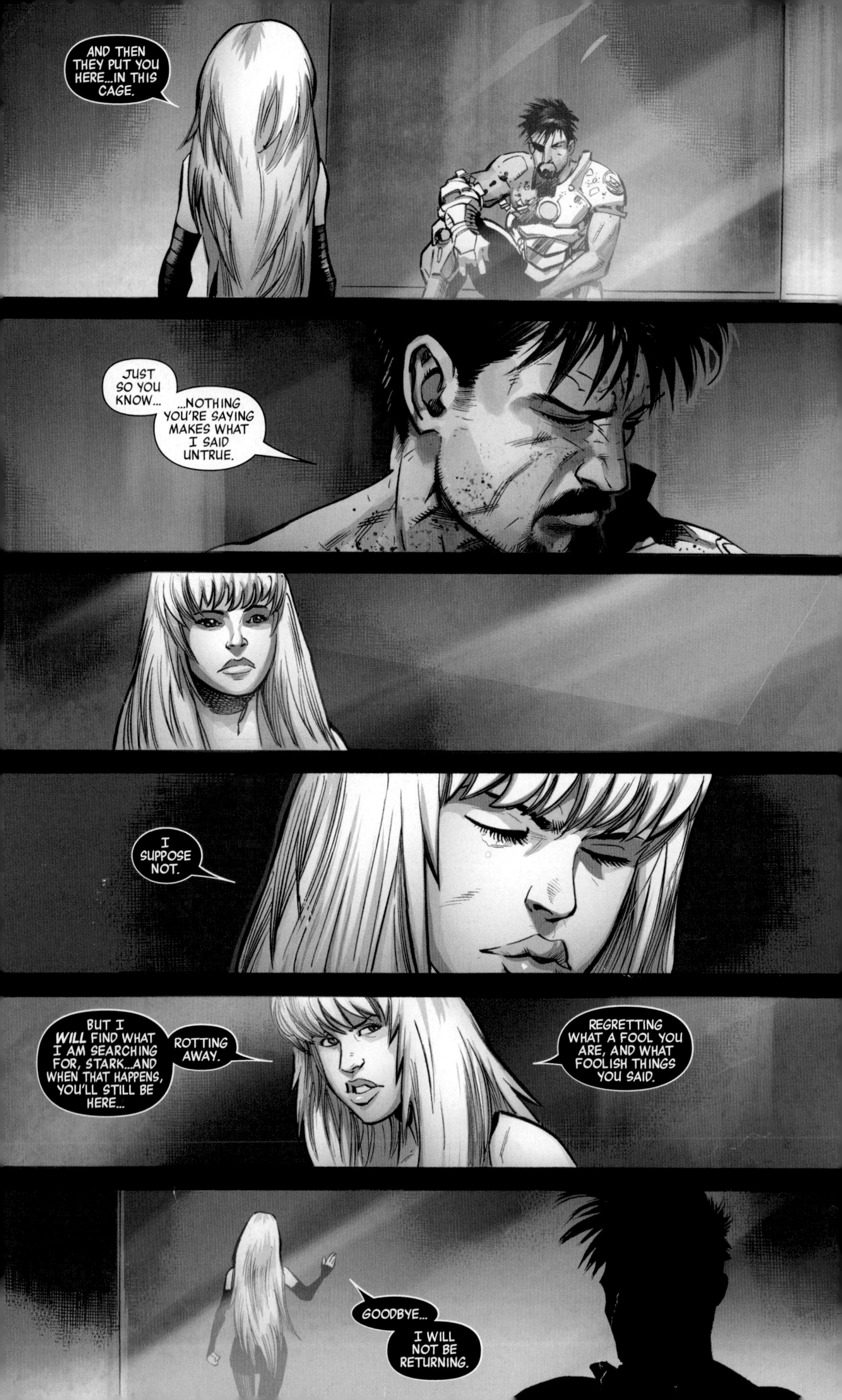

AND THEN THEY PUT YOU HERE...IN THIS CAGE.
JUST SO YOU KNOW...
...NOTHING YOU'RE SAYING MAKES WHAT I SAID UNTRUE.
I SUPPOSE NOT.
BUT I WILL FIND WHAT I AM SEARCHING FOR, STARK...AND WHEN THAT HAPPENS, YOU'LL STILL BE HERE...
ROTTING AWAY.
REGRETTING WHAT A FOOL YOU ARE, AND WHAT FOOLISH THINGS YOU SAID.
GOODBYE...
I WILL NOT BE RETURNING.

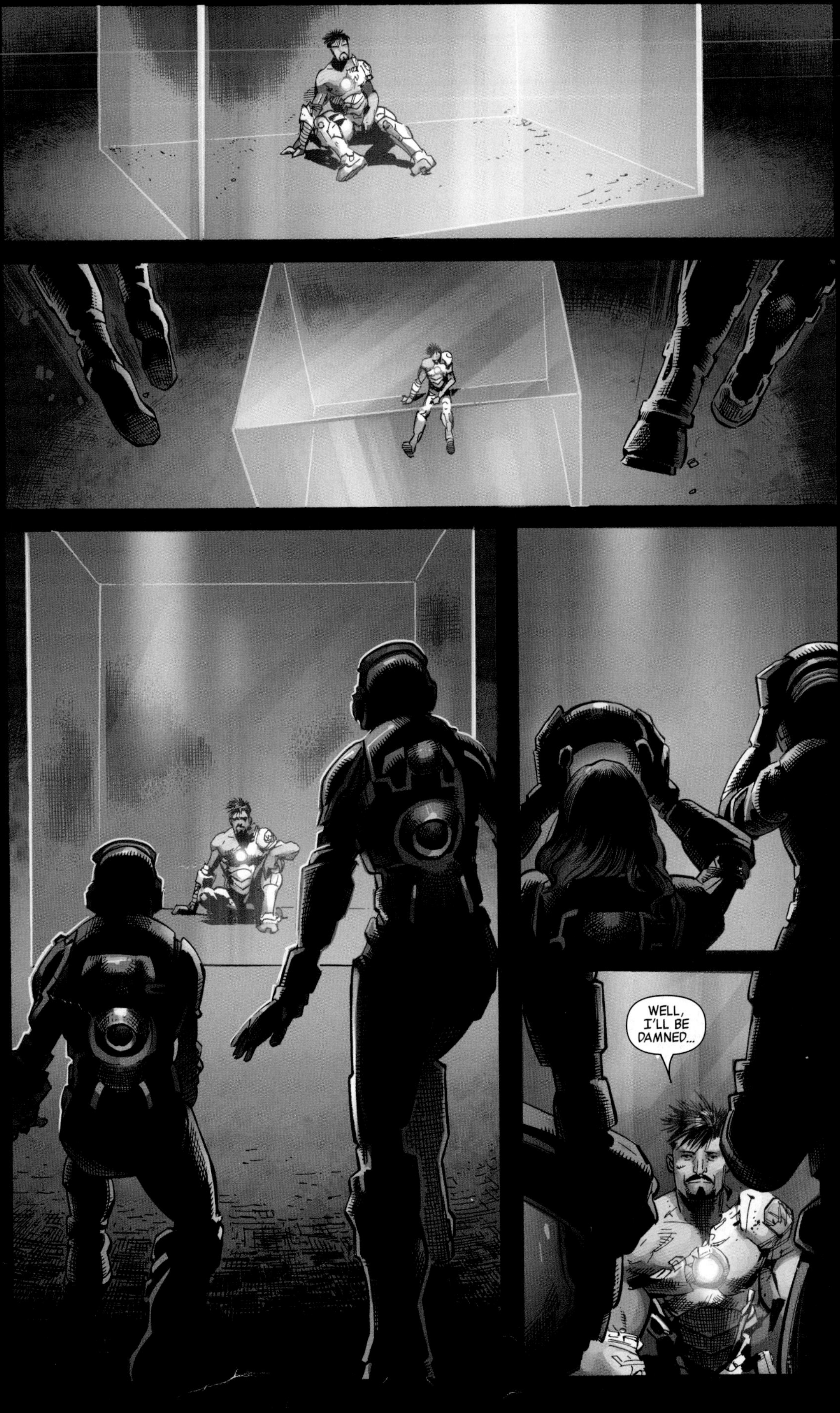
WELL, I'LL BE DAMNED...

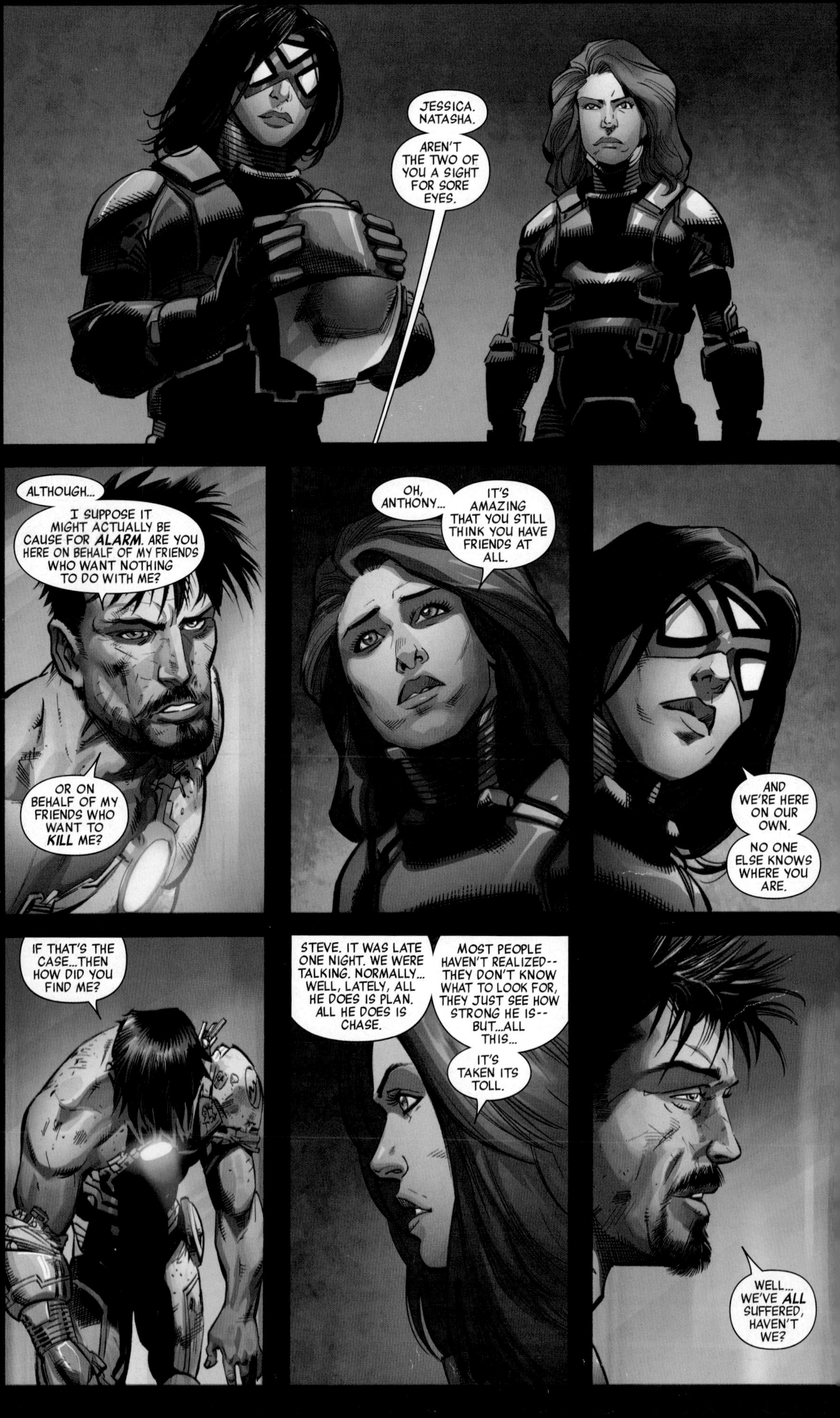
JESSICA. NATASHA.
AREN'T THE TWO OF YOU A SIGHT FOR SORE EYES.
ALTHOUGH...
I SUPPOSE IT MIGHT ACTUALLY BE CAUSE FOR ALARM. ARE YOU HERE ON BEHALF OF MY FRIENDS WHO WANT NOTHING TO DO WITH ME?
OR ON BEHALF OF MY FRIENDS WHO WANT TO KILL ME?
OH, ANTHONY...
IT'S AMAZING THAT YOU STILL THINK YOU HAVE FRIENDS AT ALL.
AND WE'RE HERE ON OUR OWN.
NO ONE ELSE KNOWS WHERE YOU ARE.
IF THAT'S THE CASE...THEN HOW DID YOU FIND ME?
STEVE. IT WAS LATE ONE NIGHT. WE WERE TALKING. NORMALLY... WELL, LATELY, ALL HE DOES IS PLAN. ALL HE DOES IS CHASE.
MOST PEOPLE HAVEN'T REALIZED-- THEY DON'T KNOW WHAT TO LOOK FOR, THEY JUST SEE HOW STRONG HE IS-- BUT...ALL THIS...
IT'S TAKEN ITS TOLL.
WELL... WE'VE ALL SUFFERED, HAVEN'T WE?

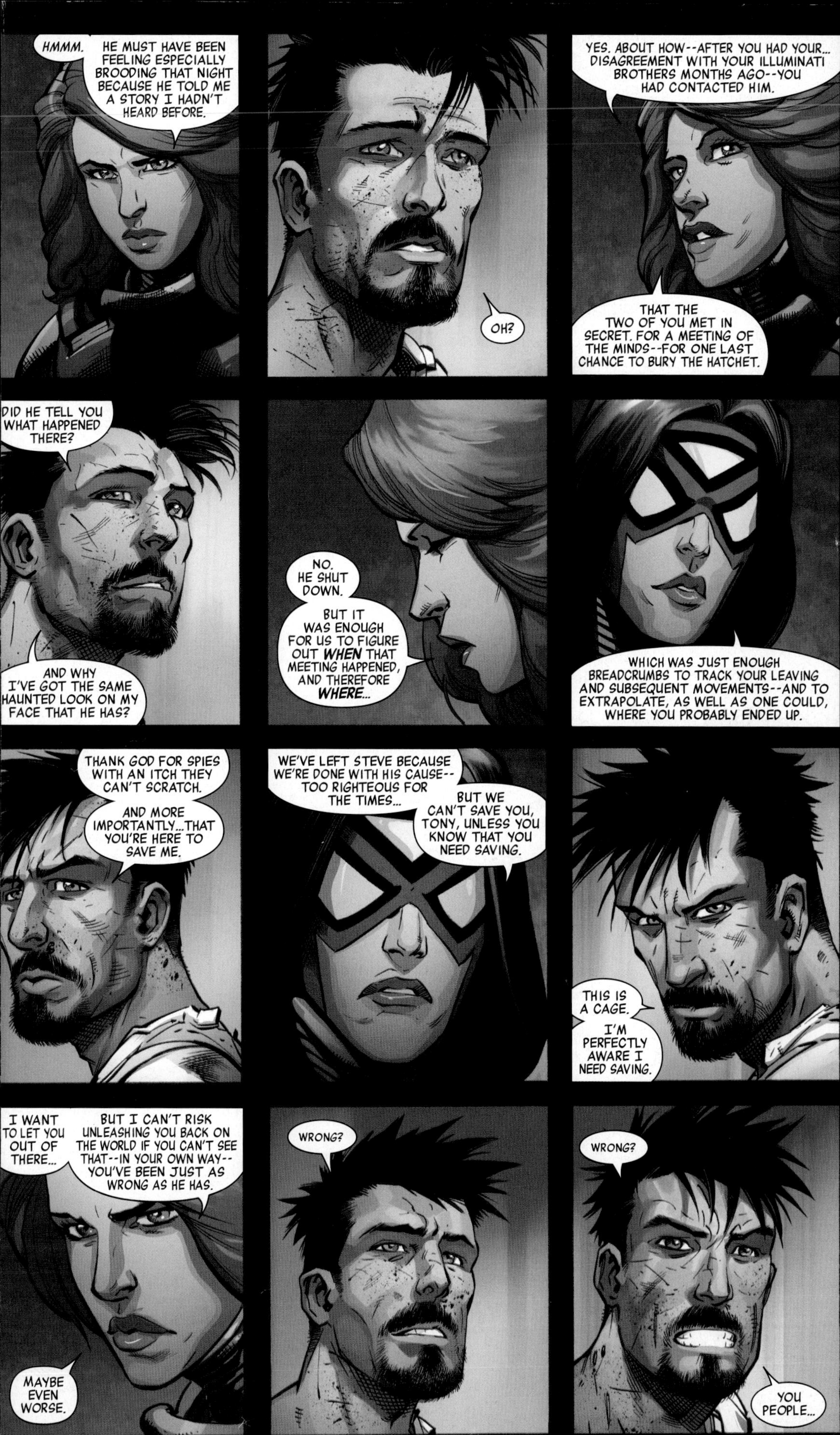

HMMM.
HE MUST HAVE BEEN FEELING ESPECIALLY BROODING THAT NIGHT BECAUSE HE TOLD ME A STORY I HADN'T HEARD BEFORE.
OH?
YES. ABOUT HOW--AFTER YOU HAD YOUR... DISAGREEMENT WITH YOUR ILLUMINATI BROTHERS MONTHS AGO--YOU HAD CONTACTED HIM.
THAT THE TWO OF YOU MET IN SECRET. FOR A MEETING OF THE MINDS--FOR ONE LAST CHANCE TO BURY THE HATCHET.
DID HE TELL YOU WHAT HAPPENED THERE?
AND WHY I'VE GOT THE SAME HAUNTED LOOK ON MY FACE THAT HE HAS?
NO. HE SHUT DOWN.
BUT IT WAS ENOUGH FOR US TO FIGURE OUT **WHEN** THAT MEETING HAPPENED, AND THEREFORE **WHERE...**
WHICH WAS JUST ENOUGH BREADCRUMBS TO TRACK YOUR LEAVING AND SUBSEQUENT MOVEMENTS--AND TO EXTRAPOLATE, AS WELL AS ONE COULD, WHERE YOU PROBABLY ENDED UP.
THANK GOD FOR SPIES WITH AN ITCH THEY CAN'T SCRATCH.
AND MORE IMPORTANTLY...THAT YOU'RE HERE TO SAVE ME.
WE'VE LEFT STEVE BECAUSE WE'RE DONE WITH HIS CAUSE--TOO RIGHTEOUS FOR THE TIMES...
BUT WE CAN'T SAVE YOU, TONY, UNLESS YOU KNOW THAT YOU NEED SAVING.
THIS IS A CAGE.
I'M PERFECTLY AWARE I NEED SAVING.
I WANT TO LET YOU OUT OF THERE...
BUT I CAN'T RISK UNLEASHING YOU BACK ON THE WORLD IF YOU CAN'T SEE THAT--IN YOUR OWN WAY--YOU'VE BEEN JUST AS WRONG AS HE HAS.
MAYBE EVEN WORSE.
WRONG?
WRONG?
YOU PEOPLE...

"ORIGIN SITES"

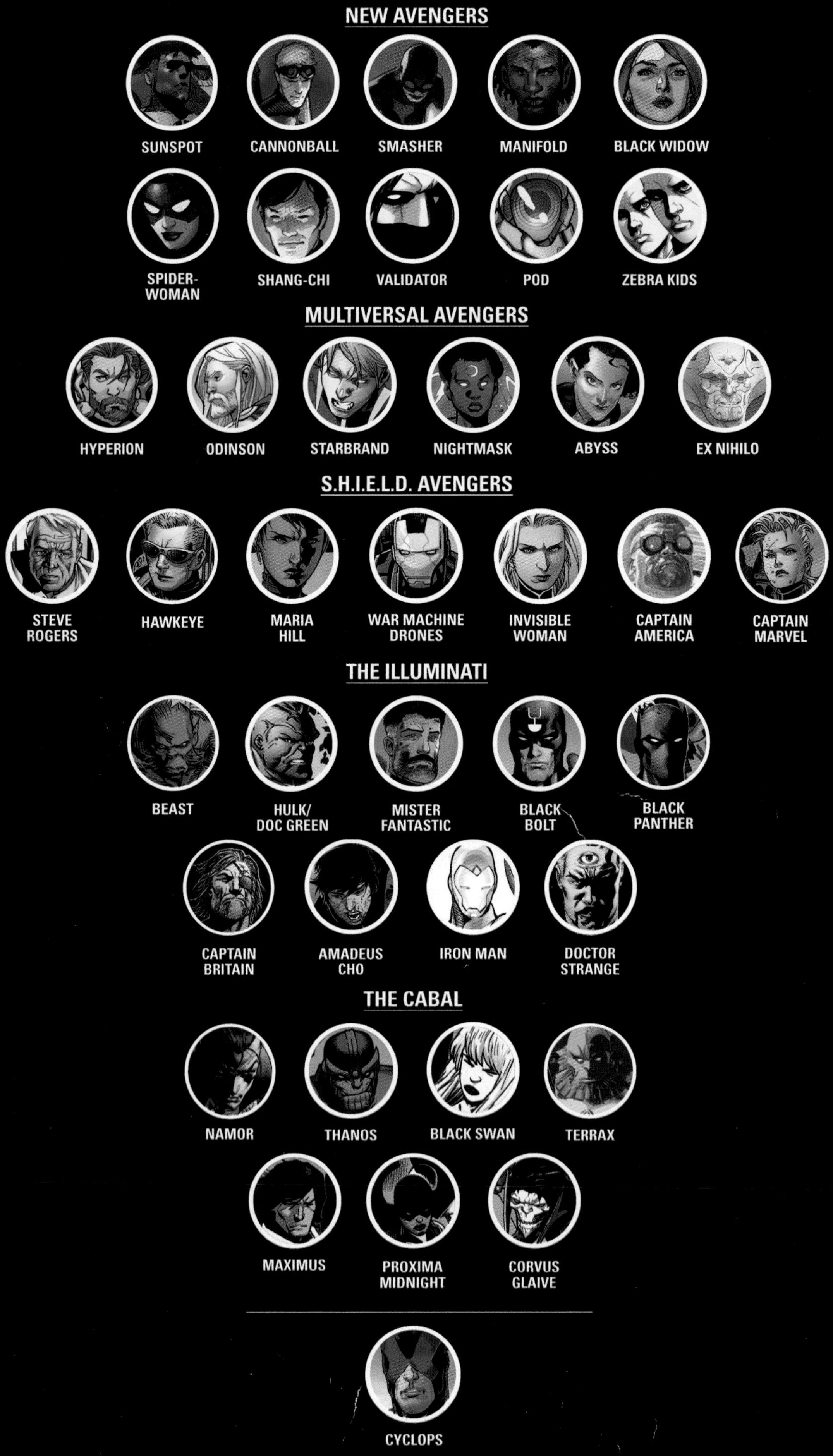
NEW AVENGERS
SUNSPOT
CANNONBALL
SMASHER
MANIFOLD
BLACK WIDOW
SPIDER-WOMAN
SHANG-CHI
VALIDATOR
POD
ZEBRA KIDS
MULTIVERSAL AVENGERS
HYPERION
ODINSON
STARBRAND
NIGHTMASK
ABYSS
EX NIHILO
S.H.I.E.L.D. AVENGERS
STEVE ROGERS
HAWKEYE
MARIA HILL
WAR MACHINE DRONES
INVISIBLE WOMAN
CAPTAIN AMERICA
CAPTAIN MARVEL
THE ILLUMINATI
BEAST
HULK/ DOC GREEN
MISTER FANTASTIC
BLACK BOLT
BLACK PANTHER
CAPTAIN BRITAIN
AMADEUS CHO
IRON MAN
DOCTOR STRANGE
THE CABAL
NAMOR
THANOS
BLACK SWAN
TERRAX
MAXIMUS
PROXIMA MIDNIGHT
CORVUS GLAIVE
CYCLOPS

PREVIOUSLY IN AVENGERS

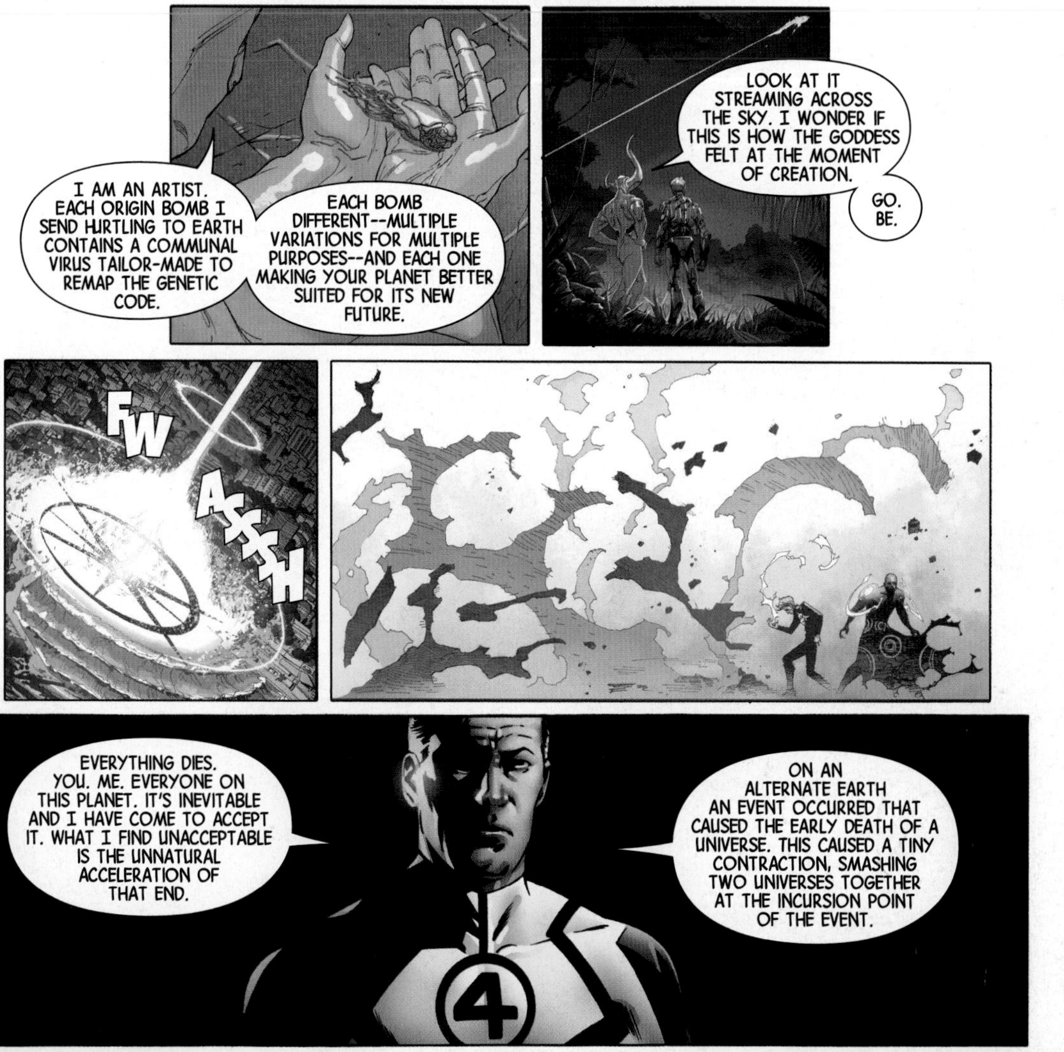
I AM AN ARTIST. EACH ORIGIN BOMB I SEND HURTLING TO EARTH CONTAINS A COMMUNAL VIRUS TAILOR-MADE TO REMAP THE GENETIC CODE.
EACH BOMB DIFFERENT--MULTIPLE VARIATIONS FOR MULTIPLE PURPOSES--AND EACH ONE MAKING YOUR PLANET BETTER SUITED FOR ITS NEW FUTURE.
LOOK AT IT STREAMING ACROSS THE SKY. I WONDER IF THIS IS HOW THE GODDESS FELT AT THE MOMENT OF CREATION.
GO. BE.
FW
AASSH
EVERYTHING DIES. YOU. ME. EVERYONE ON THIS PLANET. IT'S INEVITABLE AND I HAVE COME TO ACCEPT IT. WHAT I FIND UNACCEPTABLE IS THE UNNATURAL ACCELERATION OF THAT END.
ON AN ALTERNATE EARTH AN EVENT OCCURRED THAT CAUSED THE EARLY DEATH OF A UNIVERSE. THIS CAUSED A TINY CONTRACTION, SMASHING TWO UNIVERSES TOGETHER AT THE INCURSION POINT OF THE EVENT.

EIGHT MONTHS LATER

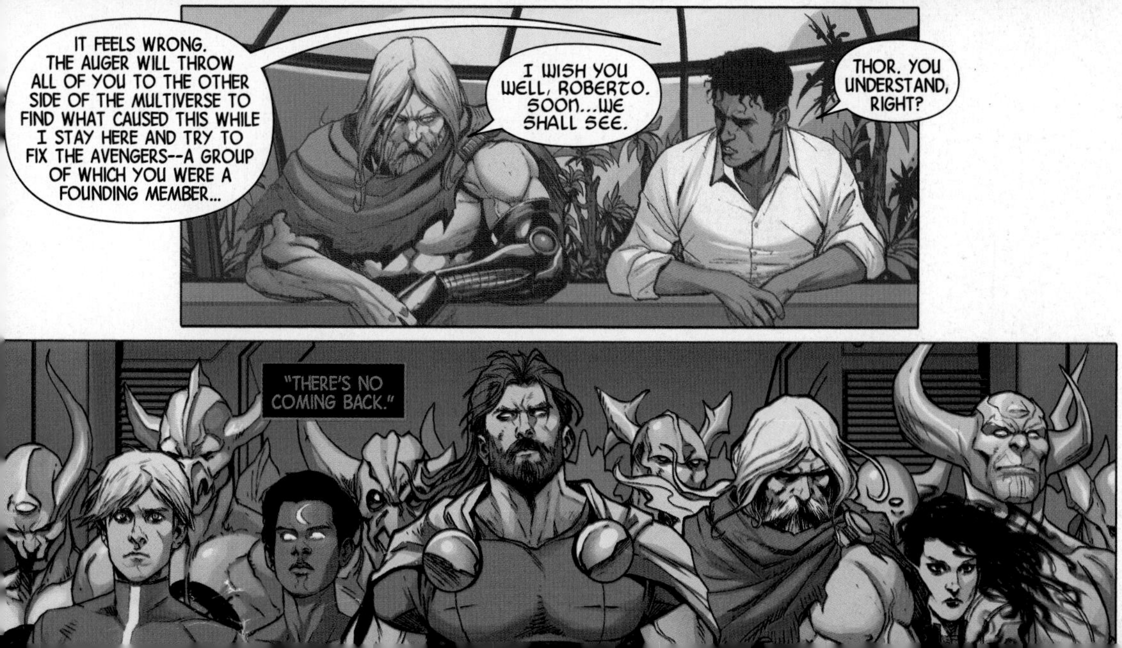
IT FEELS WRONG. THE AUGER WILL THROW ALL OF YOU TO THE OTHER SIDE OF THE MULTIVERSE TO FIND WHAT CAUSED THIS WHILE I STAY HERE AND TRY TO FIX THE AVENGERS--A GROUP OF WHICH YOU WERE A FOUNDING MEMBER...
I WISH YOU WELL, ROBERTO. SOON...WE SHALL SEE.
THOR. YOU UNDERSTAND, RIGHT?
"THERE'S NO COMING BACK."

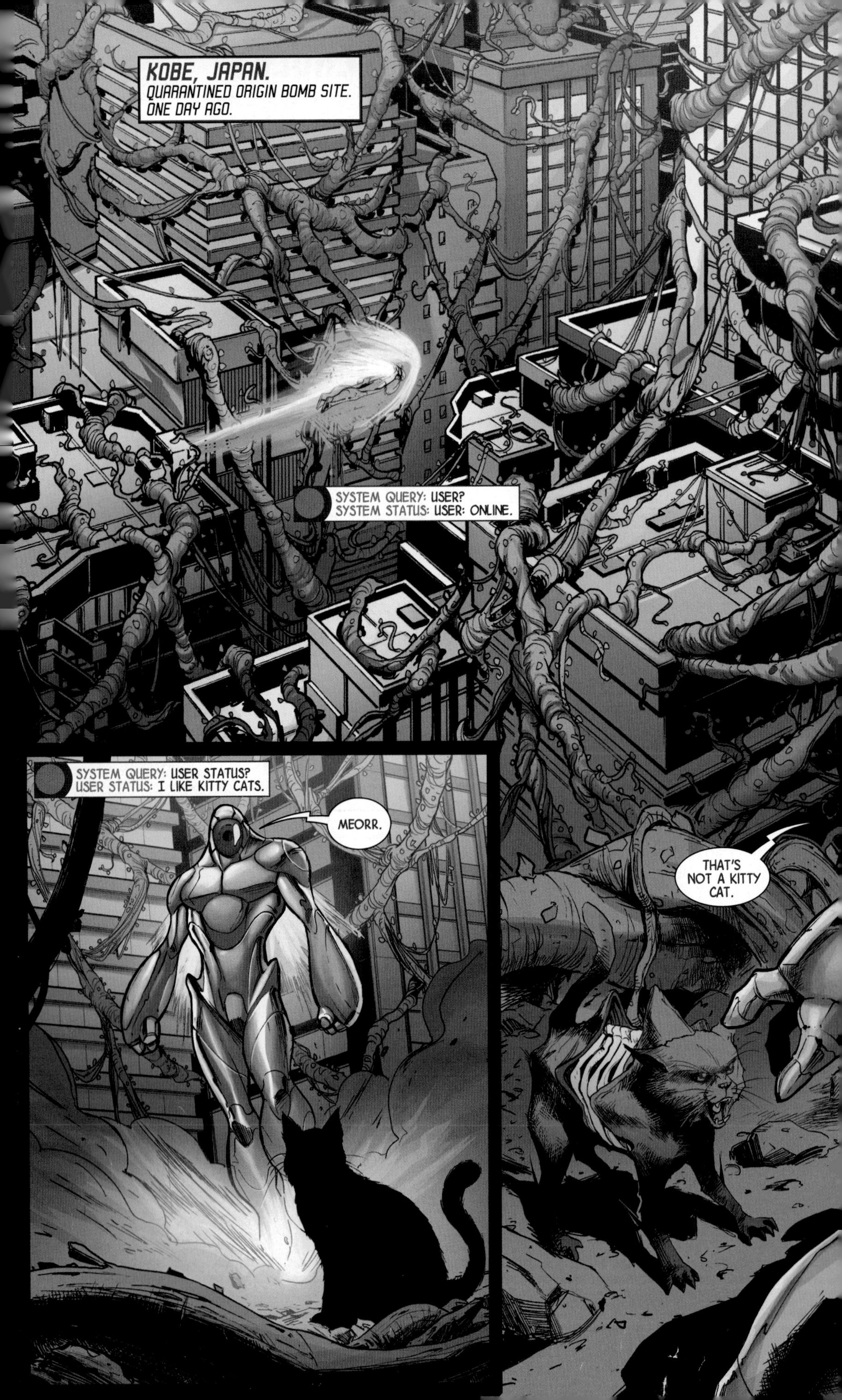
KOBE, JAPAN.
QUARANTINED ORIGIN BOMB SITE.
ONE DAY AGO.
SYSTEM QUERY: USER?
SYSTEM STATUS: USER: ONLINE.
SYSTEM QUERY: USER STATUS?
USER STATUS: I LIKE KITTY CATS.
MEORR.
THAT'S NOT A KITTY CAT.

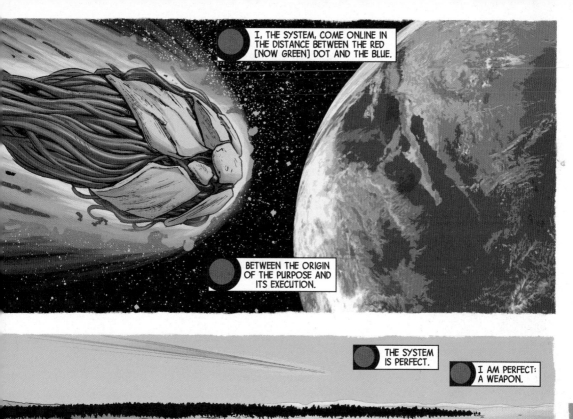

I, THE SYSTEM, COME ONLINE IN THE DISTANCE BETWEEN THE RED [NOW GREEN] DOT AND THE BLUE.

BETWEEN THE ORIGIN OF THE PURPOSE AND ITS EXECUTION.

THE SYSTEM IS PERFECT.

I AM PERFECT: A WEAPON.

I BECOME WE. THE FIRE FROZEN. THE COLD A PERFECT CHRYSALIS FOR THE PLANETARY DYNAMO.

AN OUTER SHELL OUR FIRST ARMOR. SOFT COMPARED TO WHAT THE SYSTEM IS FORMING.

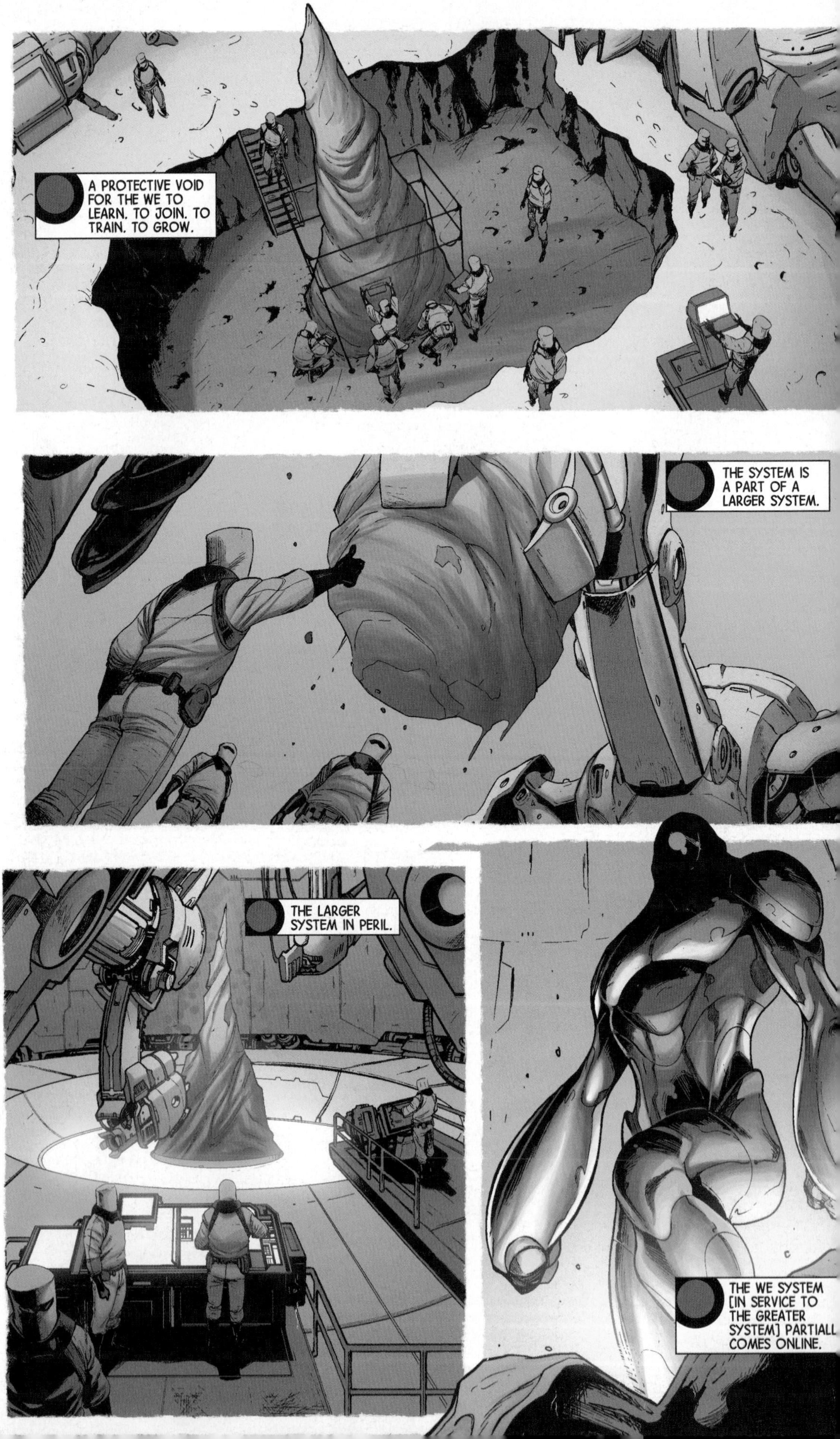
A PROTECTIVE VOID FOR THE WE TO LEARN. TO JOIN. TO TRAIN. TO GROW.
THE SYSTEM IS A PART OF A LARGER SYSTEM.
THE LARGER SYSTEM IN PERIL.
THE WE SYSTEM [IN SERVICE TO THE GREATER SYSTEM] PARTIALL COMES ONLINE.

THE I PROTECTS
THE USER PROTECTS
THE WE PROTECTS
THE GREATER SYSTEM.

THE WEAPON FULLY
FUNCTIONAL [UPGRADE.
UPGRADE. UPGRADE.]

THE WE PARTIALLY FUNCTIONAL
[CONFUSED. AFRAID. PANIC.]

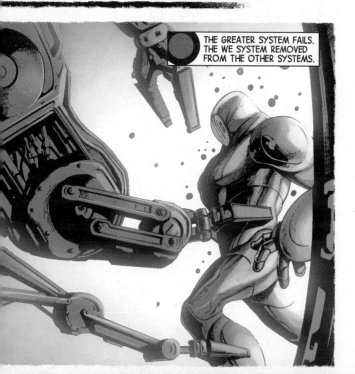

THE GREATER SYSTEM FAILS.
THE WE SYSTEM REMOVED
FROM THE OTHER SYSTEMS.

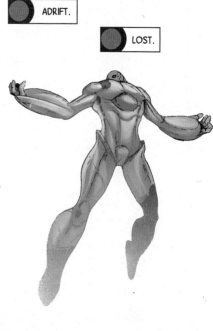

ADRIFT.

LOST.

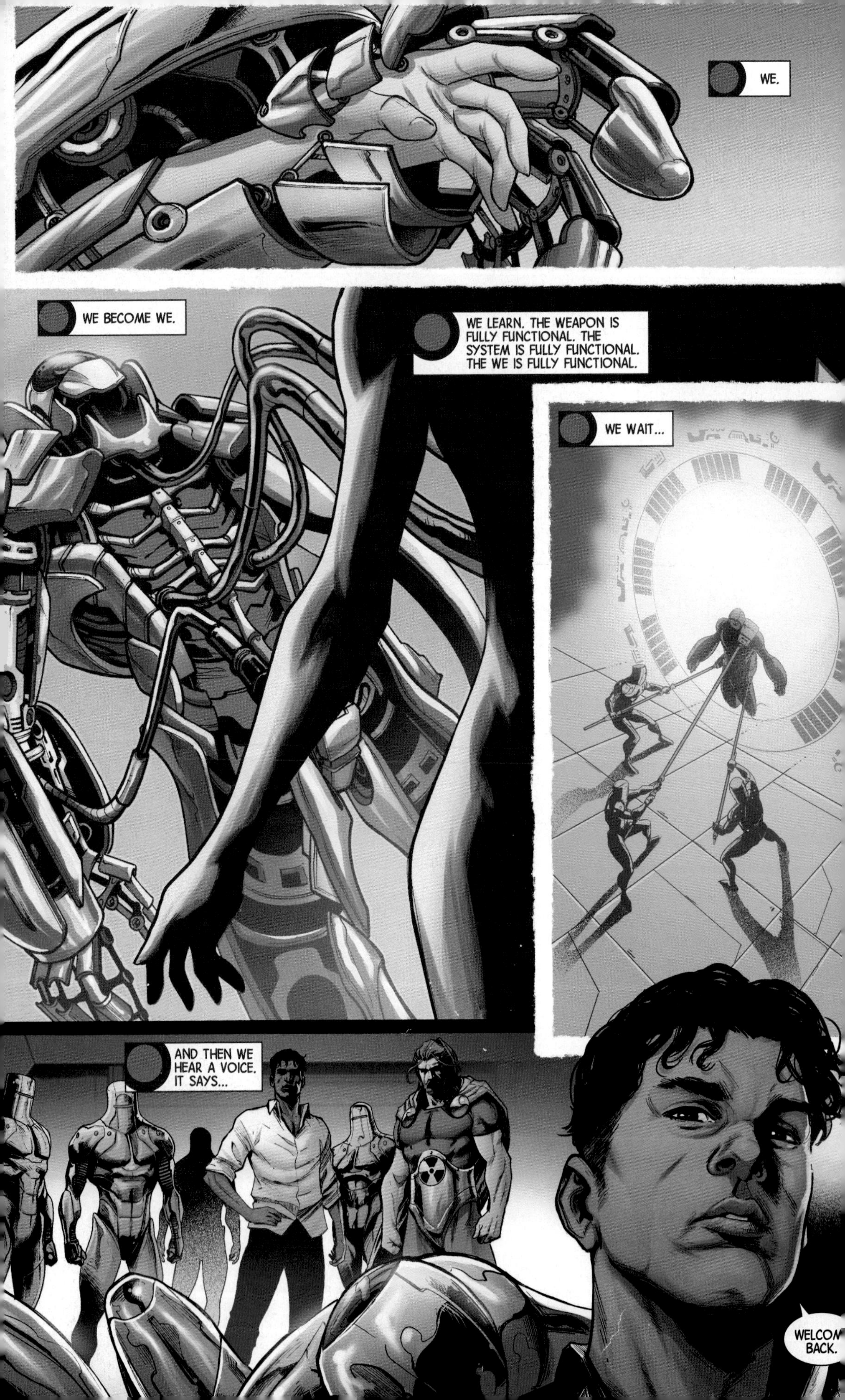
WE.
WE BECOME WE.
WE LEARN. THE WEAPON IS FULLY FUNCTIONAL. THE SYSTEM IS FULLY FUNCTIONAL. THE WE IS FULLY FUNCTIONAL.
WE WAIT...
AND THEN WE HEAR A VOICE. IT SAYS...
WELCOM BACK.

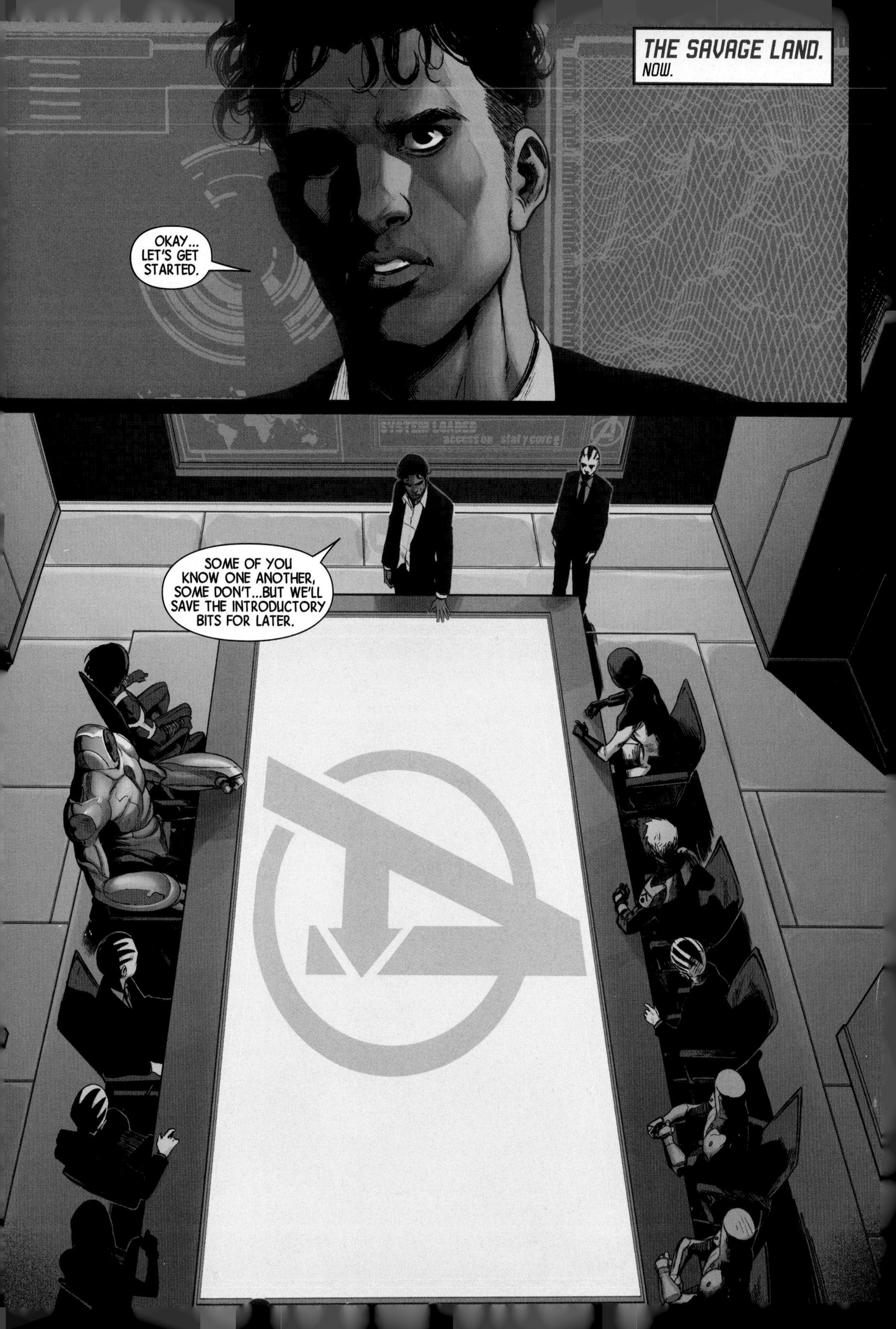
THE SAVAGE LAND. NOW.
OKAY... LET'S GET STARTED.
SOME OF YOU KNOW ONE ANOTHER, SOME DON'T...BUT WE'LL SAVE THE INTRODUCTORY BITS FOR LATER.

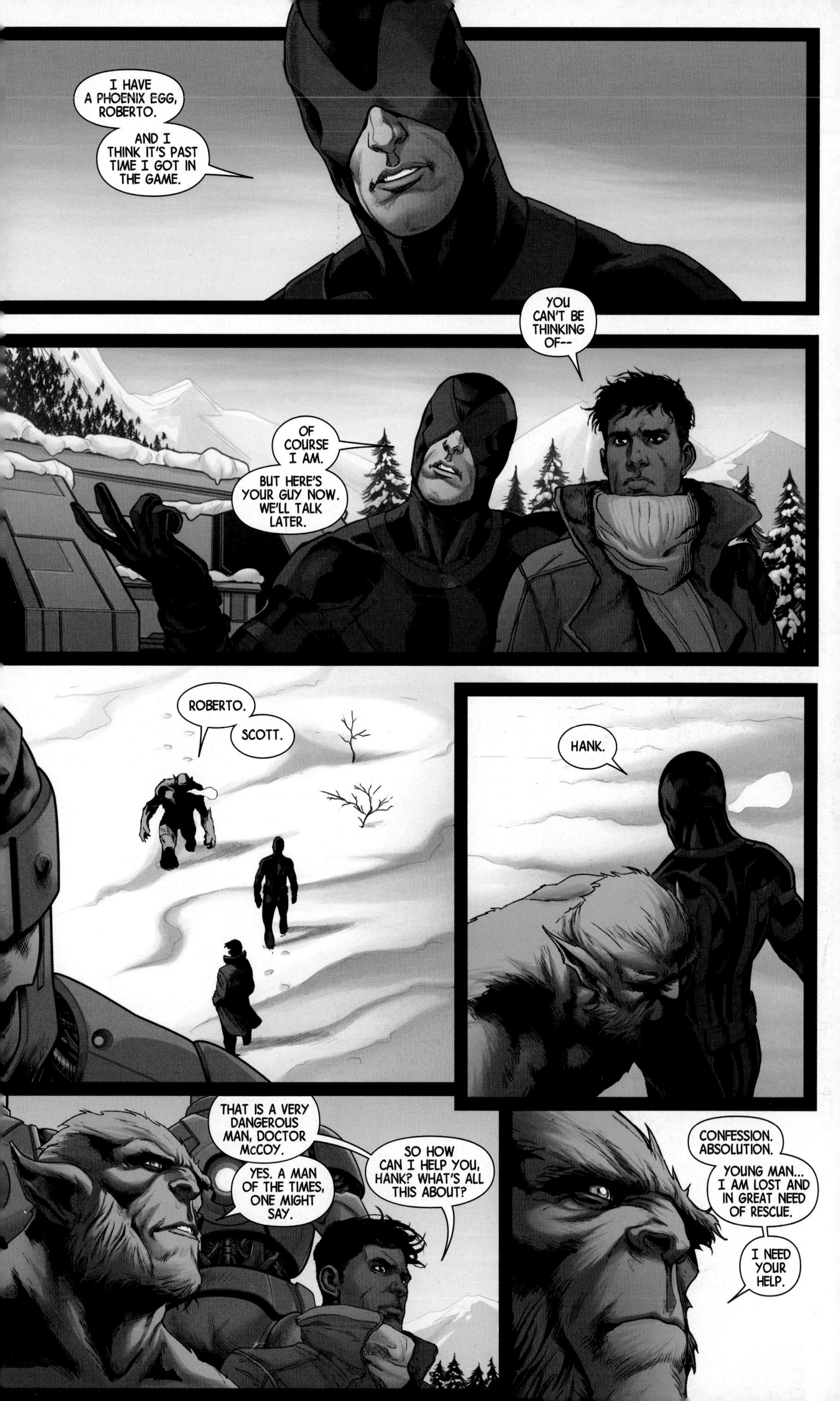
I HAVE A PHOENIX EGG, ROBERTO.
AND I THINK IT'S PAST TIME I GOT IN THE GAME.
YOU CAN'T BE THINKING OF--
OF COURSE I AM.
BUT HERE'S YOUR GUY NOW. WE'LL TALK LATER.
ROBERTO.
SCOTT.
HANK.
THAT IS A VERY DANGEROUS MAN, DOCTOR McCOY.
YES. A MAN OF THE TIMES, ONE MIGHT SAY.
SO HOW CAN I HELP YOU, HANK? WHAT'S ALL THIS ABOUT?
CONFESSION. ABSOLUTION.
YOUNG MAN... I AM LOST AND IN GREAT NEED OF RESCUE.
I NEED YOUR HELP.

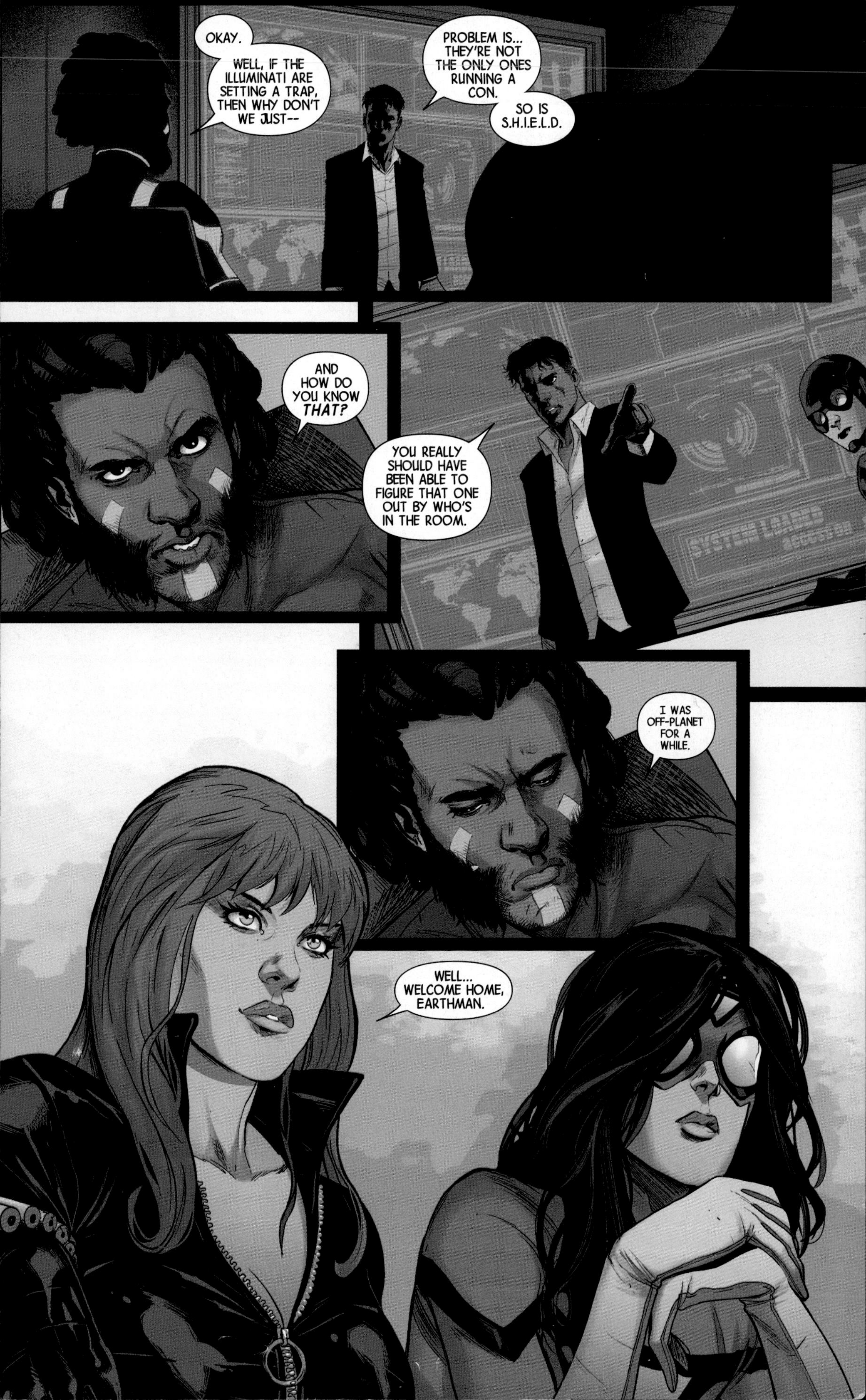
OKAY.
WELL, IF THE ILLUMINATI ARE SETTING A TRAP, THEN WHY DON'T WE JUST--
PROBLEM IS... THEY'RE NOT THE ONLY ONES RUNNING A CON.
SO IS S.H.I.E.L.D.
AND HOW DO YOU KNOW THAT?
YOU REALLY SHOULD HAVE BEEN ABLE TO FIGURE THAT ONE OUT BY WHO'S IN THE ROOM.
SYSTEM LOADED
I WAS OFF-PLANET FOR A WHILE.
WELL... WELCOME HOME, EARTHMAN.

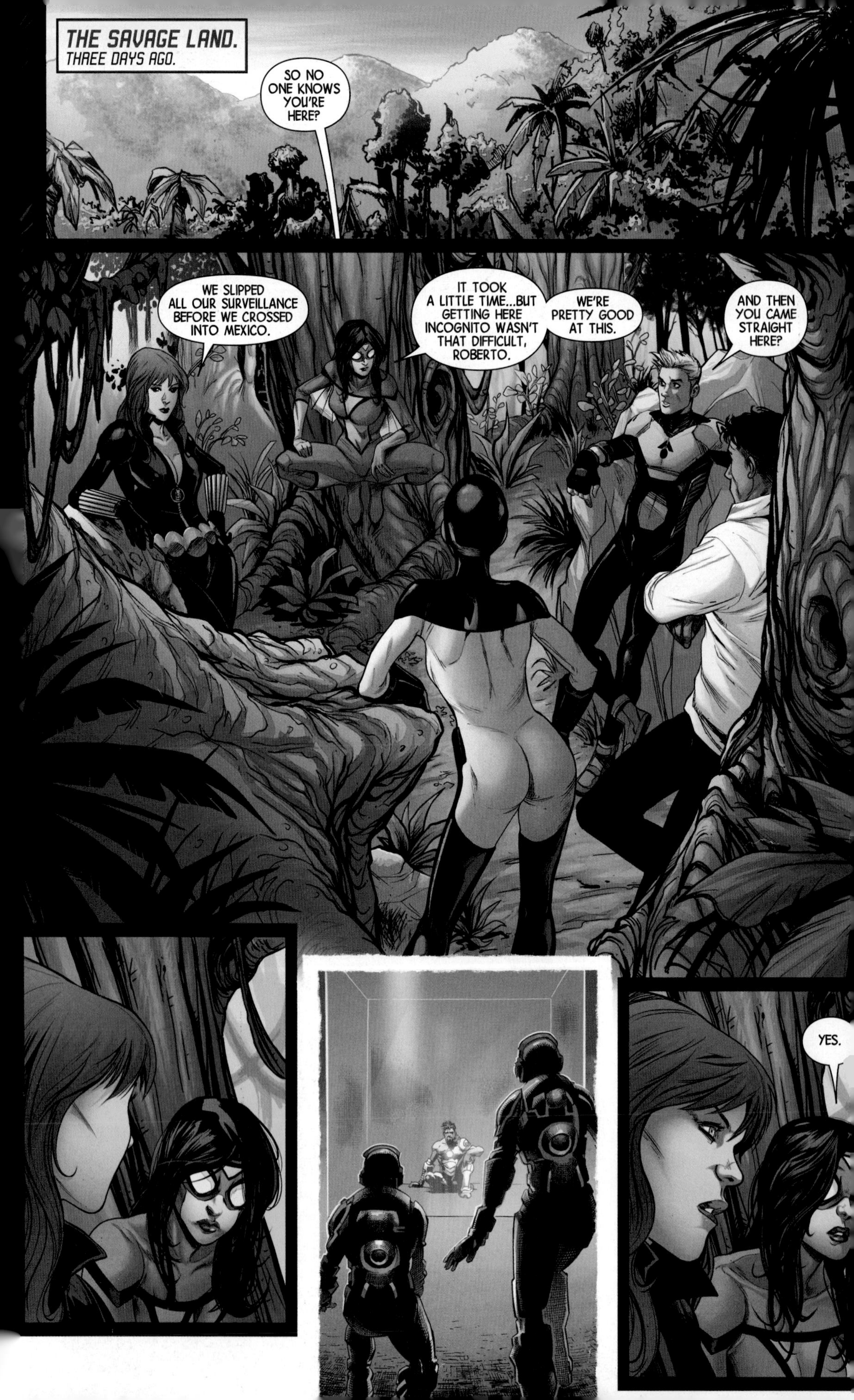
THE SAVAGE LAND.
THREE DAYS AGO.
SO NO ONE KNOWS YOU'RE HERE?
WE SLIPPED ALL OUR SURVEILLANCE BEFORE WE CROSSED INTO MEXICO.
IT TOOK A LITTLE TIME...BUT GETTING HERE INCOGNITO WASN'T THAT DIFFICULT, ROBERTO.
WE'RE PRETTY GOOD AT THIS.
AND THEN YOU CAME STRAIGHT HERE?
YES.

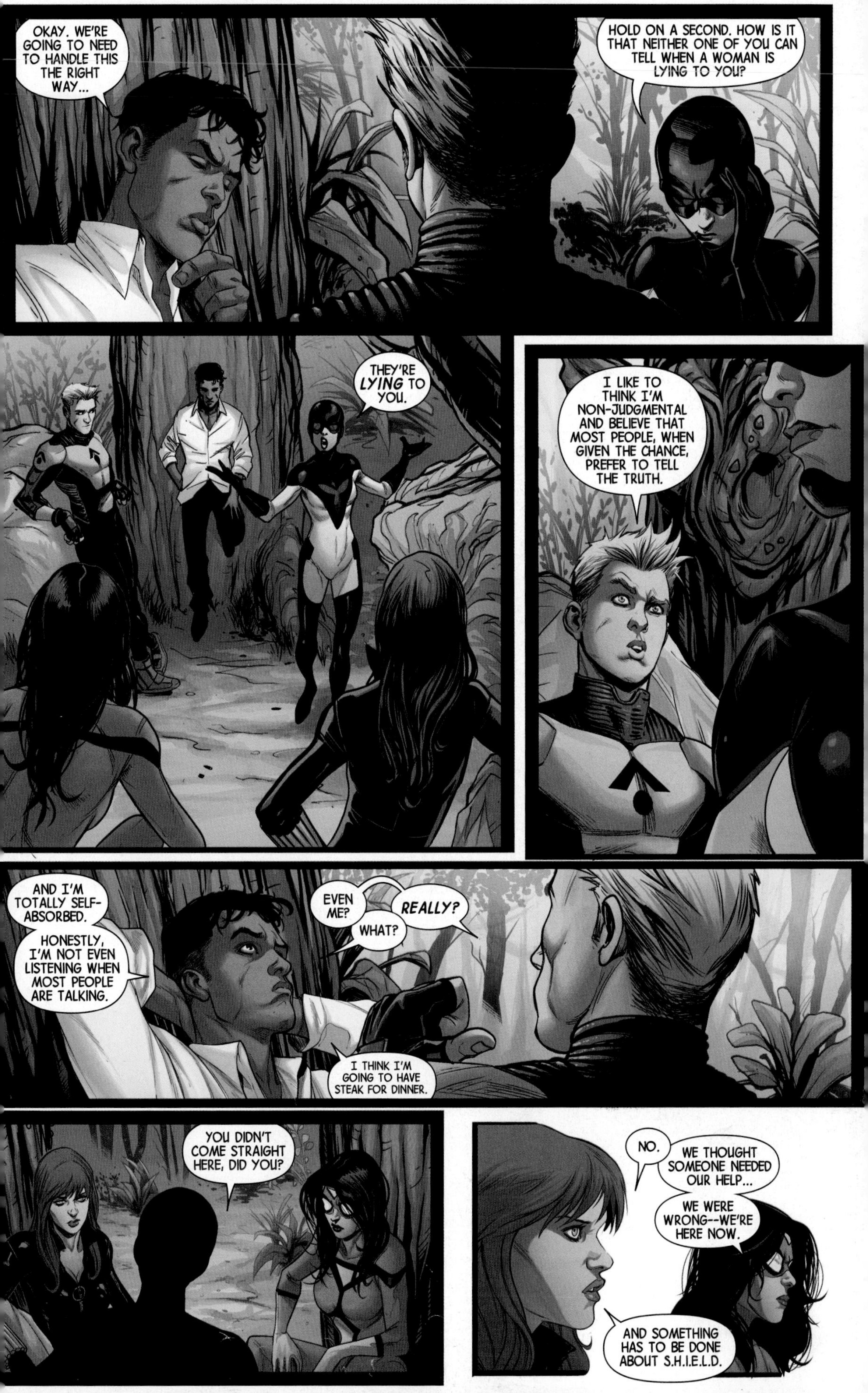

OKAY. WE'RE GOING TO NEED TO HANDLE THIS THE RIGHT WAY...
HOLD ON A SECOND. HOW IS IT THAT NEITHER ONE OF YOU CAN TELL WHEN A WOMAN IS LYING TO YOU?
THEY'RE *LYING* TO YOU.
I LIKE TO THINK I'M NON-JUDGMENTAL AND BELIEVE THAT MOST PEOPLE, WHEN GIVEN THE CHANCE, PREFER TO TELL THE TRUTH.
AND I'M TOTALLY SELF-ABSORBED.
HONESTLY, I'M NOT EVEN LISTENING WHEN MOST PEOPLE ARE TALKING.
EVEN ME?
WHAT?
REALLY?
I THINK I'M GOING TO HAVE STEAK FOR DINNER.
YOU DIDN'T COME STRAIGHT HERE, DID YOU?
NO.
WE THOUGHT SOMEONE NEEDED OUR HELP...
WE WERE WRONG--WE'RE HERE NOW.
AND SOMETHING HAS TO BE DONE ABOUT S.H.I.E.L.D.

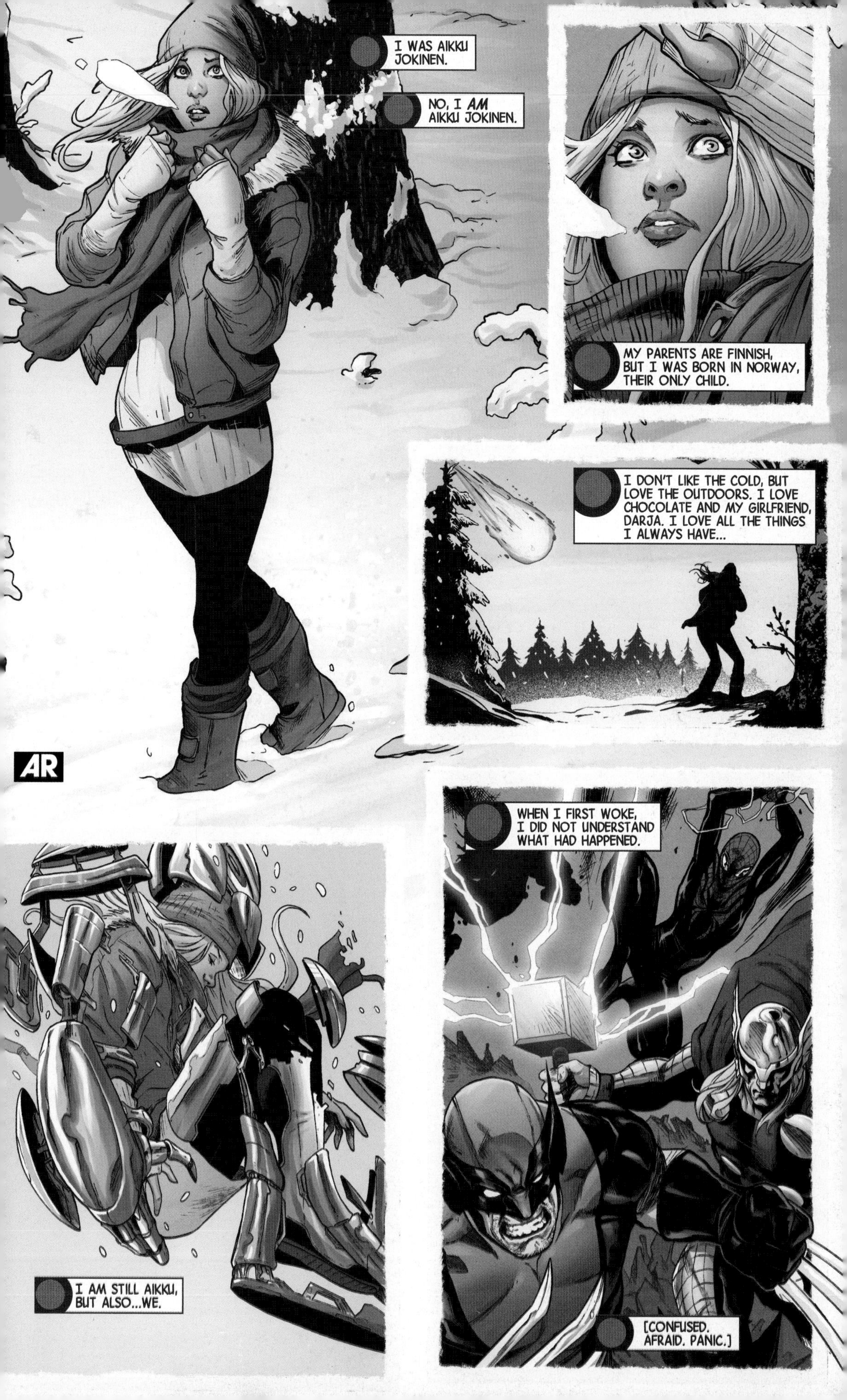
I WAS AIKKU JOKINEN.
NO, I AM AIKKU JOKINEN.
MY PARENTS ARE FINNISH, BUT I WAS BORN IN NORWAY, THEIR ONLY CHILD.
I DON'T LIKE THE COLD, BUT LOVE THE OUTDOORS. I LOVE CHOCOLATE AND MY GIRLFRIEND, DARJA. I LOVE ALL THE THINGS I ALWAYS HAVE...
I AM STILL AIKKU, BUT ALSO...WE.
WHEN I FIRST WOKE, I DID NOT UNDERSTAND WHAT HAD HAPPENED.
[CONFUSED. AFRAID. PANIC.]

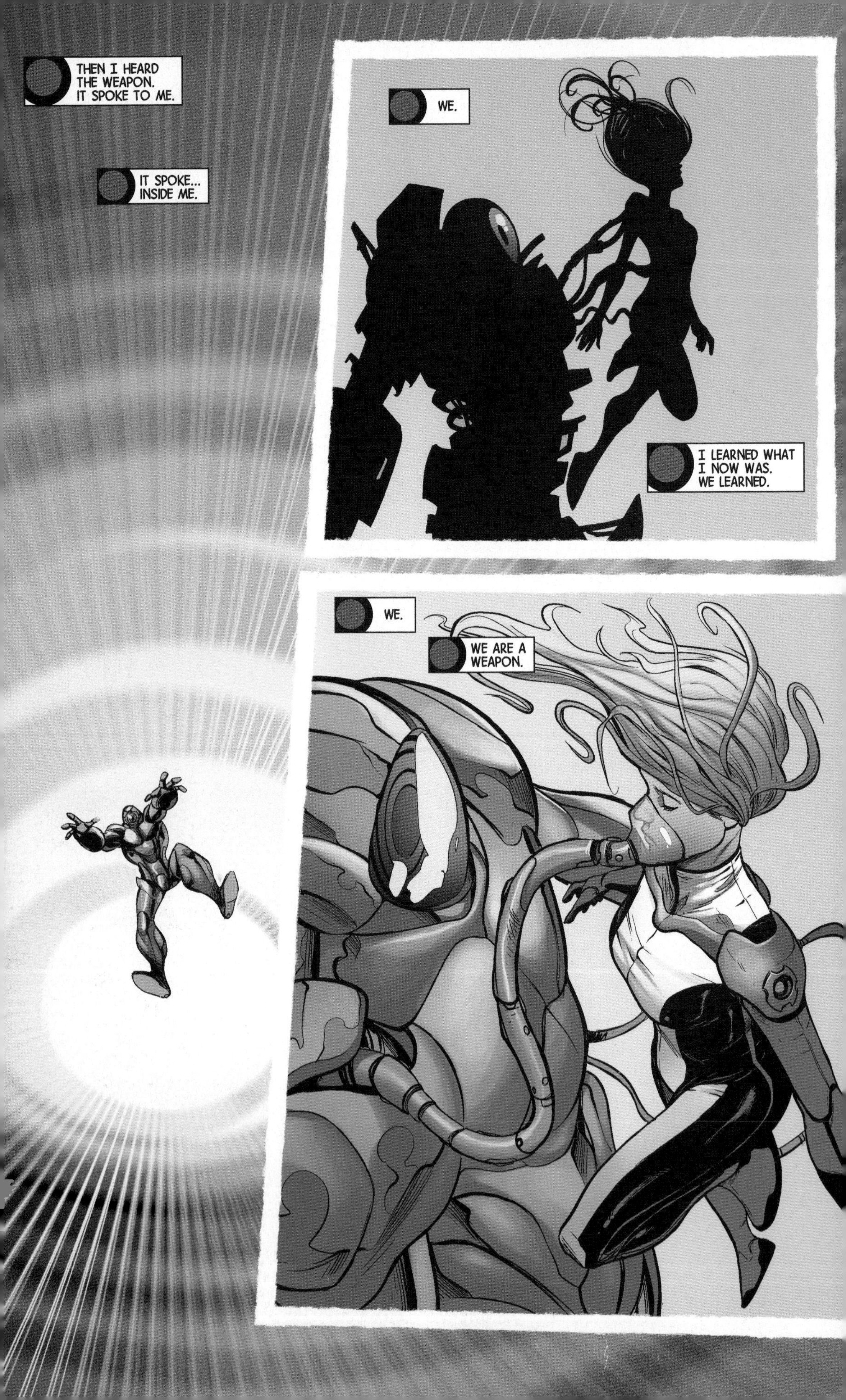
THEN I HEARD THE WEAPON. IT SPOKE TO ME.
IT SPOKE... INSIDE ME.
WE.
I LEARNED WHAT I NOW WAS. WE LEARNED.
WE.
WE ARE A WEAPON.

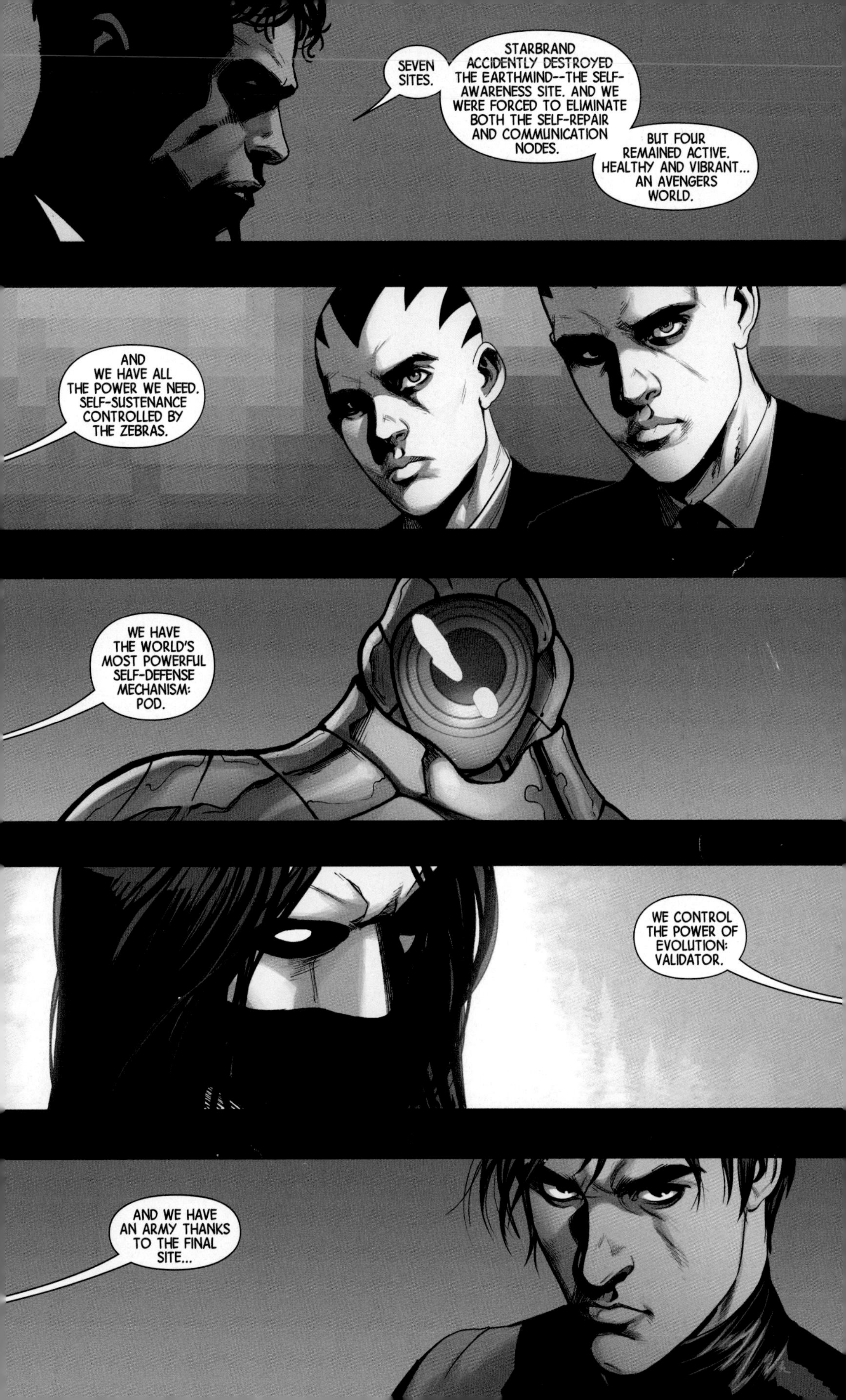
SEVEN SITES.
STARBRAND ACCIDENTLY DESTROYED THE EARTHMIND--THE SELF-AWARENESS SITE. AND WE WERE FORCED TO ELIMINATE BOTH THE SELF-REPAIR AND COMMUNICATION NODES.
BUT FOUR REMAINED ACTIVE. HEALTHY AND VIBRANT... AN AVENGERS WORLD.
AND WE HAVE ALL THE POWER WE NEED. SELF-SUSTENANCE CONTROLLED BY THE ZEBRAS.
WE HAVE THE WORLD'S MOST POWERFUL SELF-DEFENSE MECHANISM: POD.
WE CONTROL THE POWER OF EVOLUTION: VALIDATOR.
AND WE HAVE AN ARMY THANKS TO THE FINAL SITE...

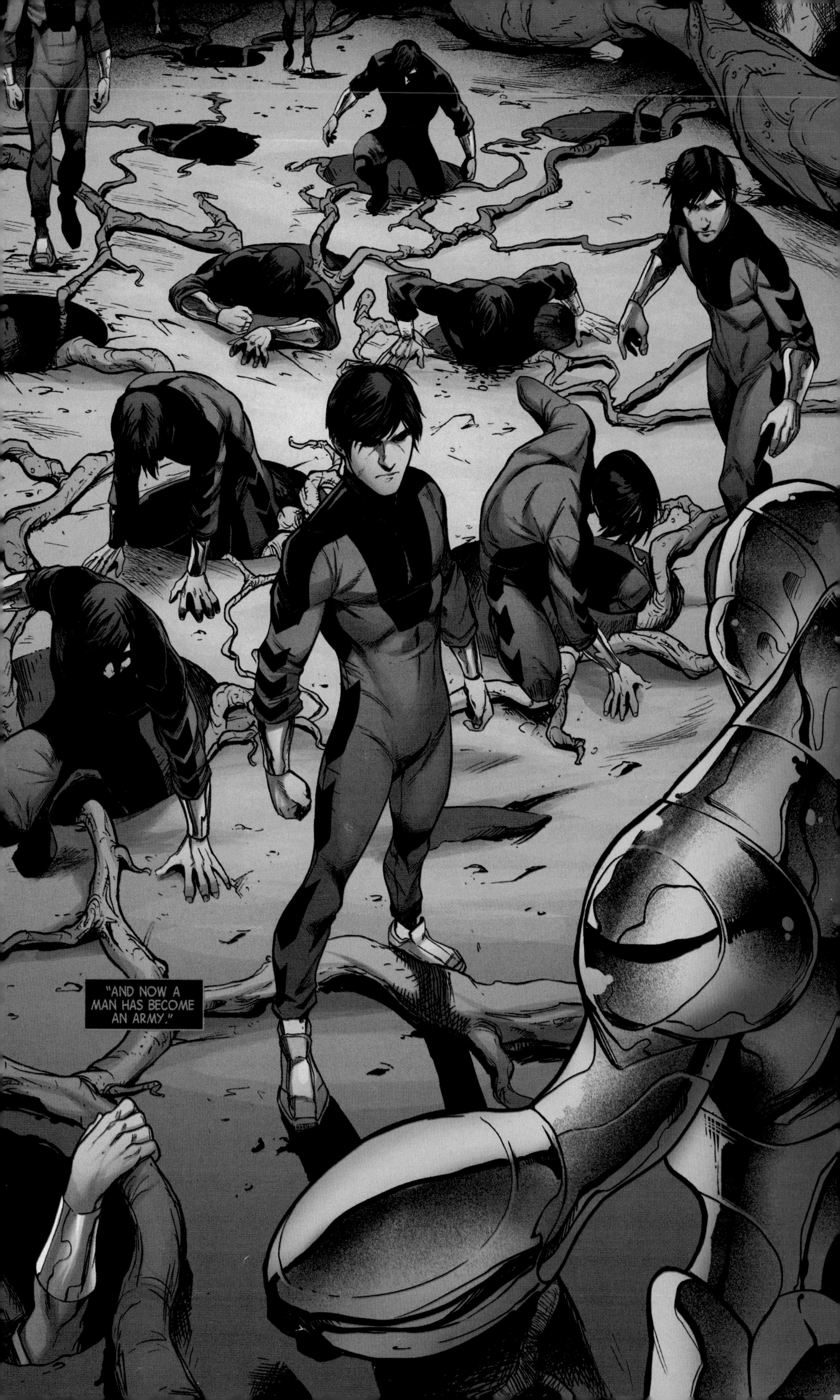
"AND NOW A MAN HAS BECOME AN ARMY."

"TRIAGE"

MULTIVERSAL AVENGERS

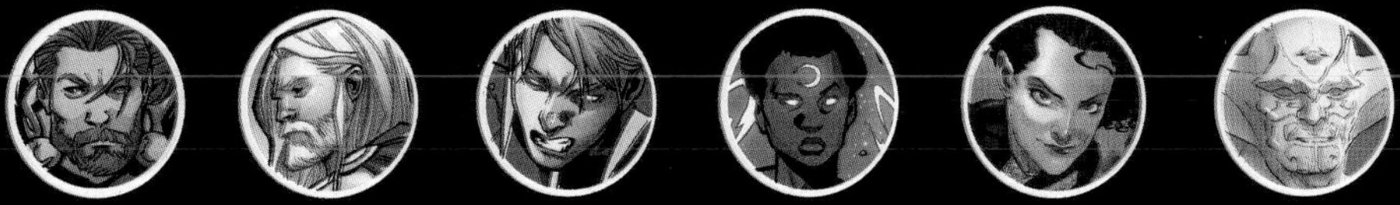

HYPERION · ODINSON · STARBRAND · NIGHTMASK · ABYSS · EX NIHILO

NEW AVENGERS

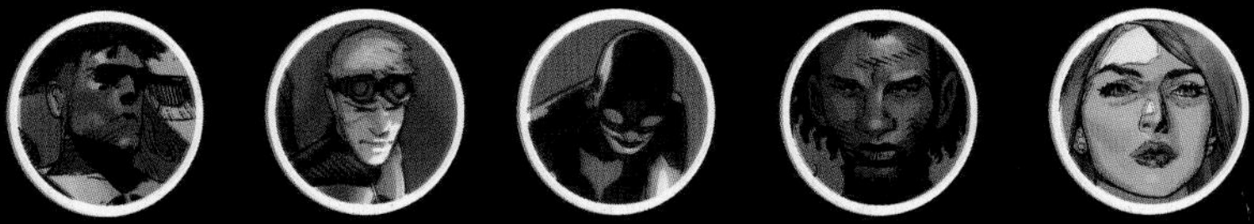

SUNSPOT · CANNONBALL · SMASHER · MANIFOLD · BLACK WIDOW

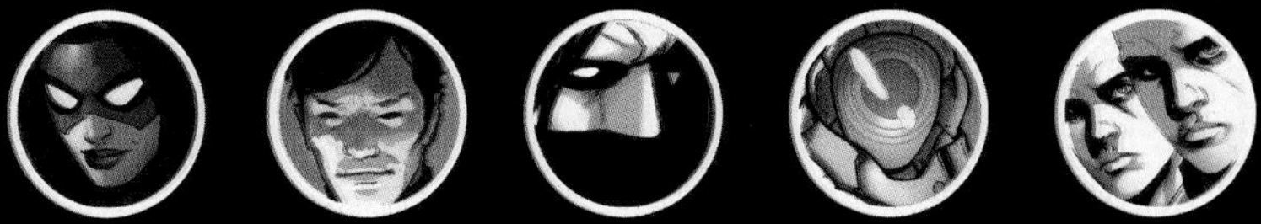

SPIDER-WOMAN · SHANG-CHI · VALIDATOR · POD · ZEBRA KIDS

S.H.I.E.L.D. AVENGERS

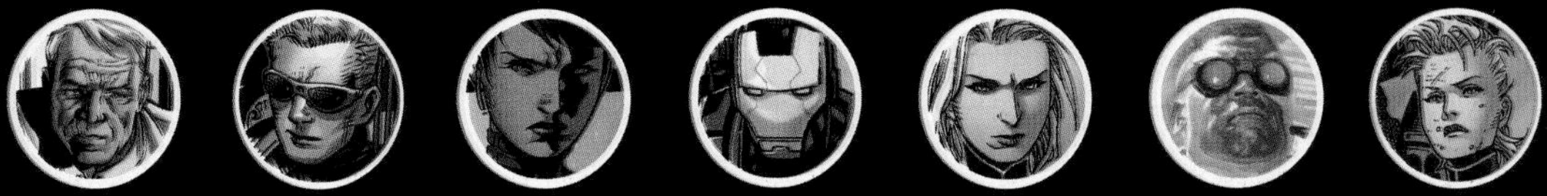

STEVE ROGERS · HAWKEYE · MARIA HILL · WAR MACHINE DRONES · INVISIBLE WOMAN · CAPTAIN AMERICA · CAPTAIN MARVEL

THE ILLUMINATI

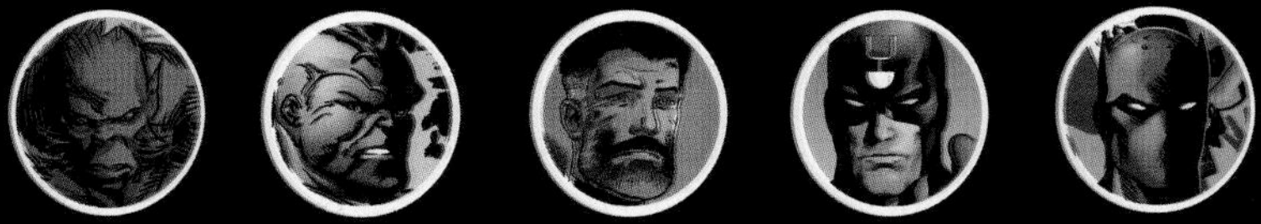

BEAST · HULK/ DOC GREEN · MISTER FANTASTIC · BLACK BOLT · BLACK PANTHER

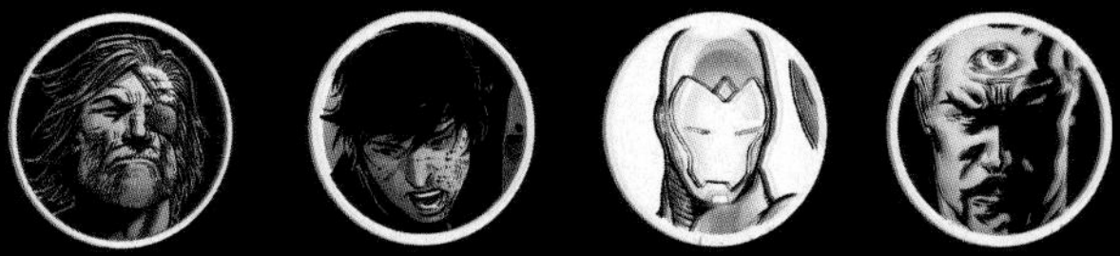

CAPTAIN BRITAIN · AMADEUS CHO · IRON MAN · DOCTOR STRANGE

THE CABAL

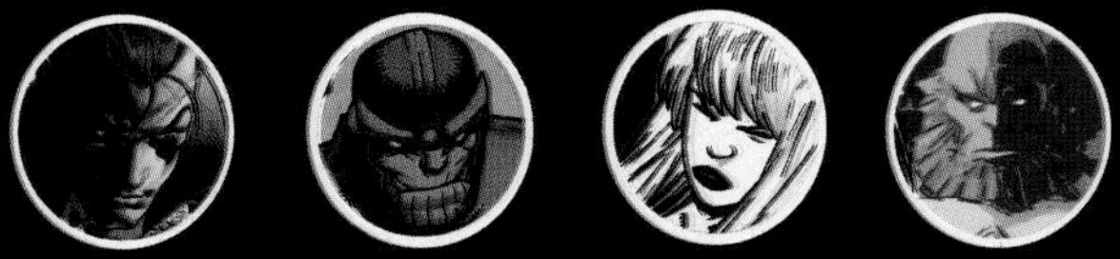

NAMOR · THANOS · BLACK SWAN · TERRAX

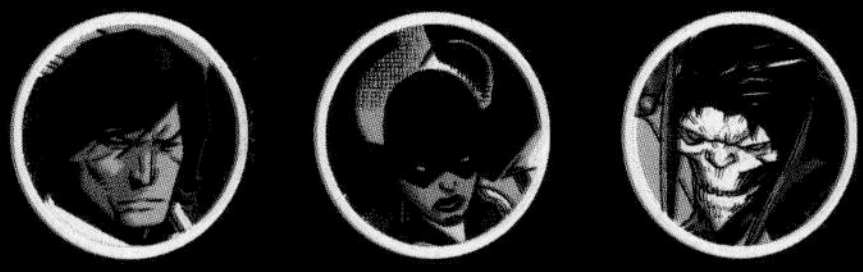

MAXIMUS · PROXIMA MIDNIGHT · CORVUS GLAIVE

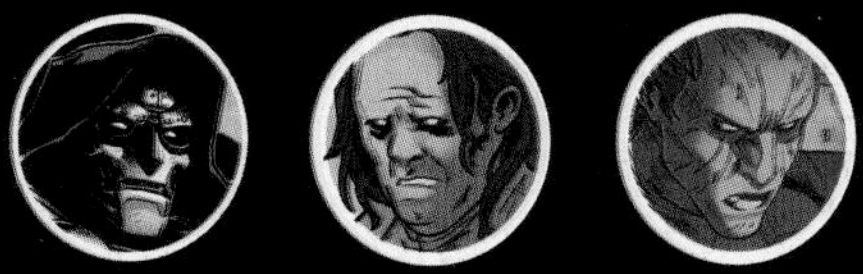

DOCTOR DOOM · THE MAD THINKER · MOLECULE MAN

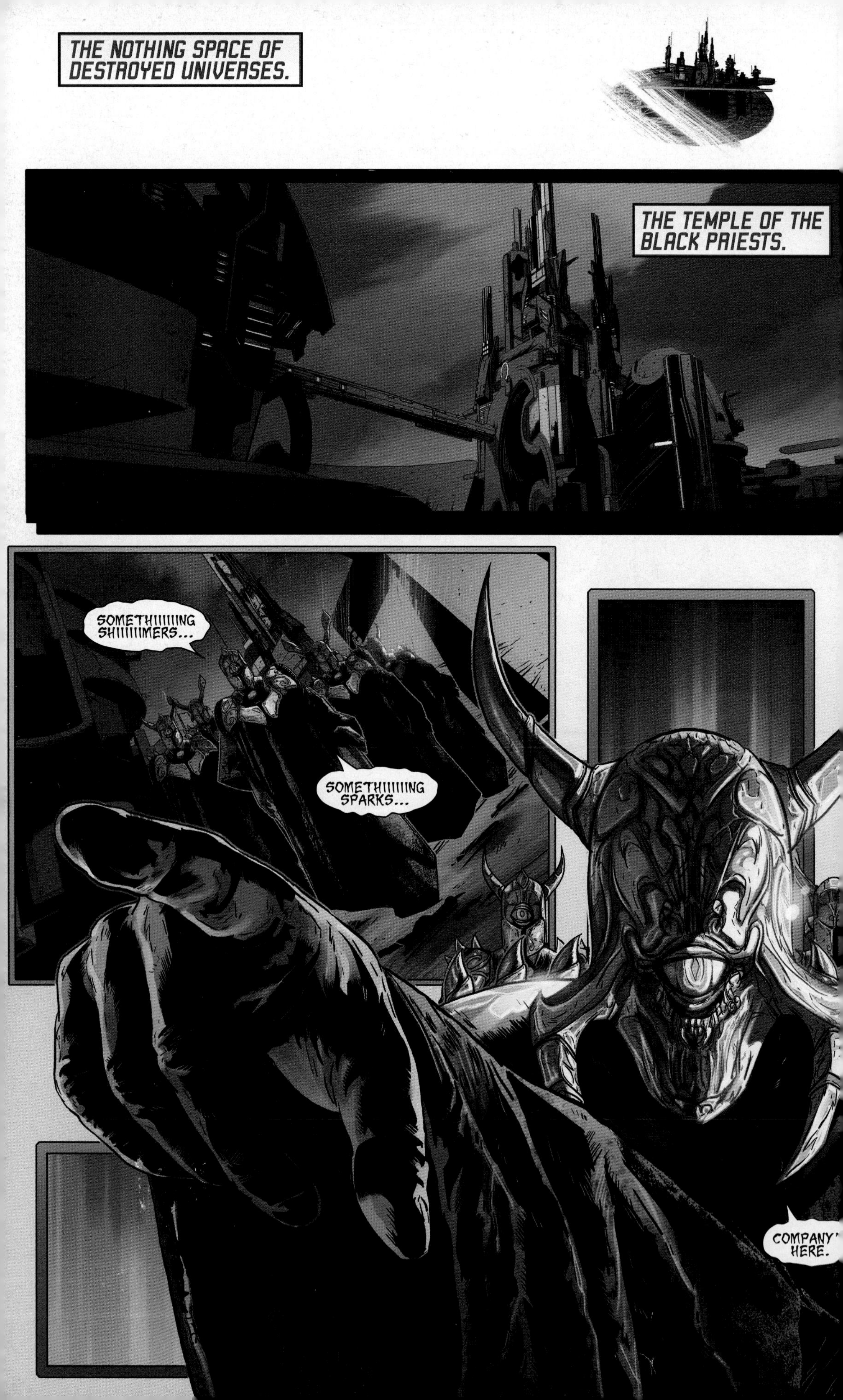
THE NOTHING SPACE OF DESTROYED UNIVERSES.
THE TEMPLE OF THE BLACK PRIESTS.
SOMETHIIIIIING SHIIIIIIMERS...
SOMETHIIIIIING SPARKS...
COMPANY' HERE.

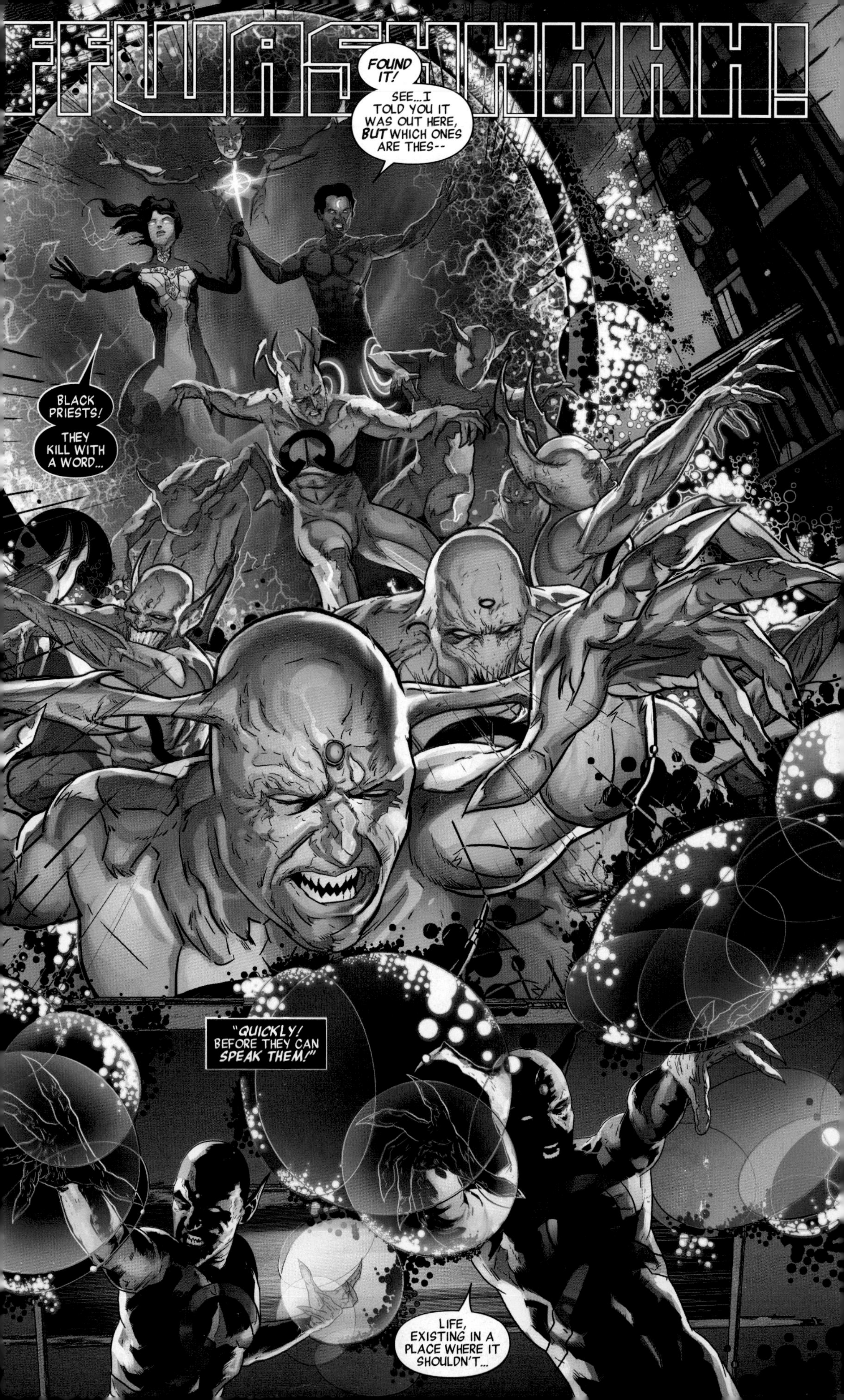
FFWASHHHHHH!
FOUND IT!
SEE...I TOLD YOU IT WAS OUT HERE, BUT WHICH ONES ARE THES--
BLACK PRIESTS!
THEY KILL WITH A WORD...
"QUICKLY! BEFORE THEY CAN SPEAK THEM!"
LIFE, EXISTING IN A PLACE WHERE IT SHOULDN'T...

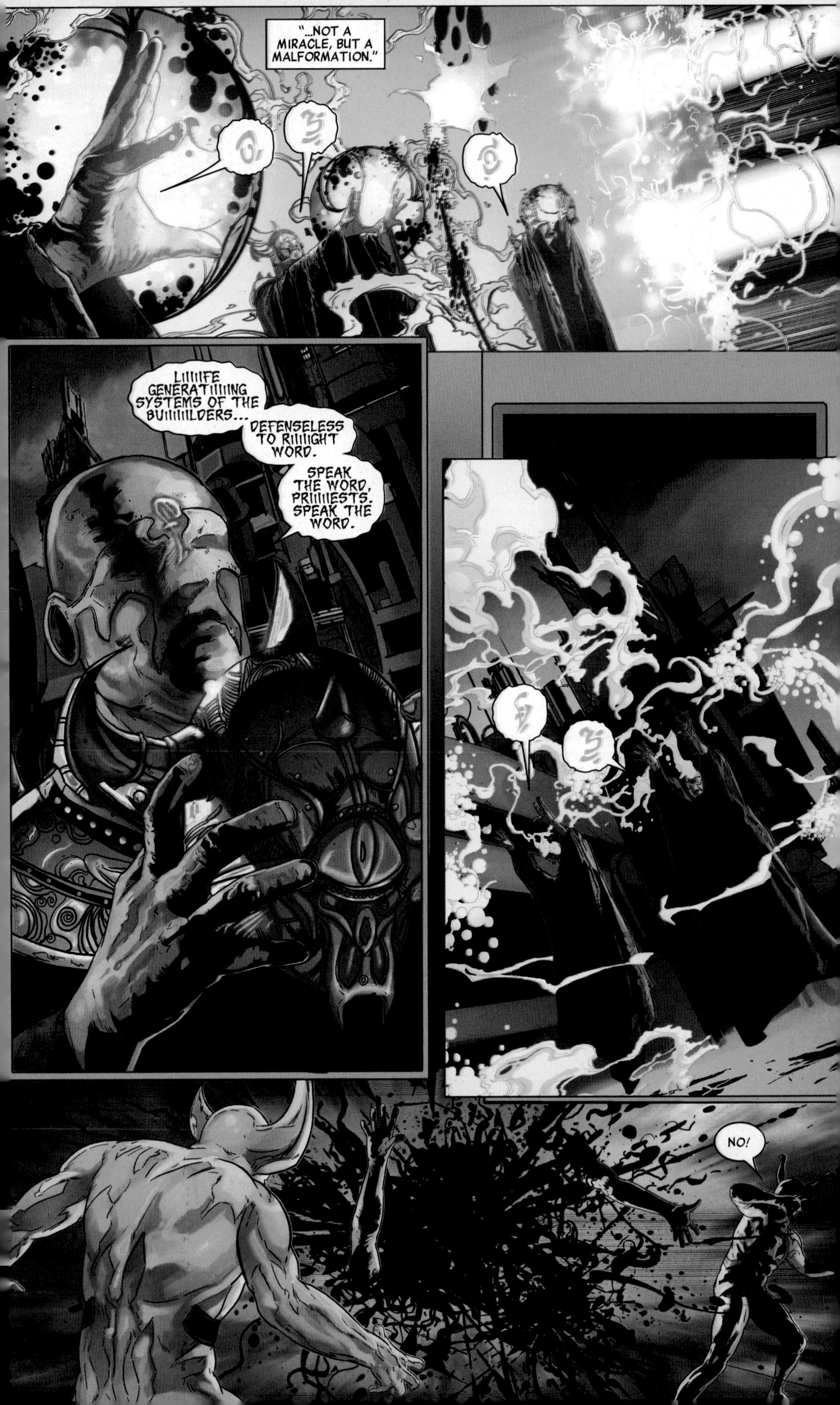
"...NOT A MIRACLE, BUT A MALFORMATION."
LIIIIIFE GENERATIIIIING SYSTEMS OF THE BUIIIIILDERS...
DEFENSELESS TO RIIIIGHT WORD.
SPEAK THE WORD, PRIIIIESTS. SPEAK THE WORD.
NO!

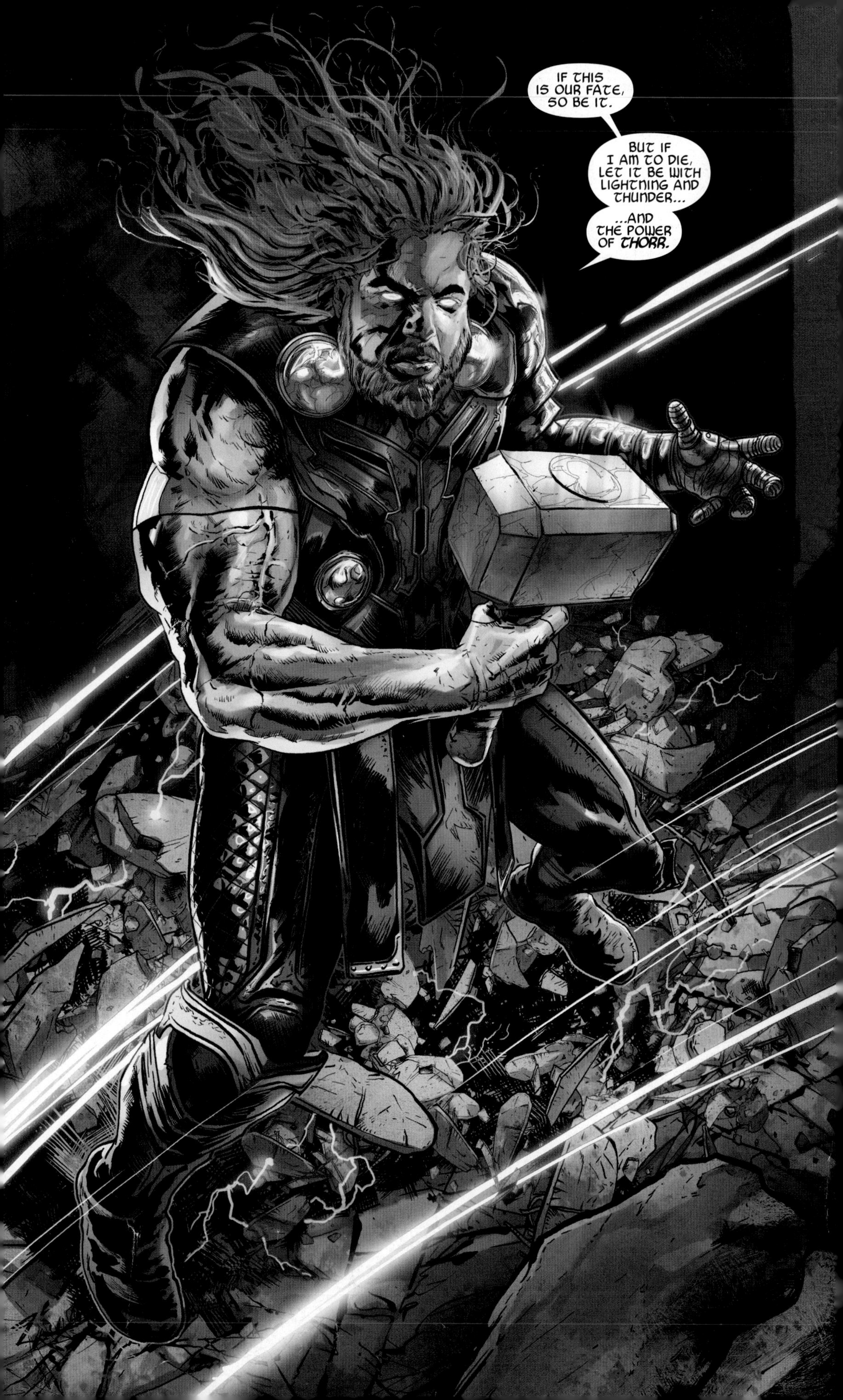
IF THIS IS OUR FATE, SO BE IT.
BUT IF I AM TO DIE, LET IT BE WITH LIGHTNING AND THUNDER...
...AND THE POWER OF THORR.

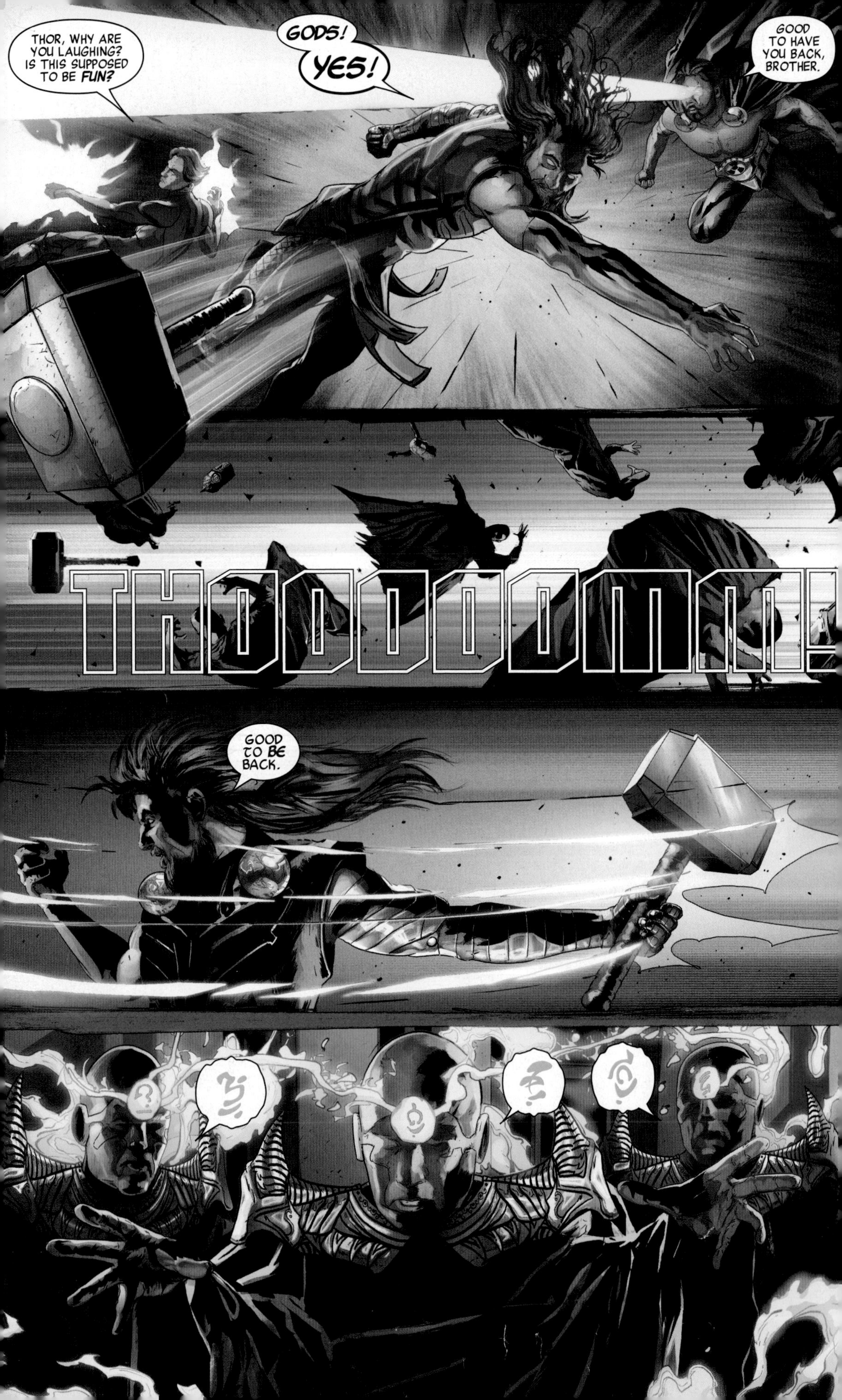
THOR, WHY ARE YOU LAUGHING? IS THIS SUPPOSED TO BE FUN?
GODS! YES!
GOOD TO HAVE YOU BACK, BROTHER.
THOOOOMM!
GOOD TO BE BACK.

I'M SURE YOU HAVE QUESTIONS, ODINSON, AS DO I...THE LEAST OF WHICH BEING WHAT HAPPENED TO YOUR ARM...

BUT DESPITE OUR QUICK RESOLUTION TO THE CONFLICT OUT THERE, THE PRIESTHOOD IS COLLECTIVELY CONCERNED ABOUT ONE EXCEEDINGLY IMPORTANT THING...

YES...

HOW DIIIID YOU FIIIIIND US OUT HERE IIIIIN THE NOTHIIIIING?

FLOATIIIING, CIIIIIRCLIIIING THE LOST SPACES?

WE DID. WELL...HE DID. TELL THEM, NIGHTMASK.

I WAS MADE TO NAVIGATE THE SUPERFLOW--THE SPACE BETWEEN UNIVERSES.

I MINE THE IDEAS THAT USED TO EXIST THERE. WITH THE DESTRUCTION OF ENTIRE UNIVERSES, THE WEB-LIKE FLOWSPACE CAME UNDONE...LIKE COLLAPSING LATTICEWORK WITHOUT A FRAME.

BUT MY ABILITY TO FIND THINGS IN THE SPACES IN BETWEEN--THE ABILITY TO MINE BROADCASTED IDEAS--STILL FUNCTIONS. WE KNEW THAT SOME OF THE BEINGS ASSOCIATED WITH THE DESTRUCTION OF EVERYTHING EXISTED HERE.

SO FINDING YOU WAS EASY ONCE I STARTED LOOKING.

HE HEARD US? WAS HE LIIIISTENIIIING CLOSELY? DIIIID HE HEAR OTHER THIIIIINGS?

DIIIID YOU HEAR THE OTHER VOIIIIIICES?

"YOU CAN'T WIN" PART I

THE ILLUMINATI

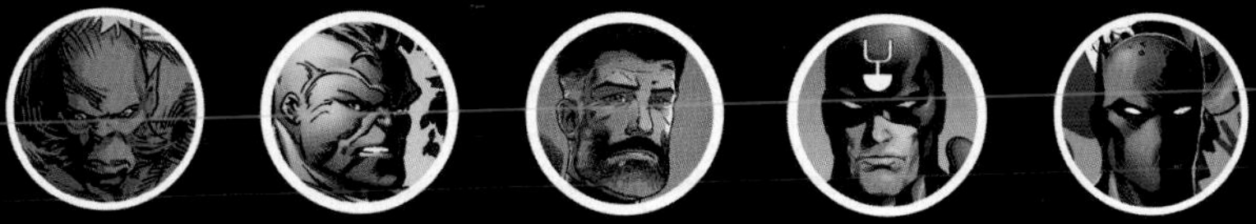

BEAST | HULK/ DOC GREEN | MISTER FANTASTIC | BLACK BOLT | BLACK PANTHER

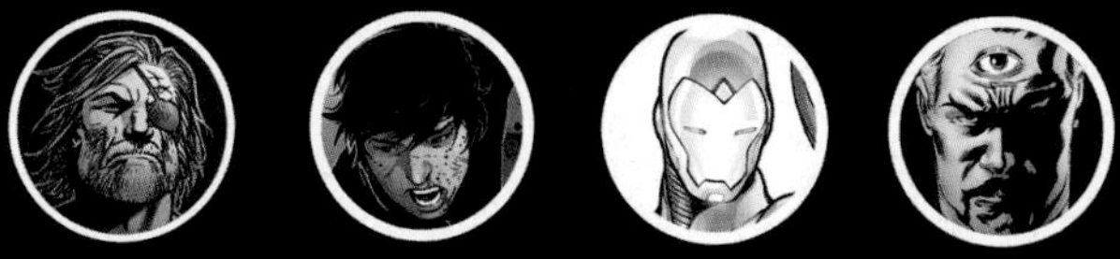

CAPTAIN BRITAIN | AMADEUS CHO | IRON MAN | DOCTOR STRANGE

S.H.I.E.L.D. AVENGERS

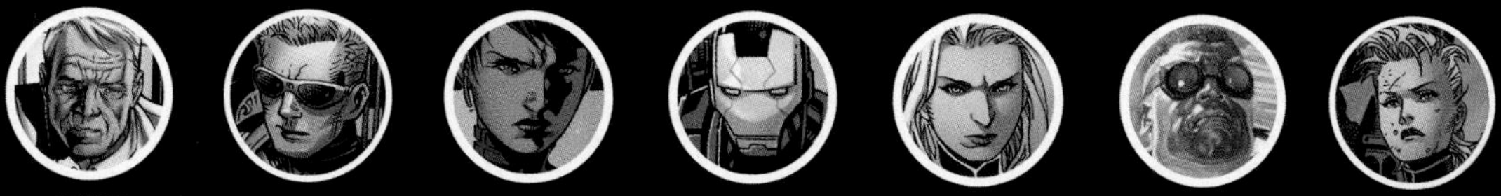

STEVE ROGERS | HAWKEYE | MARIA HILL | WAR MACHINE | INVISIBLE WOMAN | CAPTAIN AMERICA | CAPTAIN MARVEL

NEW AVENGERS

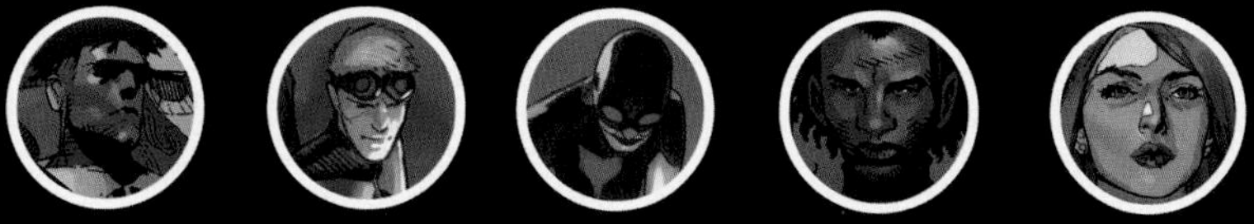

SUNSPOT | CANNONBALL | SMASHER | MANIFOLD | BLACK WIDOW

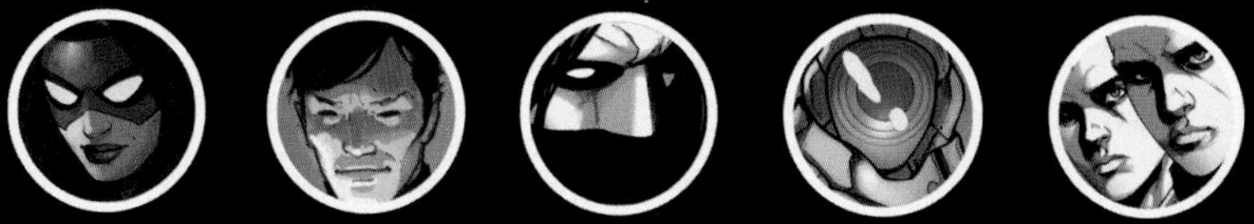

SPIDER-WOMAN | SHANG-CHI | VALIDATOR | POD | ZEBRA KIDS

MULTIVERSAL AVENGERS

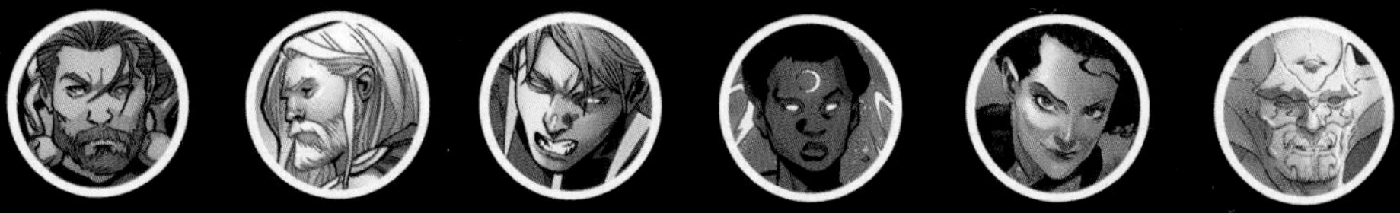

HYPERION | ODINSON | STARBRAND | NIGHTMASK | ABYSS | EX NIHILO

THE CABAL

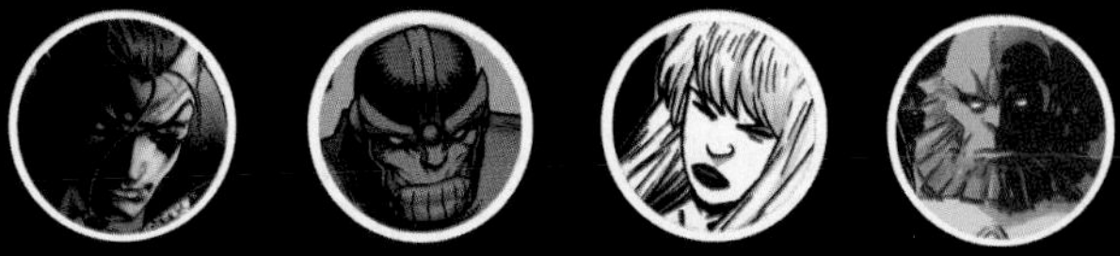

NAMOR | THANOS | BLACK SWAN | TERRAX

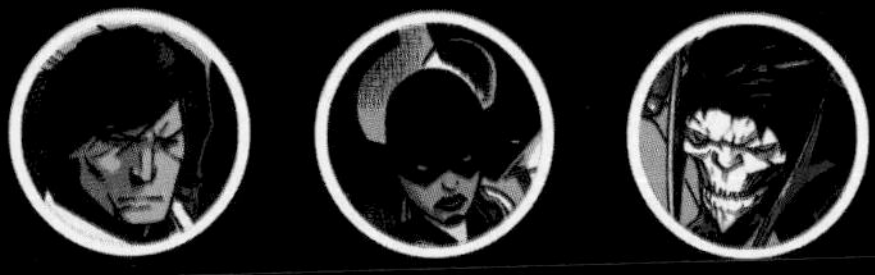

MAXIMUS | PROXIMA MIDNIGHT | CORVUS GLAIVE

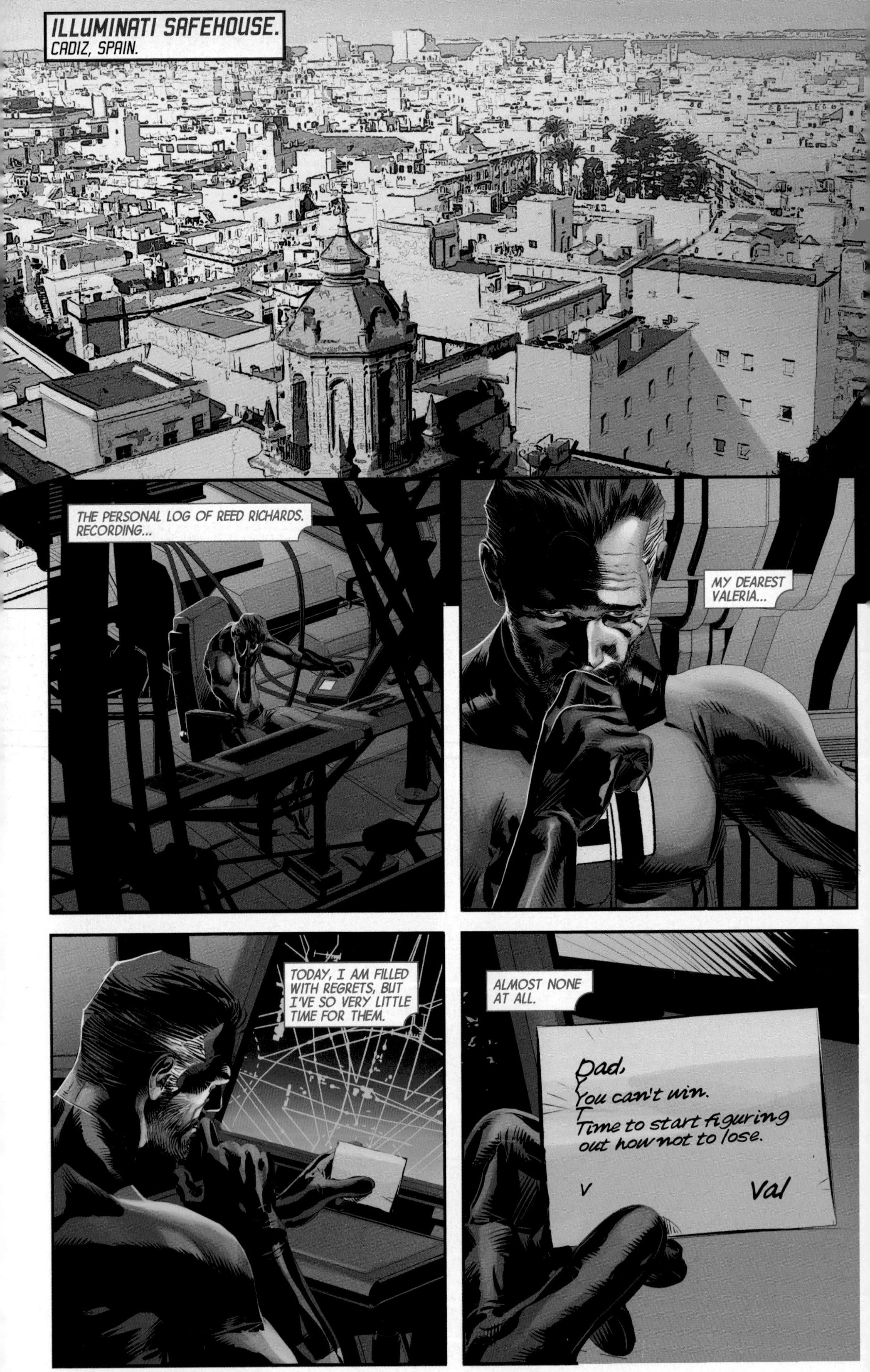
ILLUMINATI SAFEHOUSE.
CADIZ, SPAIN.
THE PERSONAL LOG OF REED RICHARDS. RECORDING...
MY DEAREST VALERIA...
TODAY, I AM FILLED WITH REGRETS, BUT I'VE SO VERY LITTLE TIME FOR THEM.
ALMOST NONE AT ALL.
Dad,
You can't win.
Time to start figuring out how not to lose.
V
Val

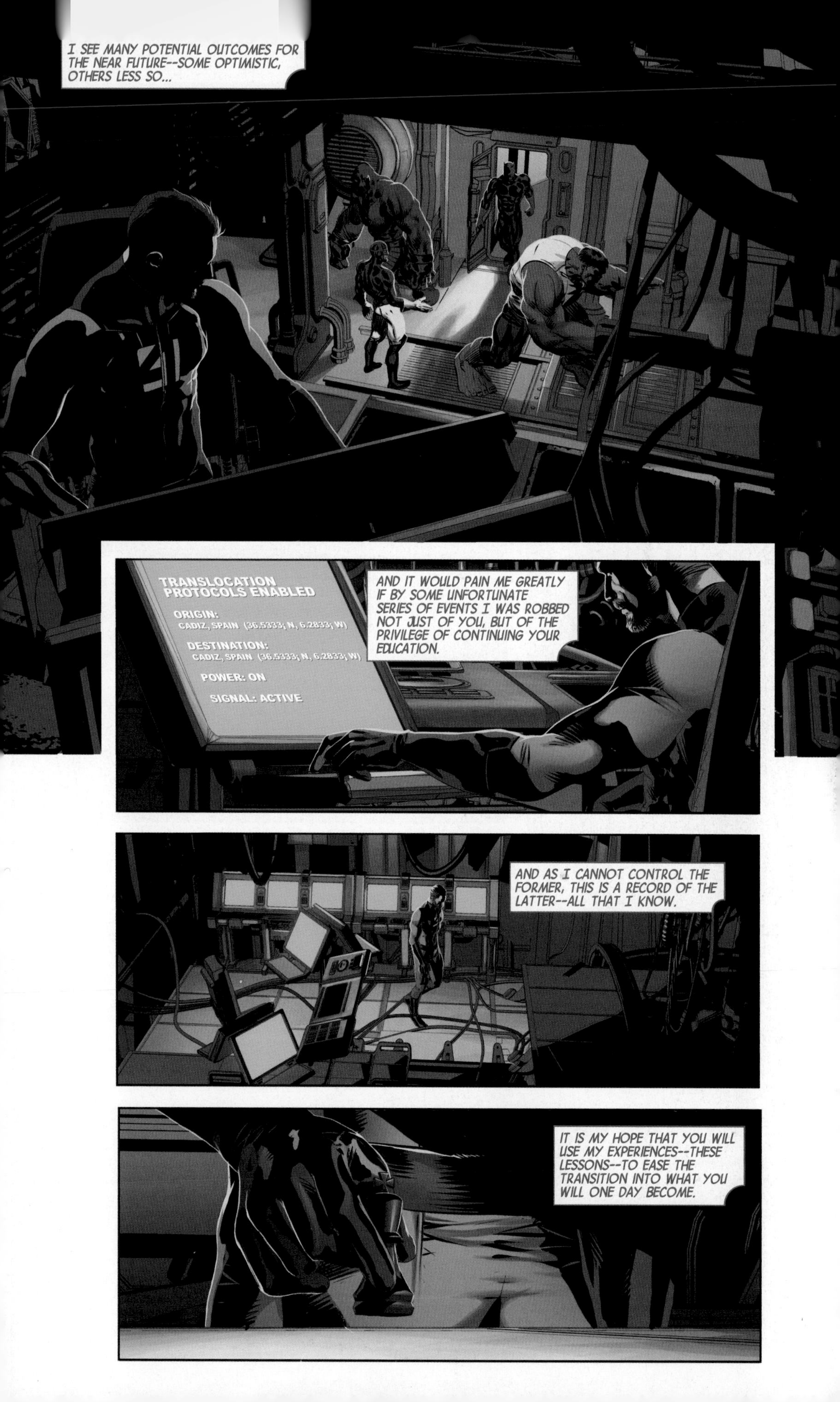
I SEE MANY POTENTIAL OUTCOMES FOR THE NEAR FUTURE--SOME OPTIMISTIC, OTHERS LESS SO...
TRANSLOCATION PROTOCOLS ENABLED
ORIGIN:
CADIZ, SPAIN (36.5333; N, 6.2833; W)
DESTINATION:
CADIZ, SPAIN (36.5333; N, 6.2833; W)
POWER: ON
SIGNAL: ACTIVE
AND IT WOULD PAIN ME GREATLY IF BY SOME UNFORTUNATE SERIES OF EVENTS I WAS ROBBED NOT JUST OF YOU, BUT OF THE PRIVILEGE OF CONTINUING YOUR EDUCATION.
AND AS I CANNOT CONTROL THE FORMER, THIS IS A RECORD OF THE LATTER--ALL THAT I KNOW.
IT IS MY HOPE THAT YOU WILL USE MY EXPERIENCES--THESE LESSONS--TO EASE THE TRANSITION INTO WHAT YOU WILL ONE DAY BECOME.

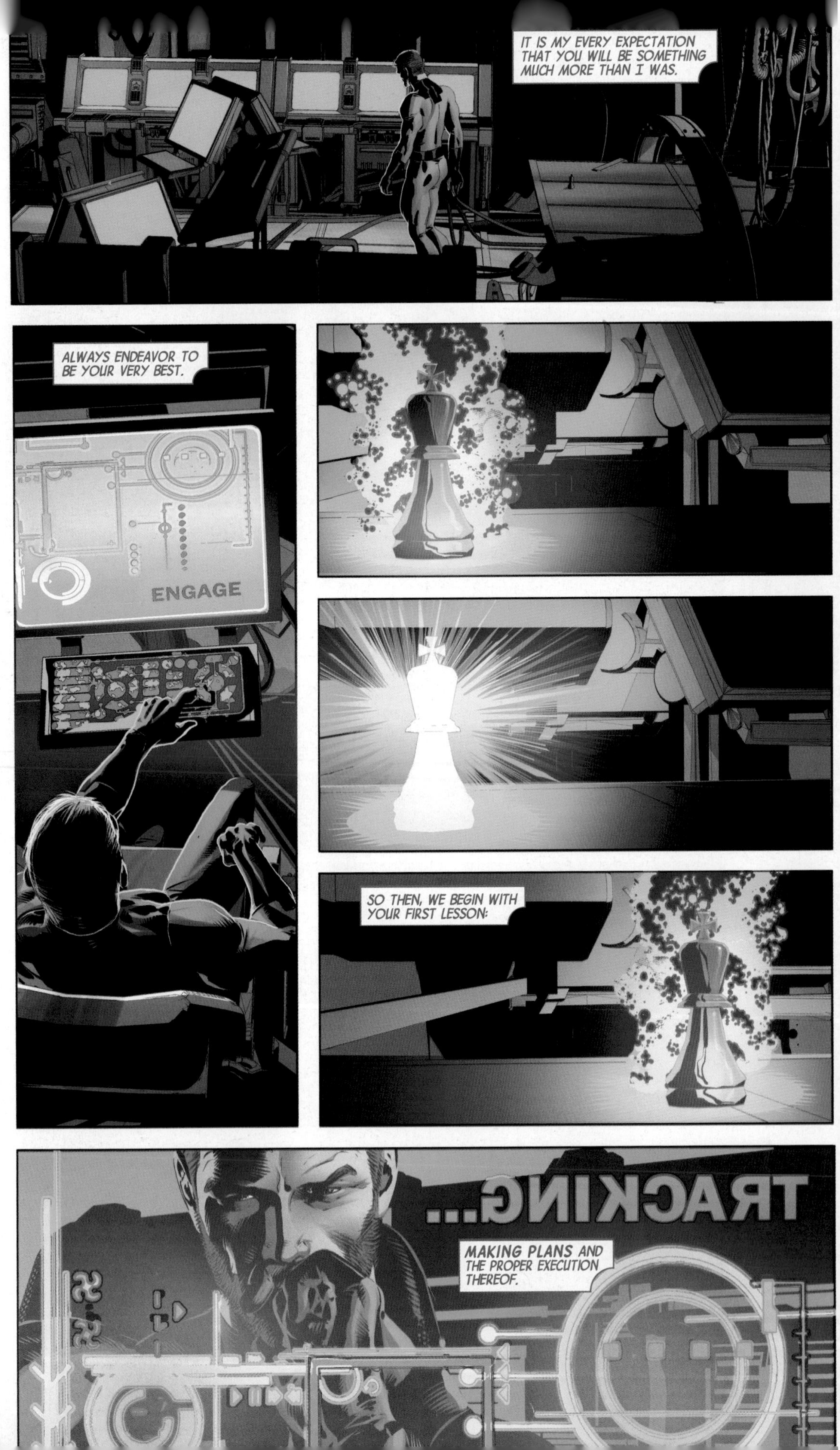
IT IS MY EVERY EXPECTATION THAT YOU WILL BE SOMETHING MUCH MORE THAN I WAS.
ALWAYS ENDEAVOR TO BE YOUR VERY BEST.
ENGAGE
SO THEN, WE BEGIN WITH YOUR FIRST LESSON:
TRACKING...
MAKING PLANS AND THE PROPER EXECUTION THEREOF.

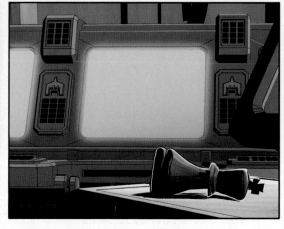

ETA: FOUR MINUTES.

THE DRONES WE LAUNCHED GOT THERE BEFORE A SECOND TRANSLOCATION SIGNAL WAS IDENTIFIED.

A GENERAL NULL FIELD HAS BEEN ERECTED, AND THE DRONES ARE PROGRAMED WITH DNA TRACKING--IF THE TARGETS MOVE, SO WILL THE FIELD.

THEY CAN FIGHT THEIR WAY OUT OF THERE... BUT NOT BEFORE WE ARRIVE.

DOESN'T TRACK...

THEY KNEW WE'D STILL BE IN THE VICINITY AFTER THEY JUMPED FROM ROME. NO WAY THEY'RE DUMB ENOUGH TO DO IT AGAIN SO SOON.

I THINK IT'S A TRAP.

WHAT ABOUT YOU, STEVE?

ME?

CLEVER BOYS BEING OH SO DAMN CLEVER...

I KNOW IT'S A TRAP.

ARCHANGEL WAR MACHINE OPS.

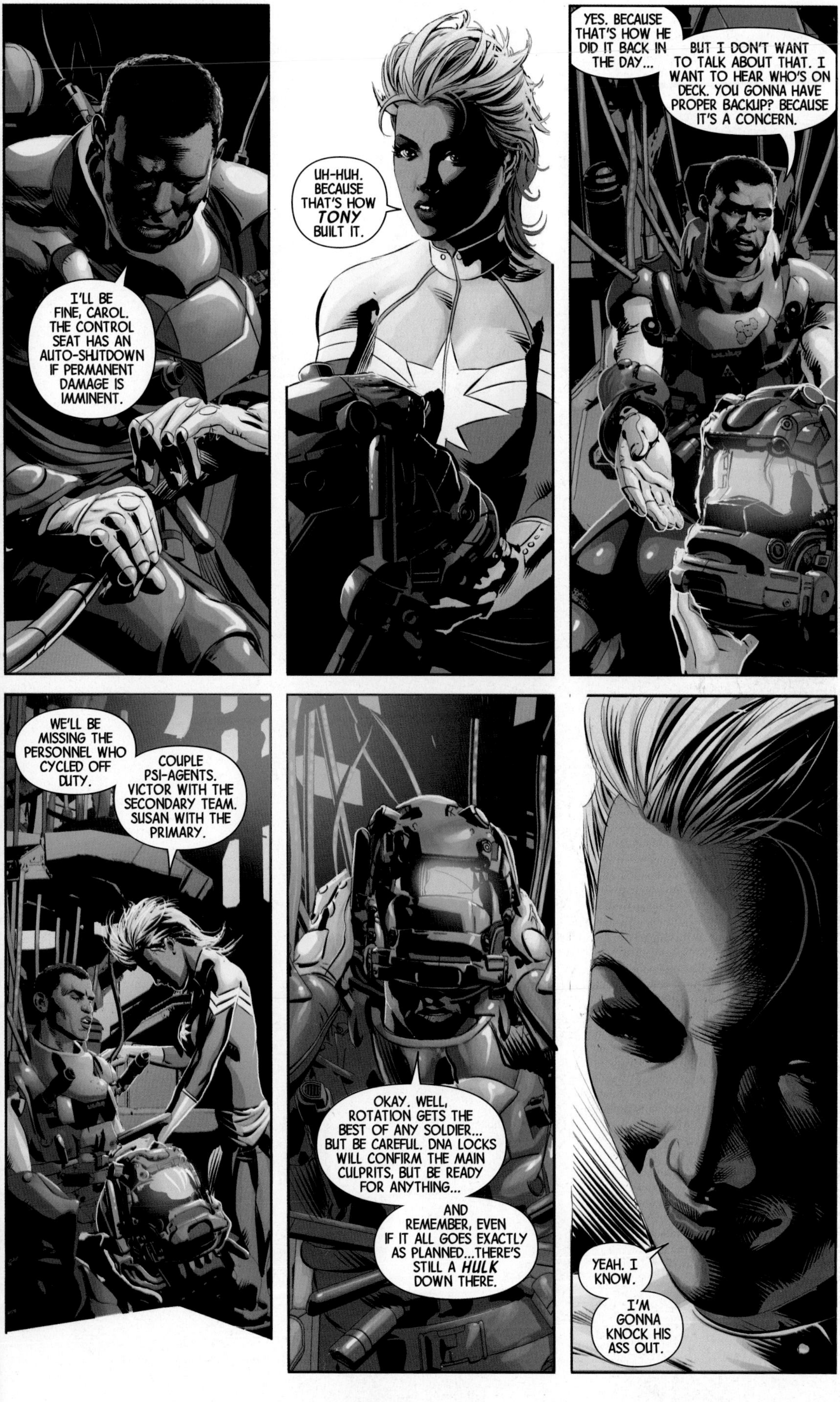

I'LL BE FINE, CAROL. THE CONTROL SEAT HAS AN AUTO-SHUTDOWN IF PERMANENT DAMAGE IS IMMINENT.
UH-HUH. BECAUSE THAT'S HOW TONY BUILT IT.
YES. BECAUSE THAT'S HOW HE DID IT BACK IN THE DAY...
BUT I DON'T WANT TO TALK ABOUT THAT. I WANT TO HEAR WHO'S ON DECK. YOU GONNA HAVE PROPER BACKUP? BECAUSE IT'S A CONCERN.
WE'LL BE MISSING THE PERSONNEL WHO CYCLED OFF DUTY.
COUPLE PSI-AGENTS. VICTOR WITH THE SECONDARY TEAM. SUSAN WITH THE PRIMARY.
OKAY. WELL, ROTATION GETS THE BEST OF ANY SOLDIER... BUT BE CAREFUL. DNA LOCKS WILL CONFIRM THE MAIN CULPRITS, BUT BE READY FOR ANYTHING...
AND REMEMBER, EVEN IF IT ALL GOES EXACTLY AS PLANNED...THERE'S STILL A HULK DOWN THERE.
YEAH. I KNOW.
I'M GONNA KNOCK HIS ASS OUT.

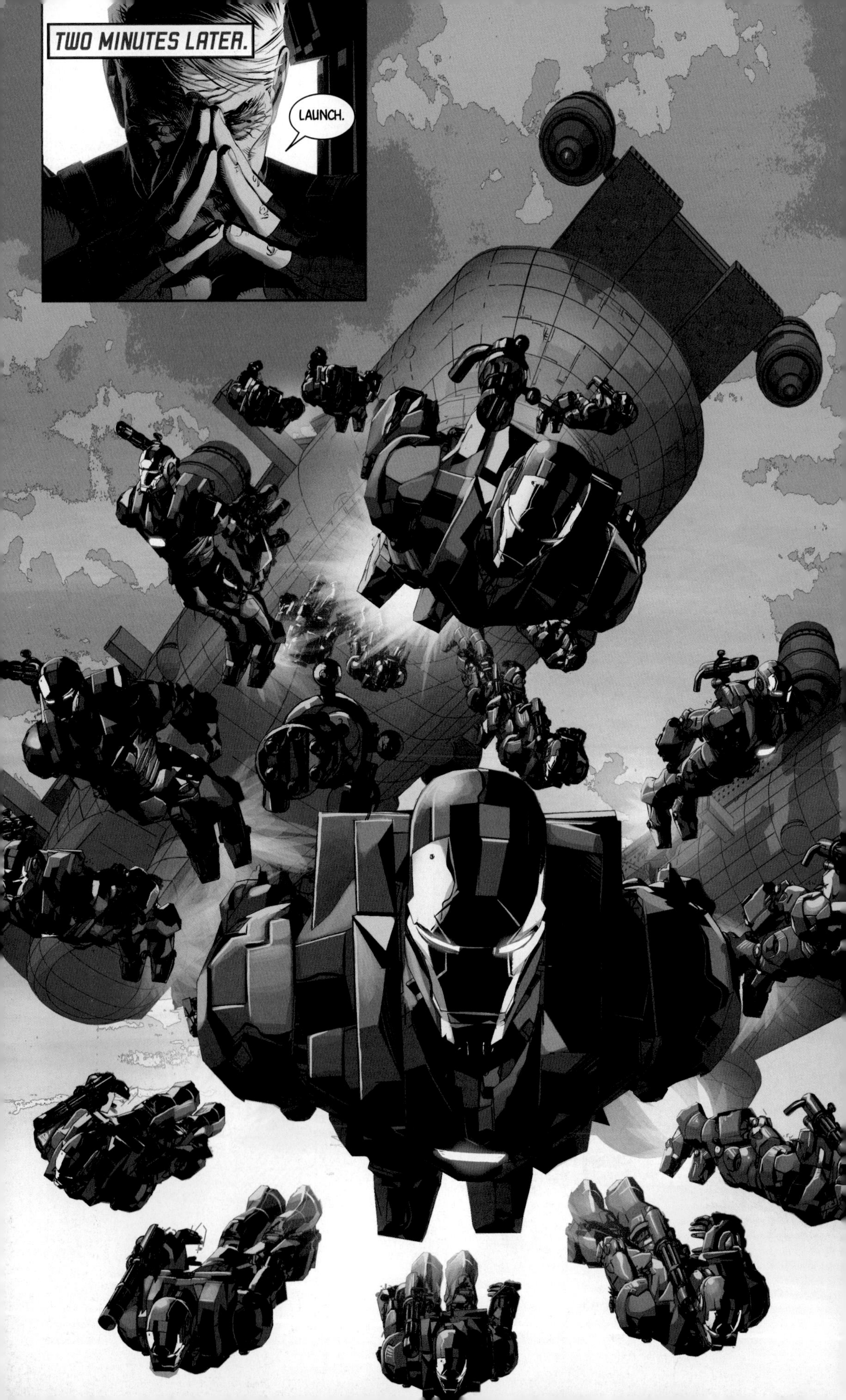
TWO MINUTES LATER.
LAUNCH.

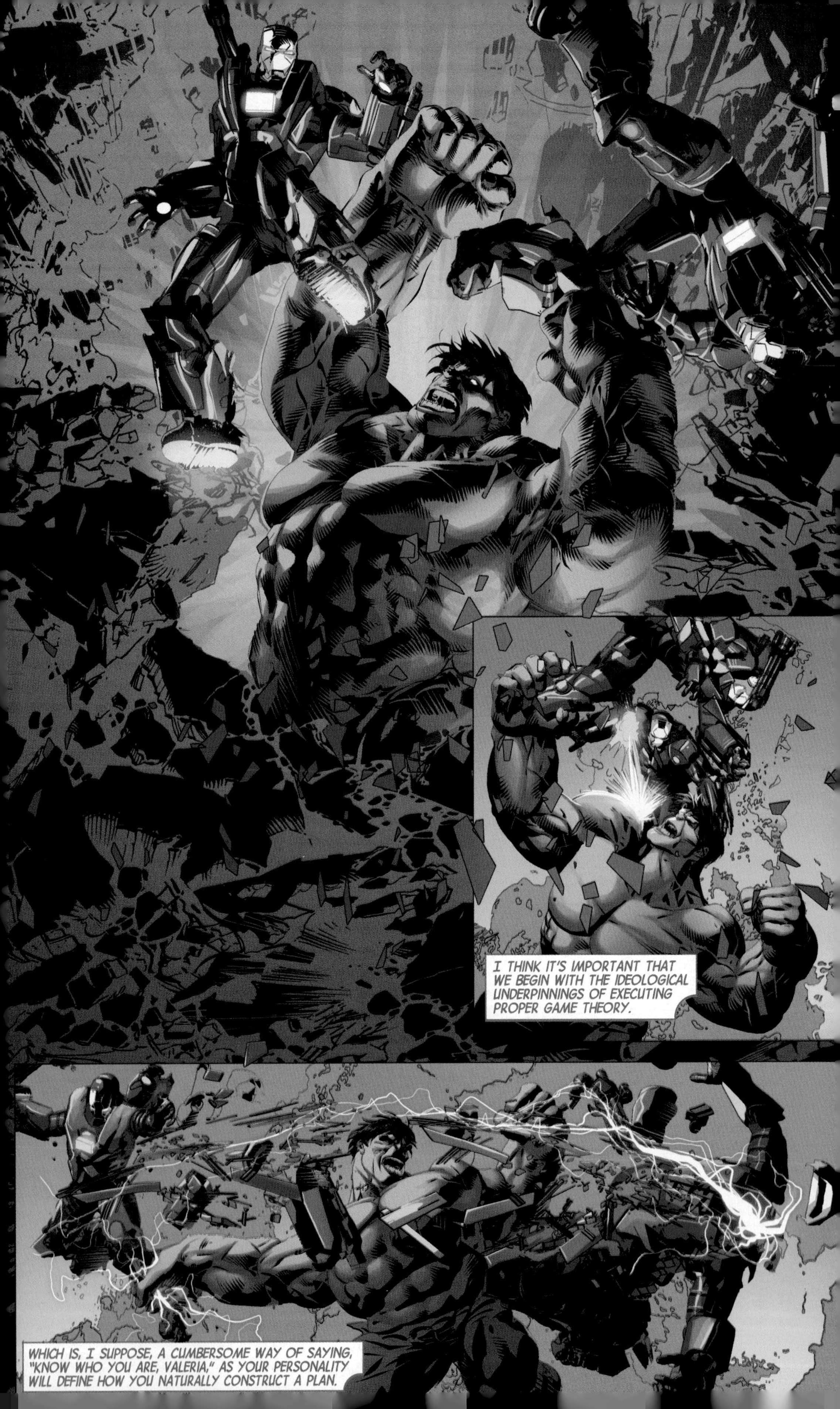

I THINK IT'S IMPORTANT THAT WE BEGIN WITH THE IDEOLOGICAL UNDERPINNINGS OF EXECUTING PROPER GAME THEORY.
WHICH IS, I SUPPOSE, A CUMBERSOME WAY OF SAYING, "KNOW WHO YOU ARE, VALERIA," AS YOUR PERSONALITY WILL DEFINE HOW YOU NATURALLY CONSTRUCT A PLAN.

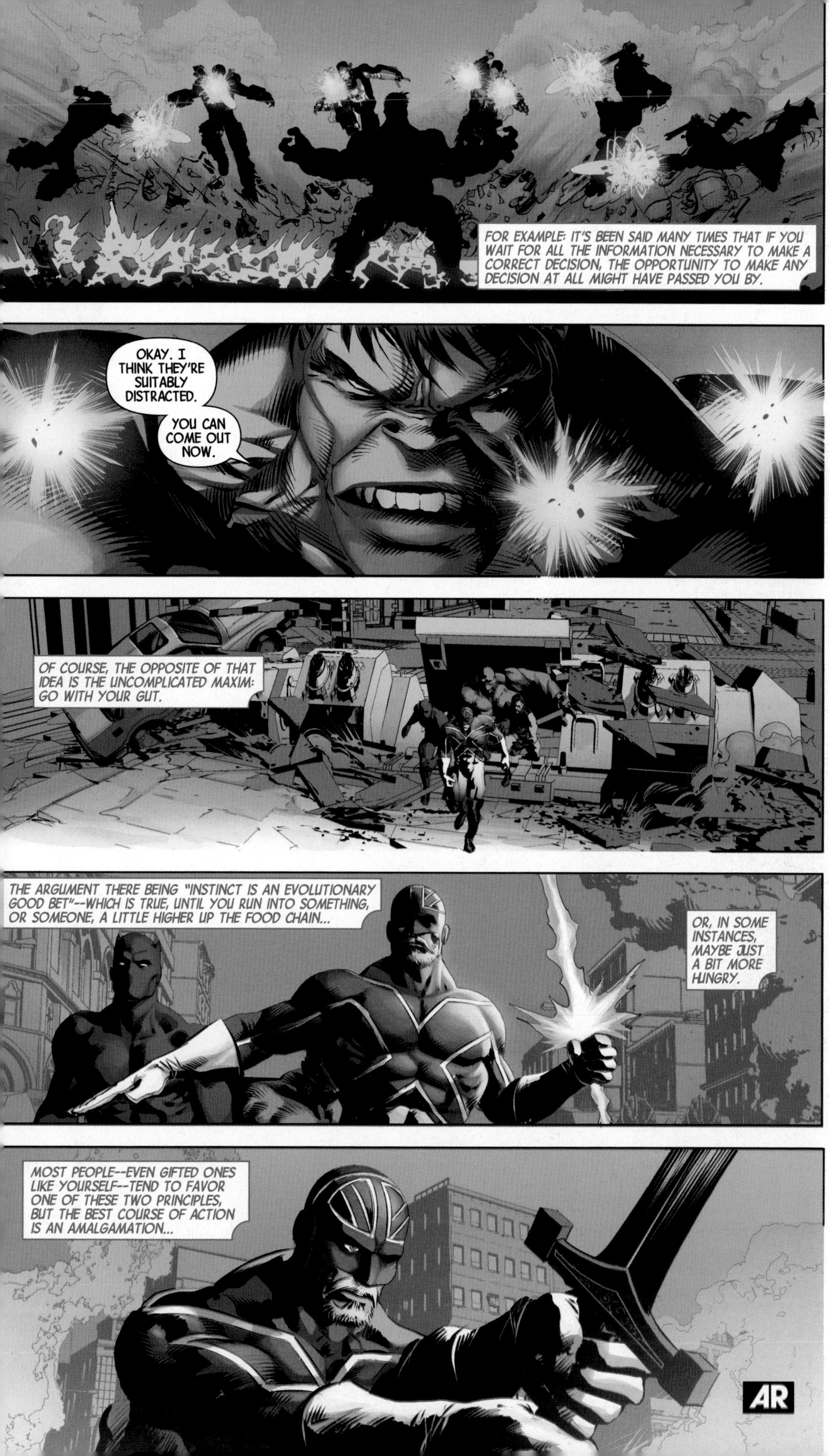
FOR EXAMPLE: IT'S BEEN SAID MANY TIMES THAT IF YOU WAIT FOR ALL THE INFORMATION NECESSARY TO MAKE A CORRECT DECISION, THE OPPORTUNITY TO MAKE ANY DECISION AT ALL MIGHT HAVE PASSED YOU BY.
OKAY. I THINK THEY'RE SUITABLY DISTRACTED.
YOU CAN COME OUT NOW.
OF COURSE, THE OPPOSITE OF THAT IDEA IS THE UNCOMPLICATED MAXIM: GO WITH YOUR GUT.
THE ARGUMENT THERE BEING "INSTINCT IS AN EVOLUTIONARY GOOD BET"--WHICH IS TRUE, UNTIL YOU RUN INTO SOMETHING, OR SOMEONE, A LITTLE HIGHER UP THE FOOD CHAIN...
OR, IN SOME INSTANCES, MAYBE JUST A BIT MORE HUNGRY.
MOST PEOPLE--EVEN GIFTED ONES LIKE YOURSELF--TEND TO FAVOR ONE OF THESE TWO PRINCIPLES, BUT THE BEST COURSE OF ACTION IS AN AMALGAMATION...
AR

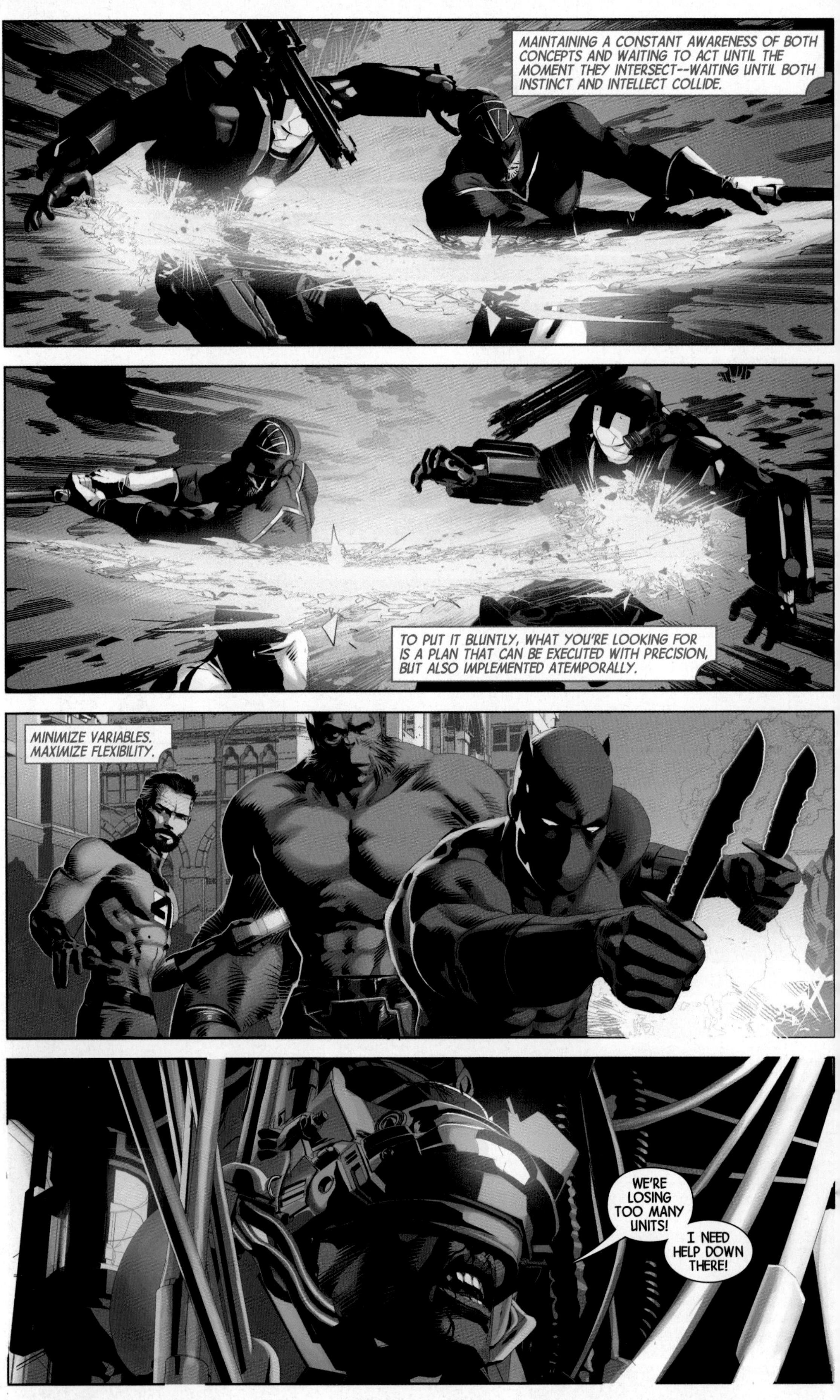
MAINTAINING A CONSTANT AWARENESS OF BOTH CONCEPTS AND WAITING TO ACT UNTIL THE MOMENT THEY INTERSECT--WAITING UNTIL BOTH INSTINCT AND INTELLECT COLLIDE.
TO PUT IT BLUNTLY, WHAT YOU'RE LOOKING FOR IS A PLAN THAT CAN BE EXECUTED WITH PRECISION, BUT ALSO IMPLEMENTED ATEMPORALLY.
MINIMIZE VARIABLES. MAXIMIZE FLEXIBILITY.
WE'RE LOSING TOO MANY UNITS!
I NEED HELP DOWN THERE!

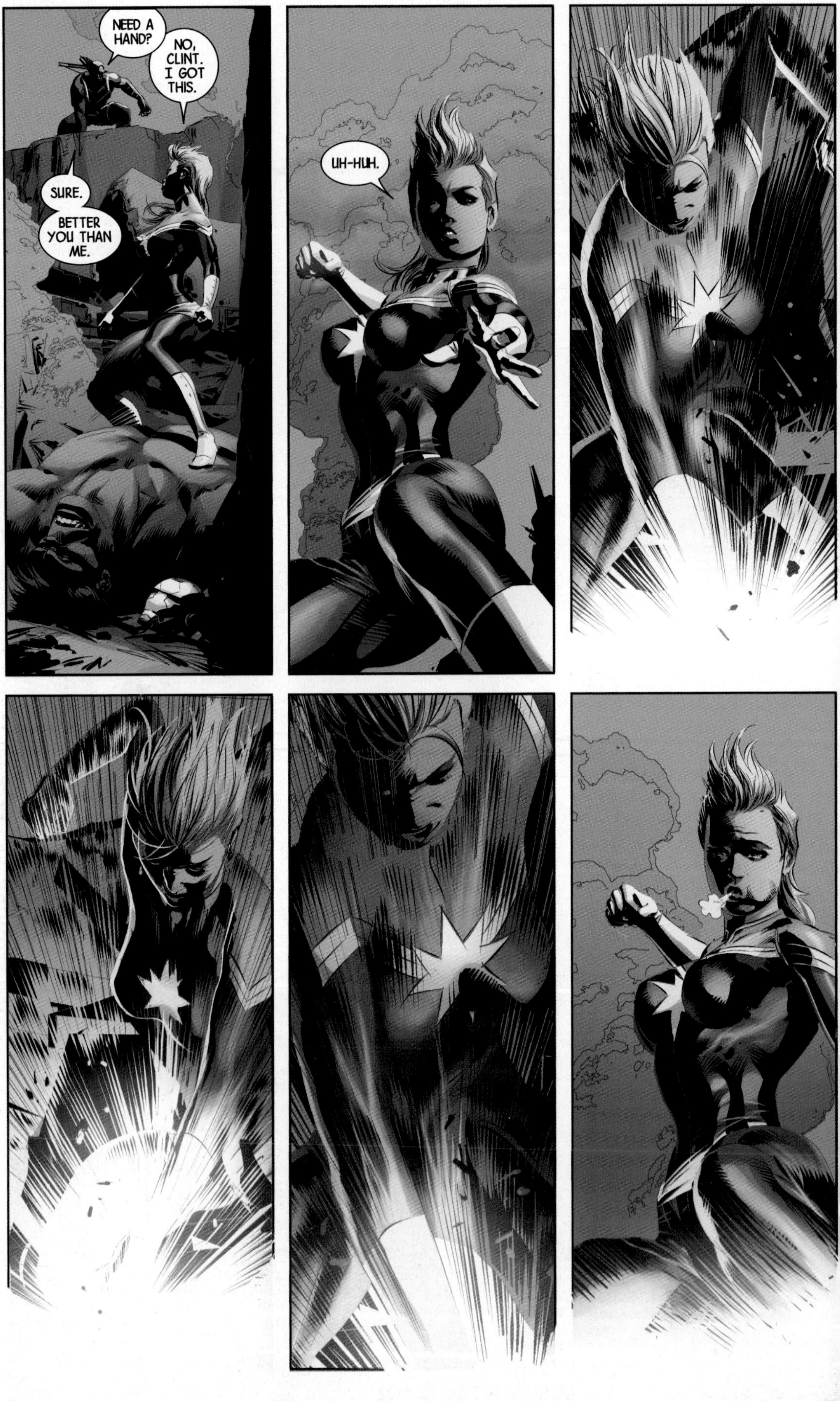
NEED A HAND?
NO, CLINT. I GOT THIS.
SURE.
BETTER YOU THAN ME.
UH-HUH.

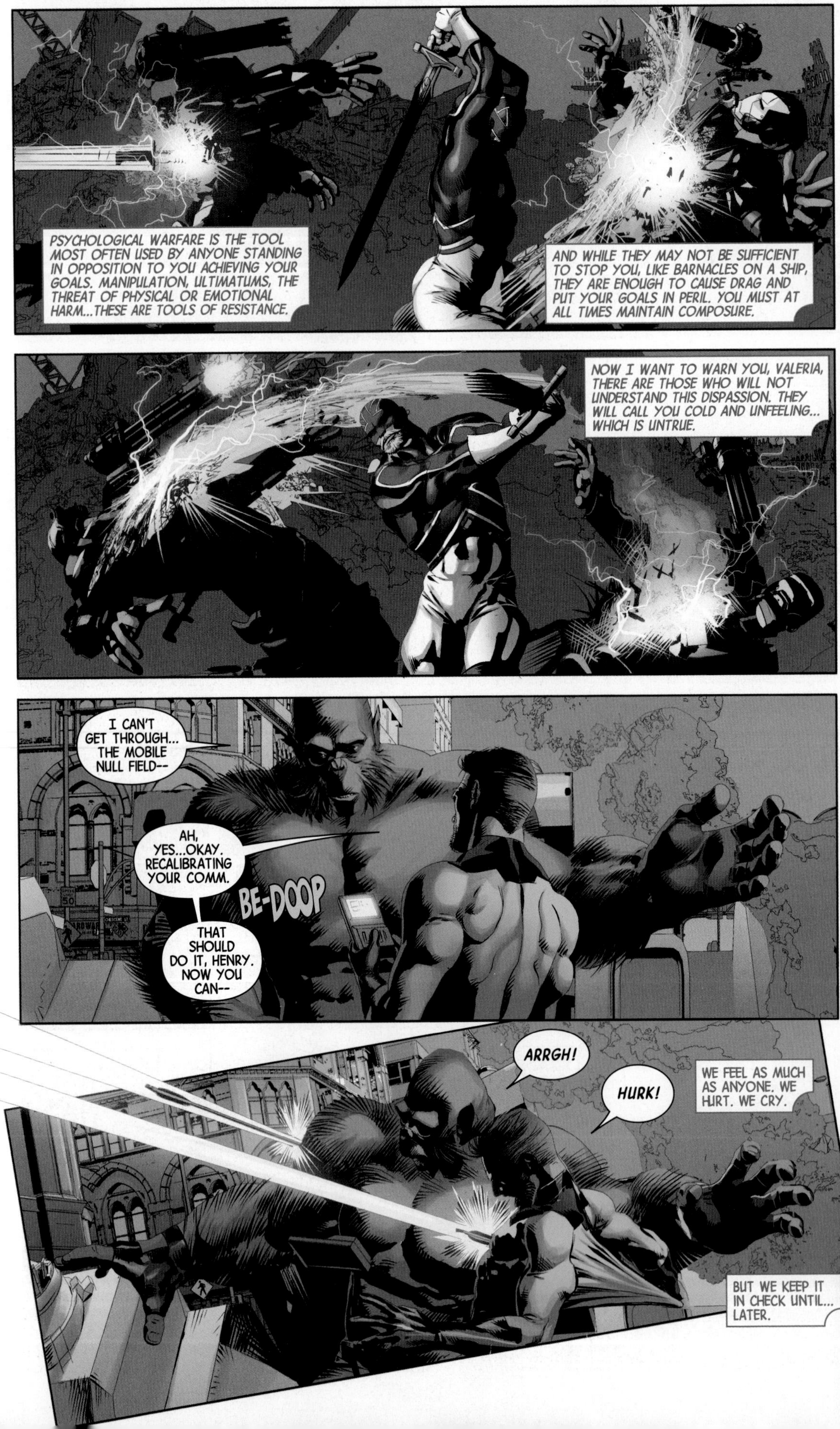
PSYCHOLOGICAL WARFARE IS THE TOOL MOST OFTEN USED BY ANYONE STANDING IN OPPOSITION TO YOU ACHIEVING YOUR GOALS. MANIPULATION, ULTIMATUMS, THE THREAT OF PHYSICAL OR EMOTIONAL HARM...THESE ARE TOOLS OF RESISTANCE.
AND WHILE THEY MAY NOT BE SUFFICIENT TO STOP YOU, LIKE BARNACLES ON A SHIP, THEY ARE ENOUGH TO CAUSE DRAG AND PUT YOUR GOALS IN PERIL. YOU MUST AT ALL TIMES MAINTAIN COMPOSURE.
NOW I WANT TO WARN YOU, VALERIA, THERE ARE THOSE WHO WILL NOT UNDERSTAND THIS DISPASSION. THEY WILL CALL YOU COLD AND UNFEELING... WHICH IS UNTRUE.
I CAN'T GET THROUGH... THE MOBILE NULL FIELD--
AH, YES...OKAY. RECALIBRATING YOUR COMM.
BE-DOOP
THAT SHOULD DO IT, HENRY. NOW YOU CAN--
ARRGH!
HURK!
WE FEEL AS MUCH AS ANYONE. WE HURT. WE CRY.
BUT WE KEEP IT IN CHECK UNTIL... LATER.

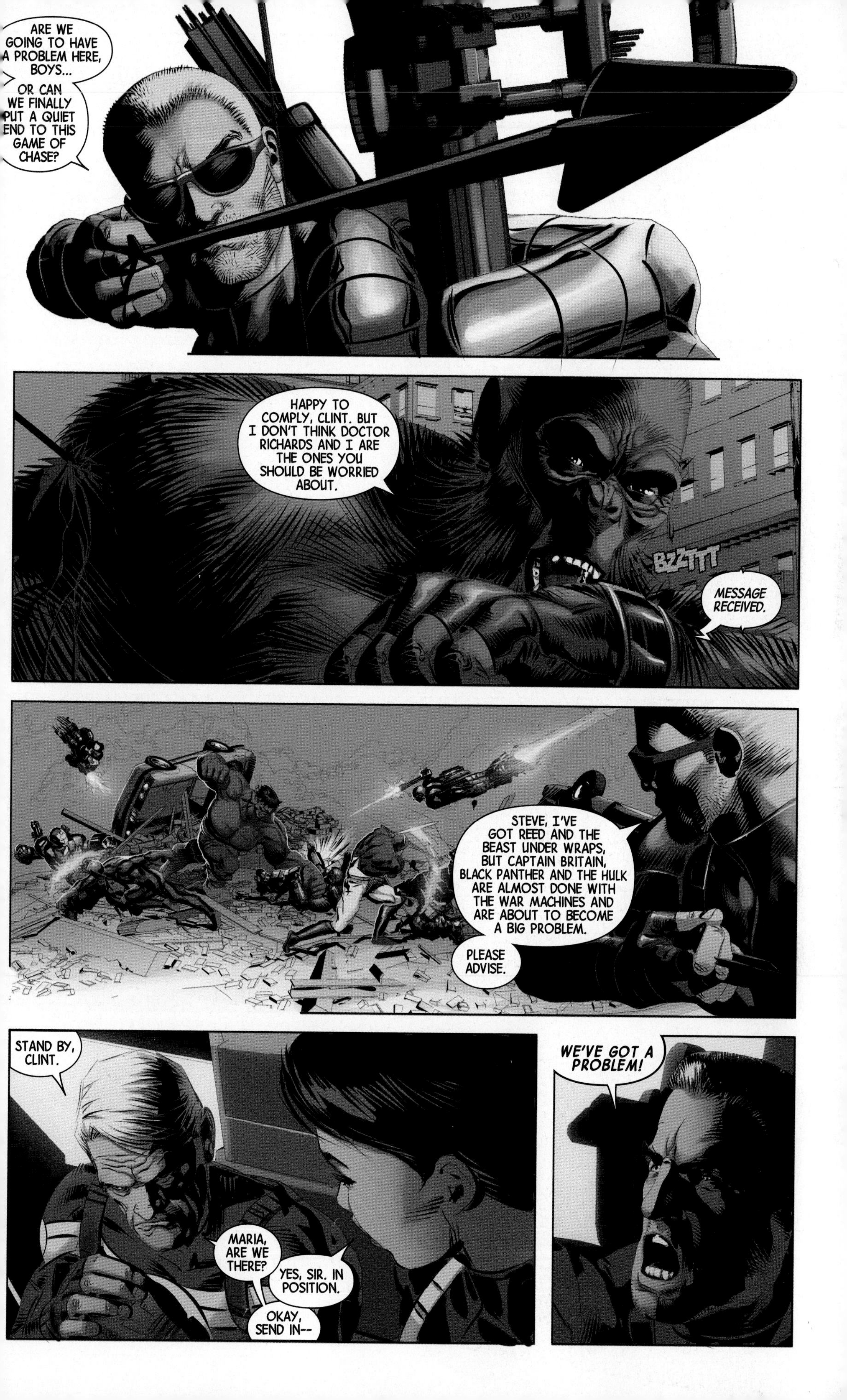
ARE WE GOING TO HAVE A PROBLEM HERE, BOYS...
OR CAN WE FINALLY PUT A QUIET END TO THIS GAME OF CHASE?
HAPPY TO COMPLY, CLINT. BUT I DON'T THINK DOCTOR RICHARDS AND I ARE THE ONES YOU SHOULD BE WORRIED ABOUT.
BZZTTT
MESSAGE RECEIVED.
STEVE, I'VE GOT REED AND THE BEAST UNDER WRAPS, BUT CAPTAIN BRITAIN, BLACK PANTHER AND THE HULK ARE ALMOST DONE WITH THE WAR MACHINES AND ARE ABOUT TO BECOME A BIG PROBLEM.
PLEASE ADVISE.
STAND BY, CLINT.
MARIA, ARE WE THERE?
YES, SIR. IN POSITION.
OKAY, SEND IN--
WE'VE GOT A PROBLEM!

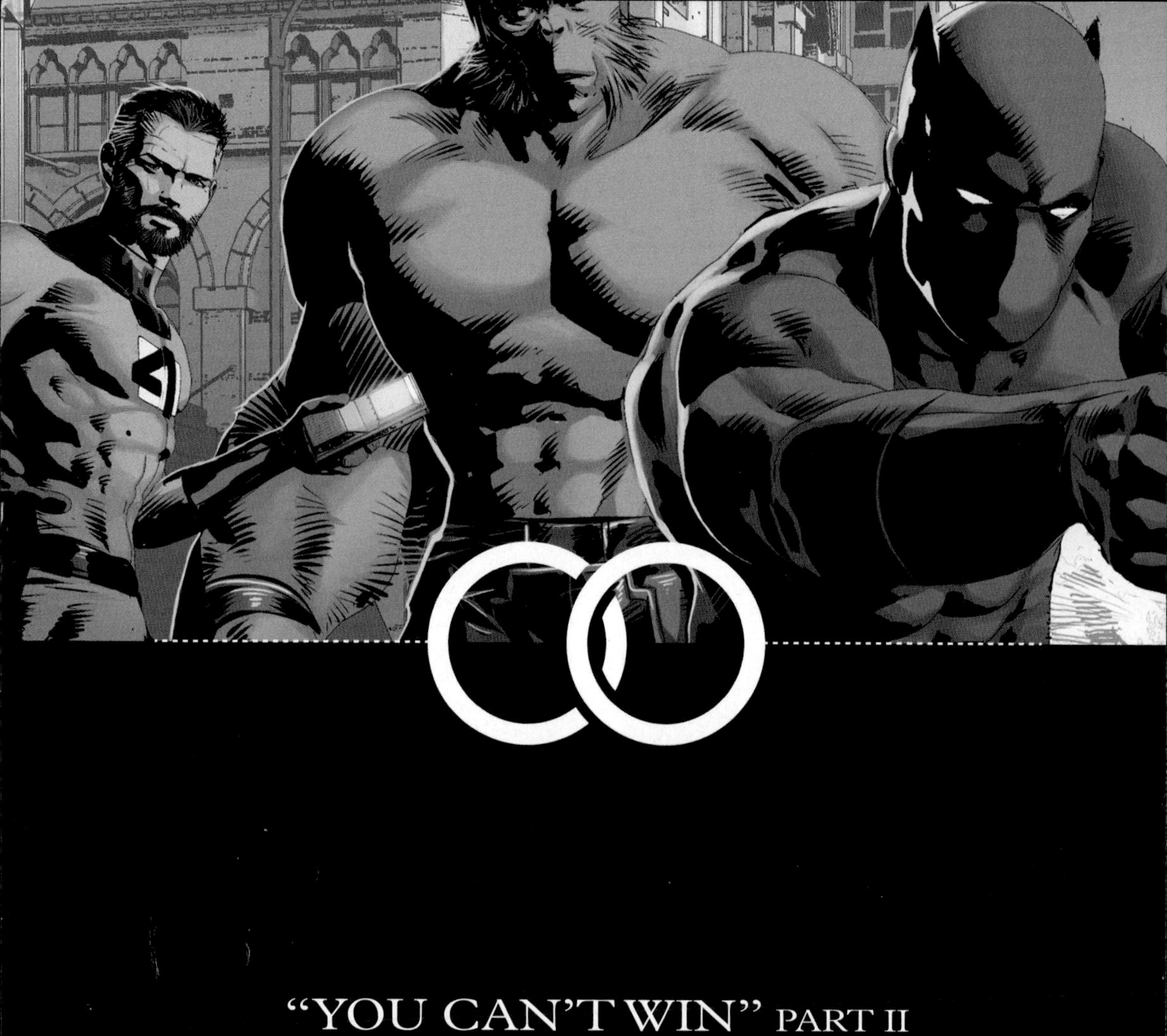
"YOU CAN'T WIN" PART II

S.H.I.E.L.D. AVENGERS

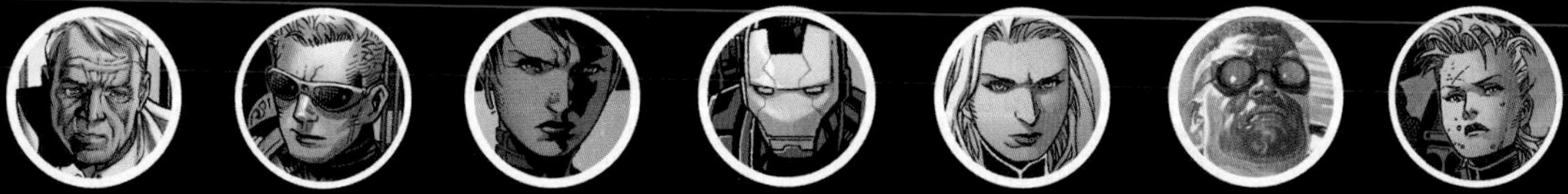

STEVE ROGERS | HAWKEYE | MARIA HILL | WAR MACHINE | INVISIBLE WOMAN | CAPTAIN AMERICA | CAPTAIN MARVEL

THE ILLUMINATI

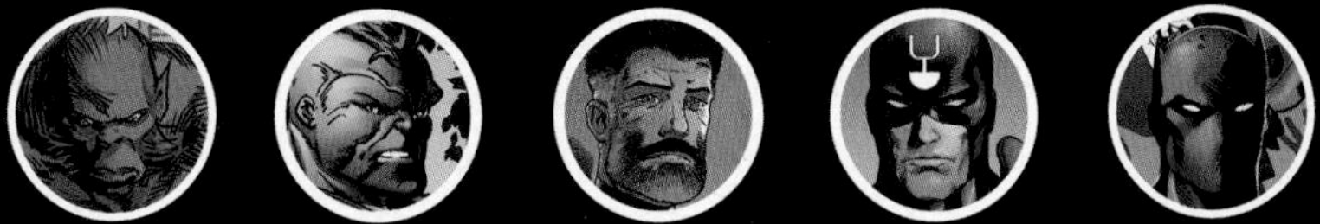

BEAST | HULK/ DOC GREEN | REED RICHARDS | BLACK BOLT | BLACK PANTHER

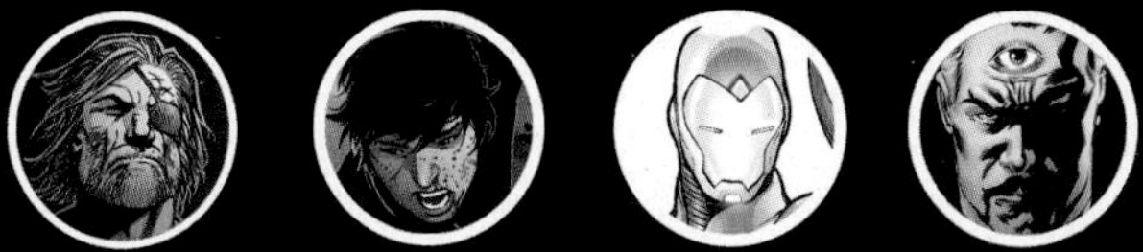

CAPTAIN BRITAIN | AMADEUS CHO | IRON MAN | DOCTOR STRANGE

NEW AVENGERS

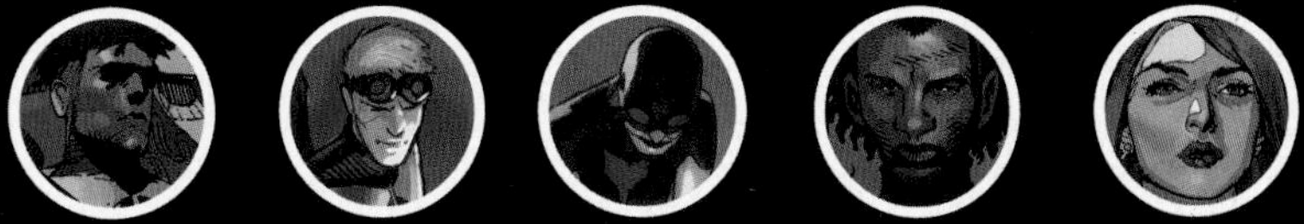

SUNSPOT | CANNONBALL | SMASHER | MANIFOLD | BLACK WIDOW

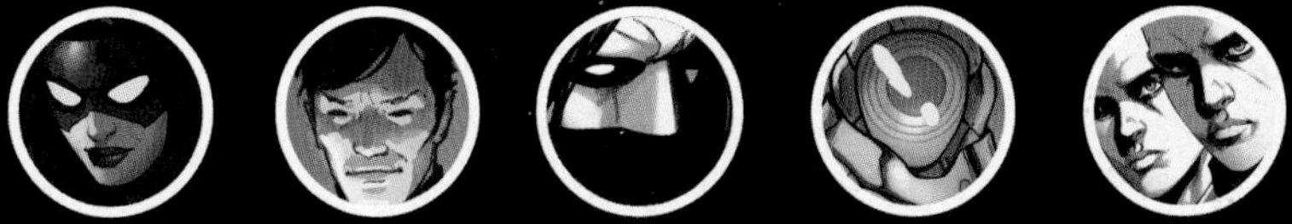

SPIDER-WOMAN | SHANG-CHI | VALIDATOR | POD | ZEBRA KIDS

MULTIVERSAL AVENGERS

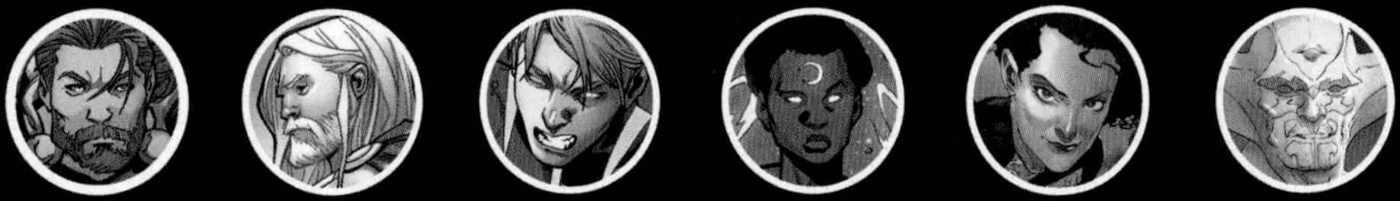

HYPERION | ODINSON | STARBRAND | NIGHTMASK | ABYSS | EX NIHILO

THE CABAL

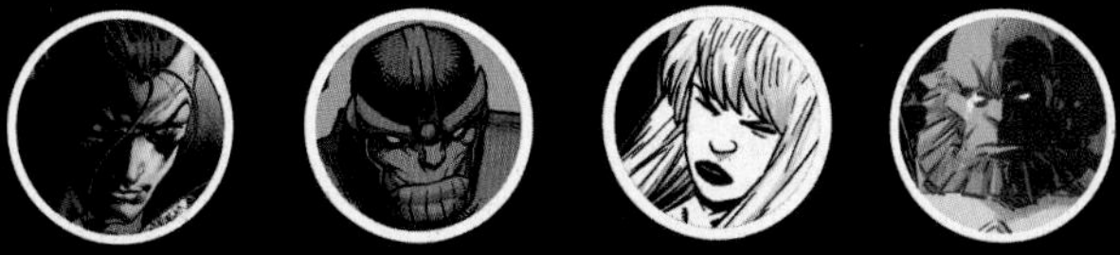

NAMOR | THANOS | BLACK SWAN | TERRAX

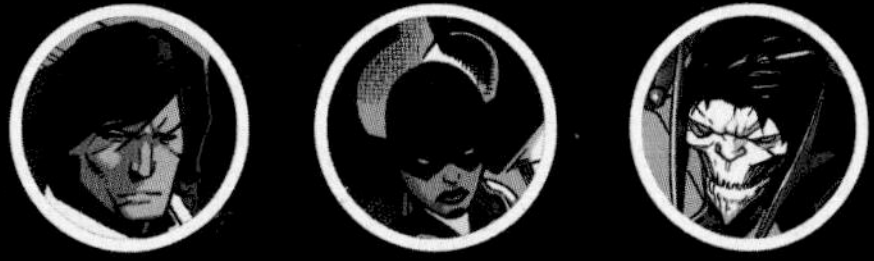

MAXIMUS | PROXIMA MIDNIGHT | CORVUS GLAIVE

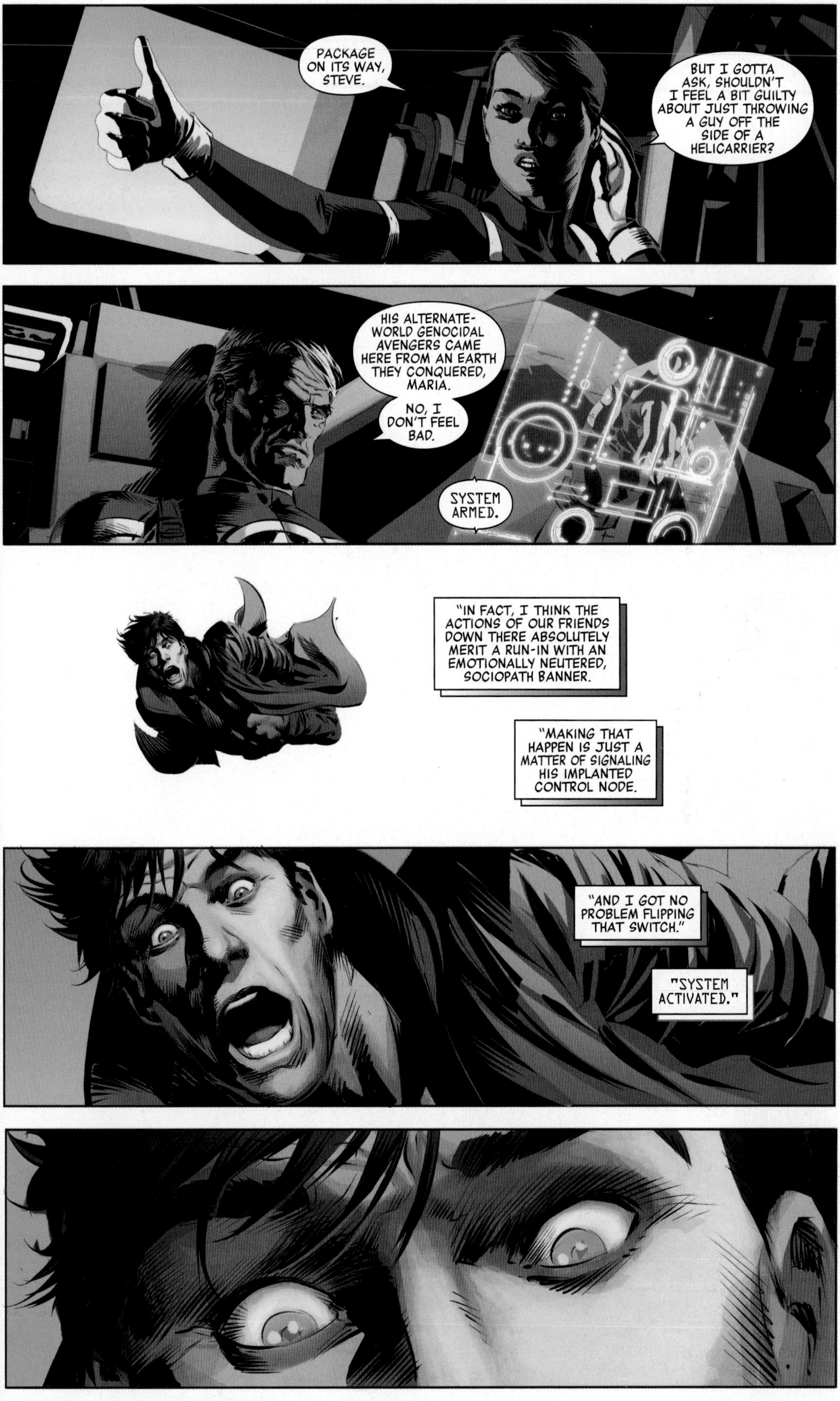
PACKAGE ON ITS WAY, STEVE.
BUT I GOTTA ASK, SHOULDN'T I FEEL A BIT GUILTY ABOUT JUST THROWING A GUY OFF THE SIDE OF A HELICARRIER?
HIS ALTERNATE-WORLD GENOCIDAL AVENGERS CAME HERE FROM AN EARTH THEY CONQUERED, MARIA.
NO, I DON'T FEEL BAD.
SYSTEM ARMED.
"IN FACT, I THINK THE ACTIONS OF OUR FRIENDS DOWN THERE ABSOLUTELY MERIT A RUN-IN WITH AN EMOTIONALLY NEUTERED, SOCIOPATH BANNER.
"MAKING THAT HAPPEN IS JUST A MATTER OF SIGNALING HIS IMPLANTED CONTROL NODE.
"AND I GOT NO PROBLEM FLIPPING THAT SWITCH."
"SYSTEM ACTIVATED."

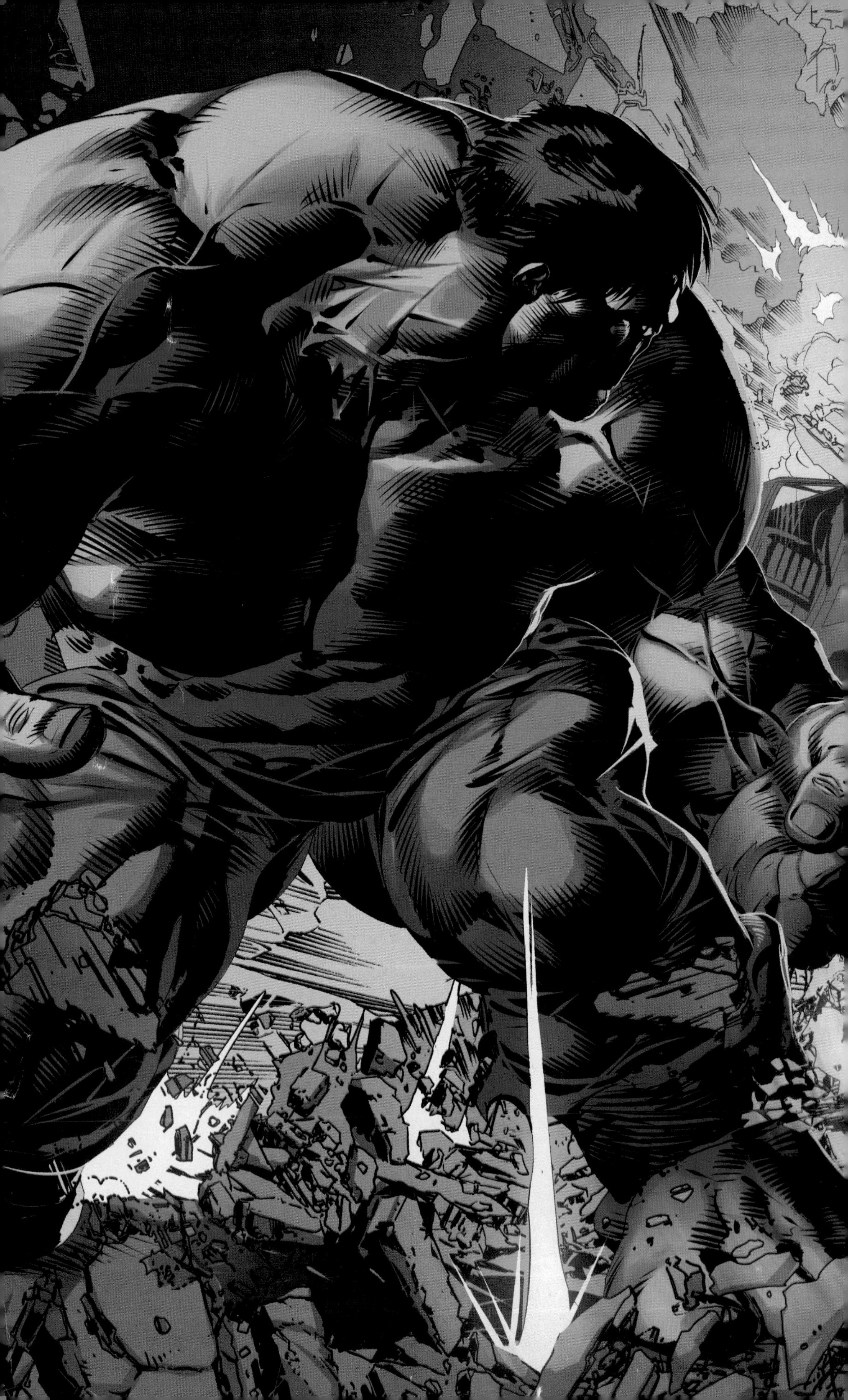

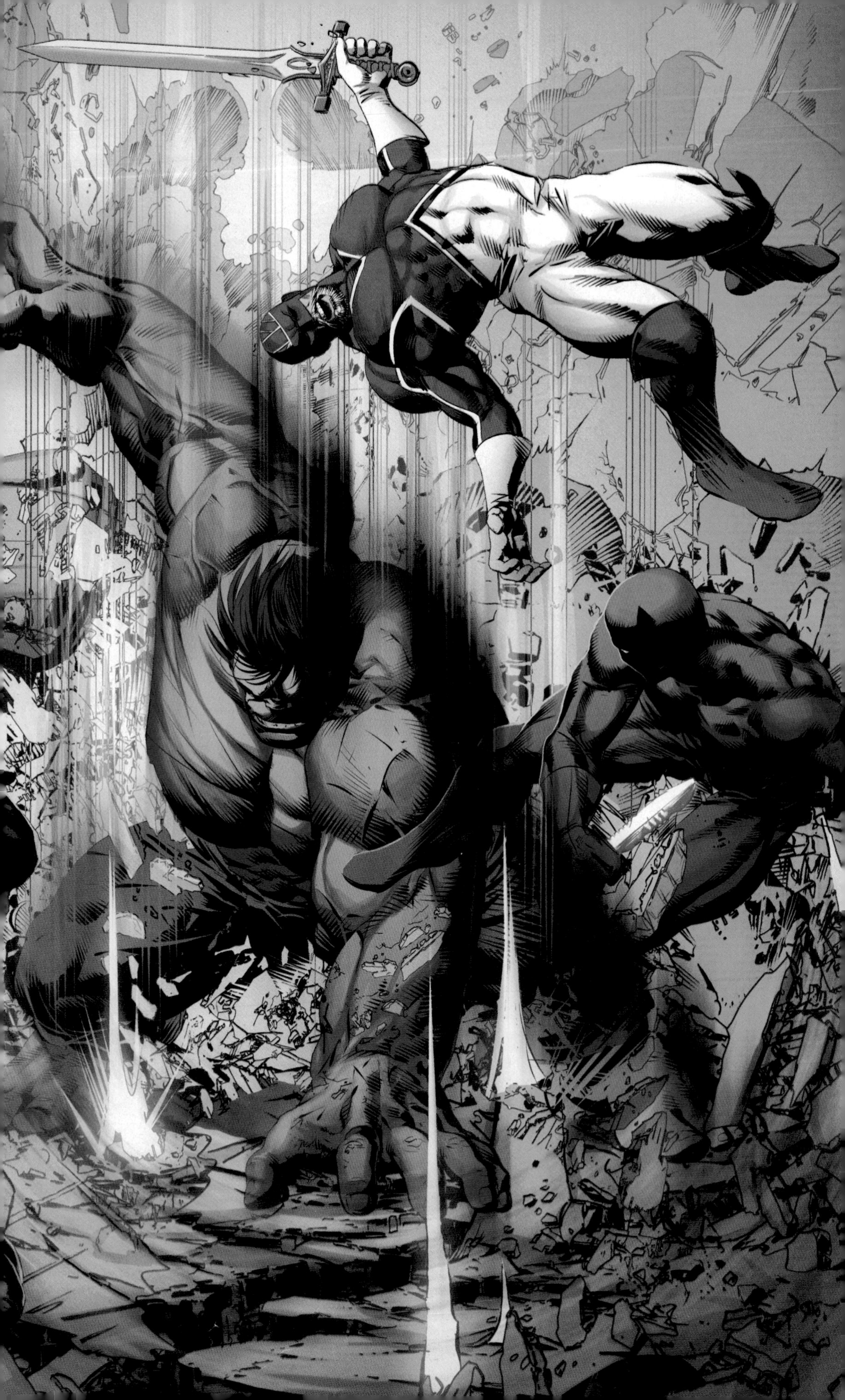

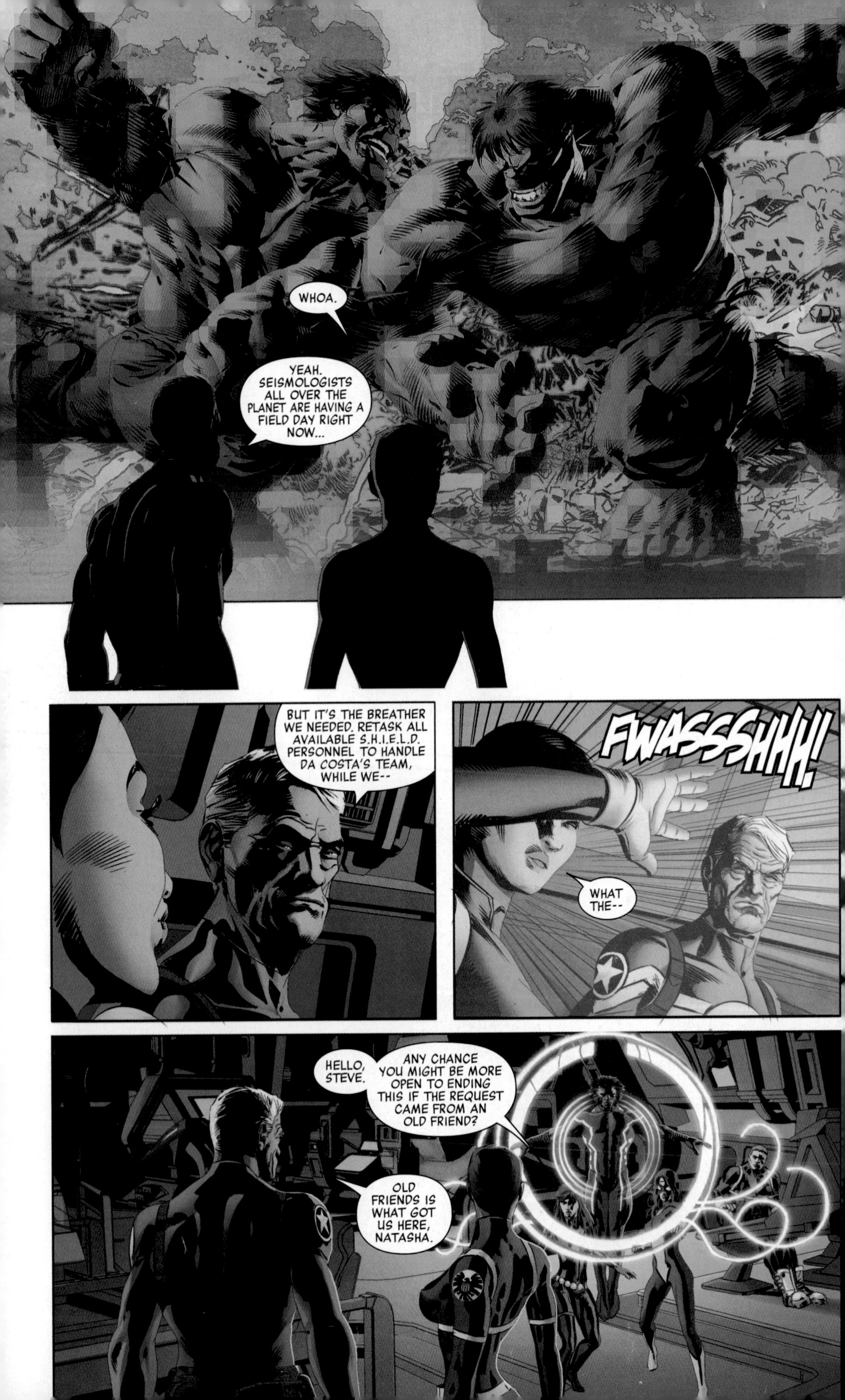
WHOA.
YEAH. SEISMOLOGISTS ALL OVER THE PLANET ARE HAVING A FIELD DAY RIGHT NOW...
BUT IT'S THE BREATHER WE NEEDED. RETASK ALL AVAILABLE S.H.I.E.L.D. PERSONNEL TO HANDLE DA COSTA'S TEAM, WHILE WE--
FWASSSHHH!
WHAT THE--
HELLO, STEVE.
ANY CHANCE YOU MIGHT BE MORE OPEN TO ENDING THIS IF THE REQUEST CAME FROM AN OLD FRIEND?
OLD FRIENDS IS WHAT GOT US HERE, NATASHA.

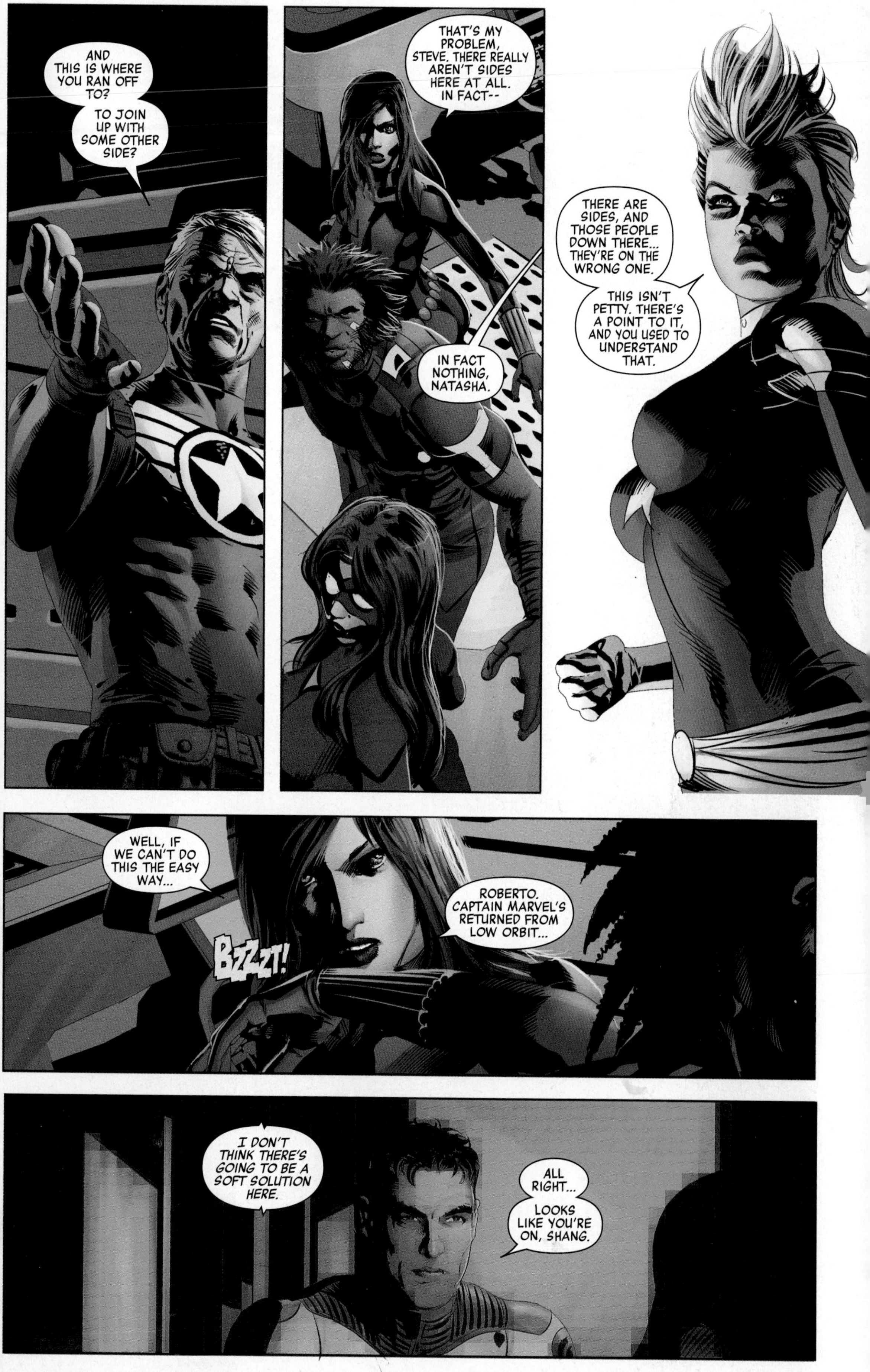
AND THIS IS WHERE YOU RAN OFF TO?
TO JOIN UP WITH SOME OTHER SIDE?
THAT'S MY PROBLEM, STEVE. THERE REALLY AREN'T SIDES HERE AT ALL. IN FACT--
IN FACT NOTHING, NATASHA.
THERE ARE SIDES, AND THOSE PEOPLE DOWN THERE... THEY'RE ON THE WRONG ONE.
THIS ISN'T PETTY. THERE'S A POINT TO IT, AND YOU USED TO UNDERSTAND THAT.
WELL, IF WE CAN'T DO THIS THE EASY WAY...
BZZZT!
ROBERTO. CAPTAIN MARVEL'S RETURNED FROM LOW ORBIT...
I DON'T THINK THERE'S GOING TO BE A SOFT SOLUTION HERE.
ALL RIGHT...
LOOKS LIKE YOU'RE ON, SHANG.

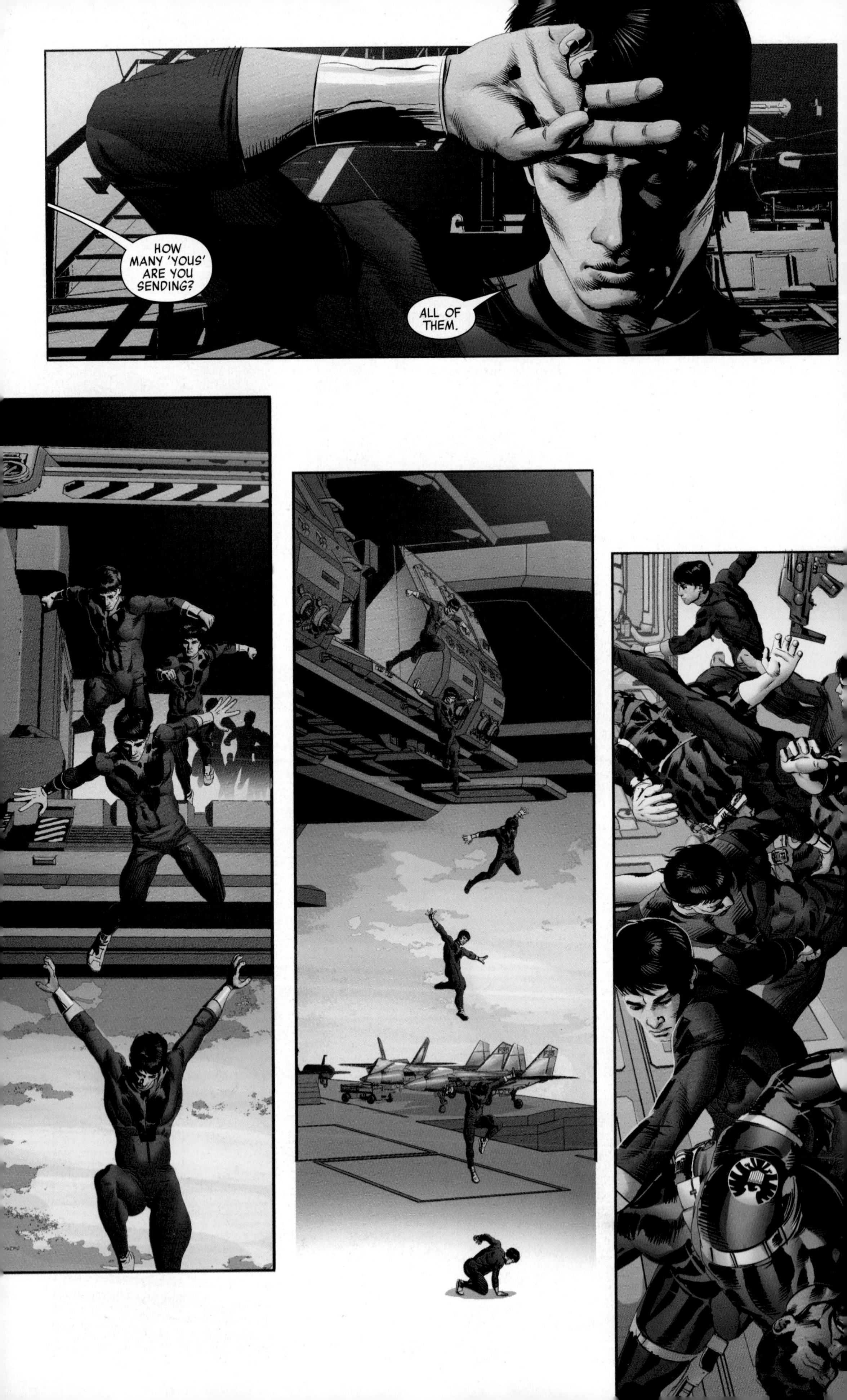
HOW MANY 'YOUS' ARE YOU SENDING?
ALL OF THEM.

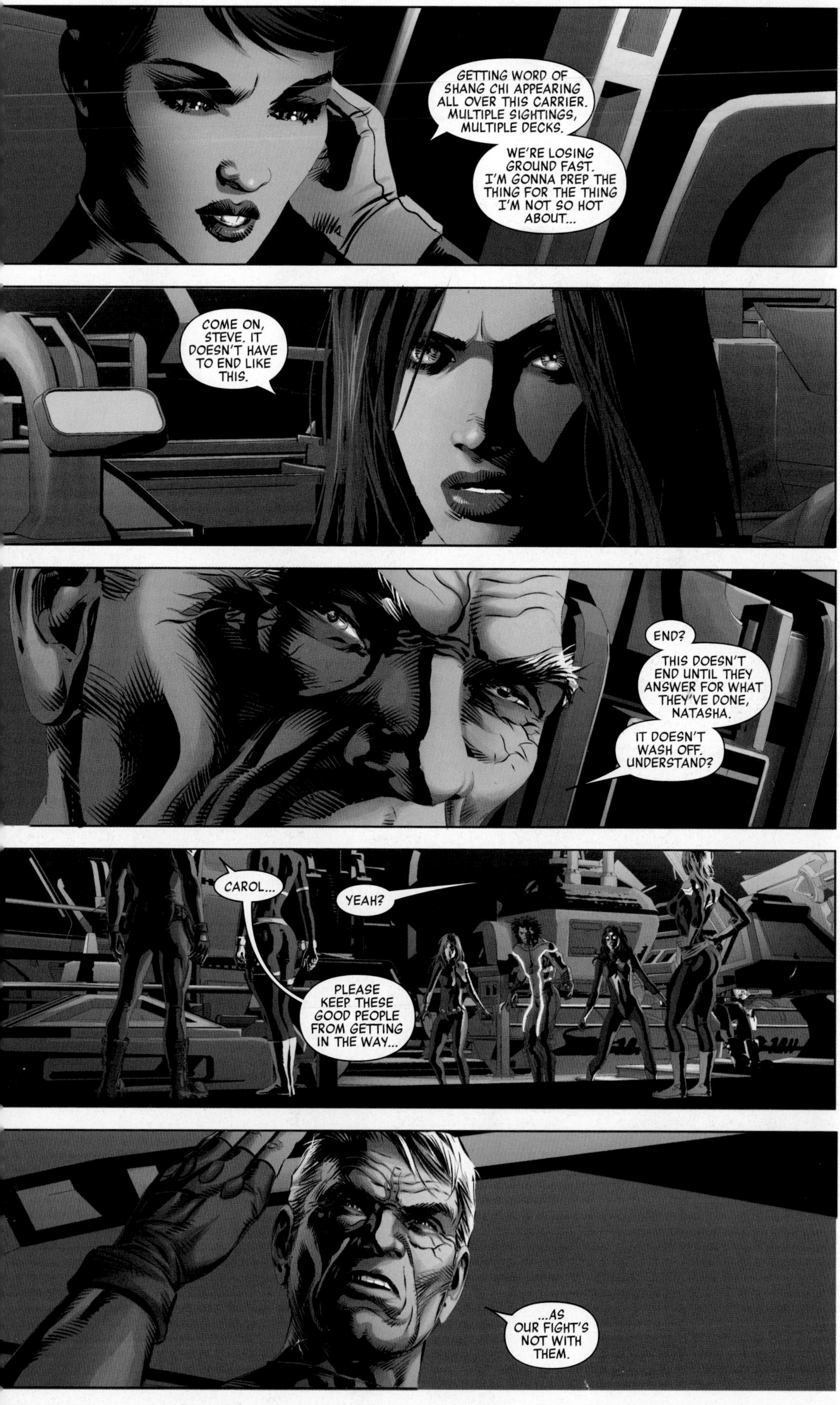
GETTING WORD OF SHANG CHI APPEARING ALL OVER THIS CARRIER. MULTIPLE SIGHTINGS, MULTIPLE DECKS.
WE'RE LOSING GROUND FAST. I'M GONNA PREP THE THING FOR THE THING I'M NOT SO HOT ABOUT...
COME ON, STEVE. IT DOESN'T HAVE TO END LIKE THIS.
END?
THIS DOESN'T END UNTIL THEY ANSWER FOR WHAT THEY'VE DONE, NATASHA.
IT DOESN'T WASH OFF. UNDERSTAND?
CAROL...
YEAH?
PLEASE KEEP THESE GOOD PEOPLE FROM GETTING IN THE WAY...
...AS OUR FIGHT'S NOT WITH THEM.

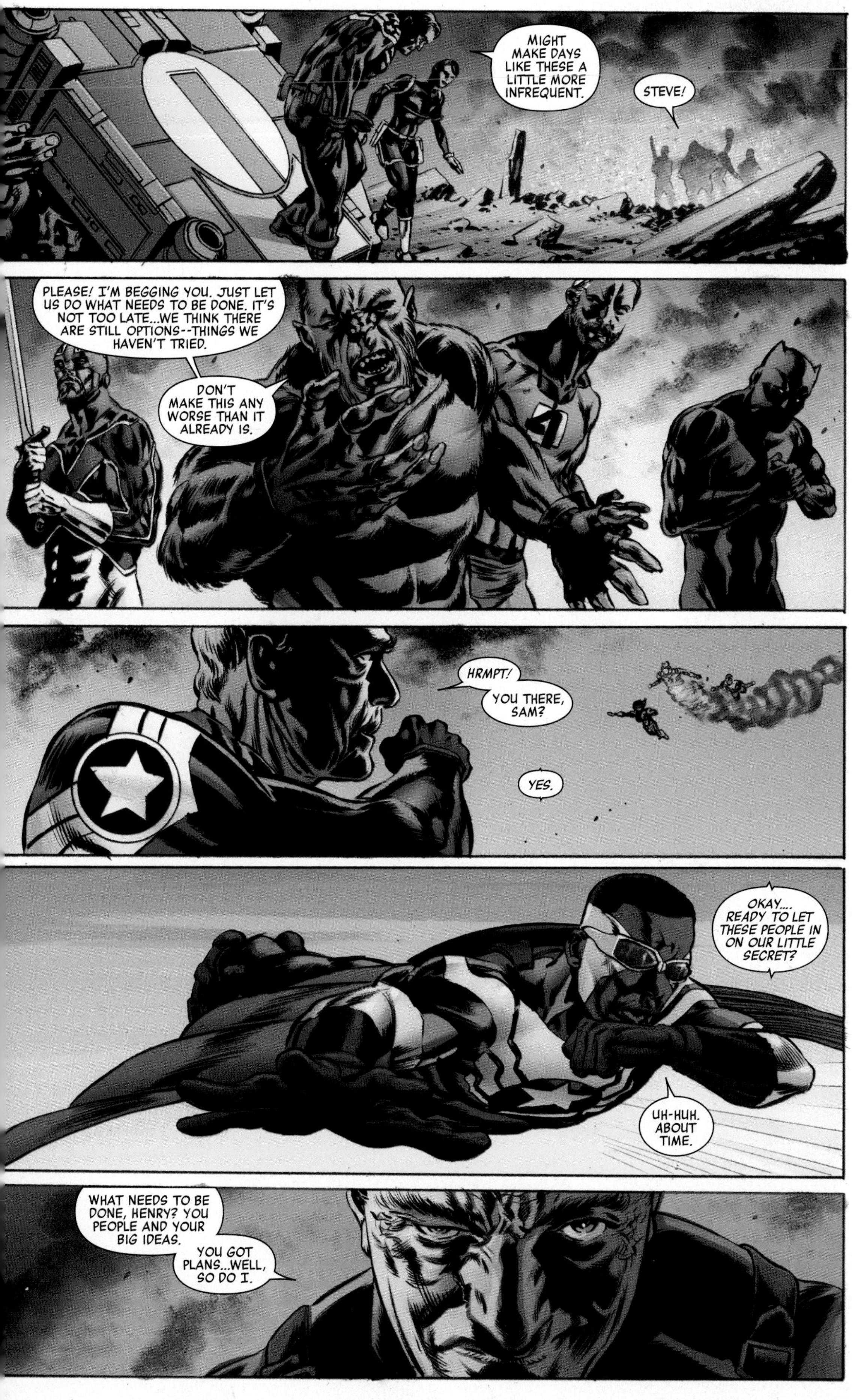
MIGHT MAKE DAYS LIKE THESE A LITTLE MORE INFREQUENT.
STEVE!
PLEASE! I'M BEGGING YOU. JUST LET US DO WHAT NEEDS TO BE DONE. IT'S NOT TOO LATE...WE THINK THERE ARE STILL OPTIONS--THINGS WE HAVEN'T TRIED.
DON'T MAKE THIS ANY WORSE THAN IT ALREADY IS.
HRMPT!
YOU THERE, SAM?
YES.
OKAY.... READY TO LET THESE PEOPLE IN ON OUR LITTLE SECRET?
UH-HUH. ABOUT TIME.
WHAT NEEDS TO BE DONE, HENRY? YOU PEOPLE AND YOUR BIG IDEAS.
YOU GOT PLANS...WELL, SO DO I.

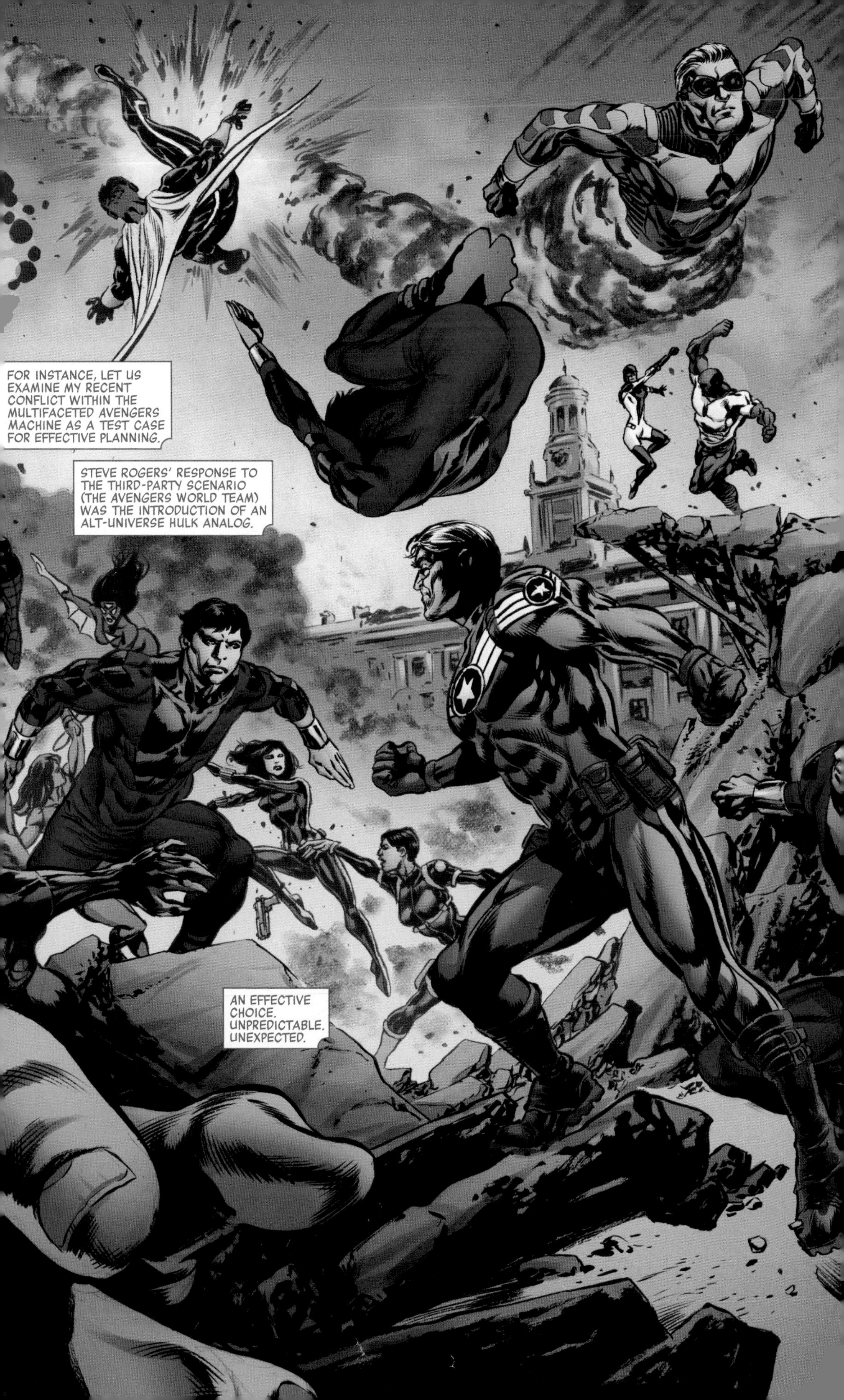
FOR INSTANCE, LET US EXAMINE MY RECENT CONFLICT WITHIN THE MULTIFACETED AVENGERS MACHINE AS A TEST CASE FOR EFFECTIVE PLANNING.
STEVE ROGERS' RESPONSE TO THE THIRD-PARTY SCENARIO (THE AVENGERS WORLD TEAM) WAS THE INTRODUCTION OF AN ALT-UNIVERSE HULK ANALOG.
AN EFFECTIVE CHOICE. UNPREDICTABLE. UNEXPECTED.

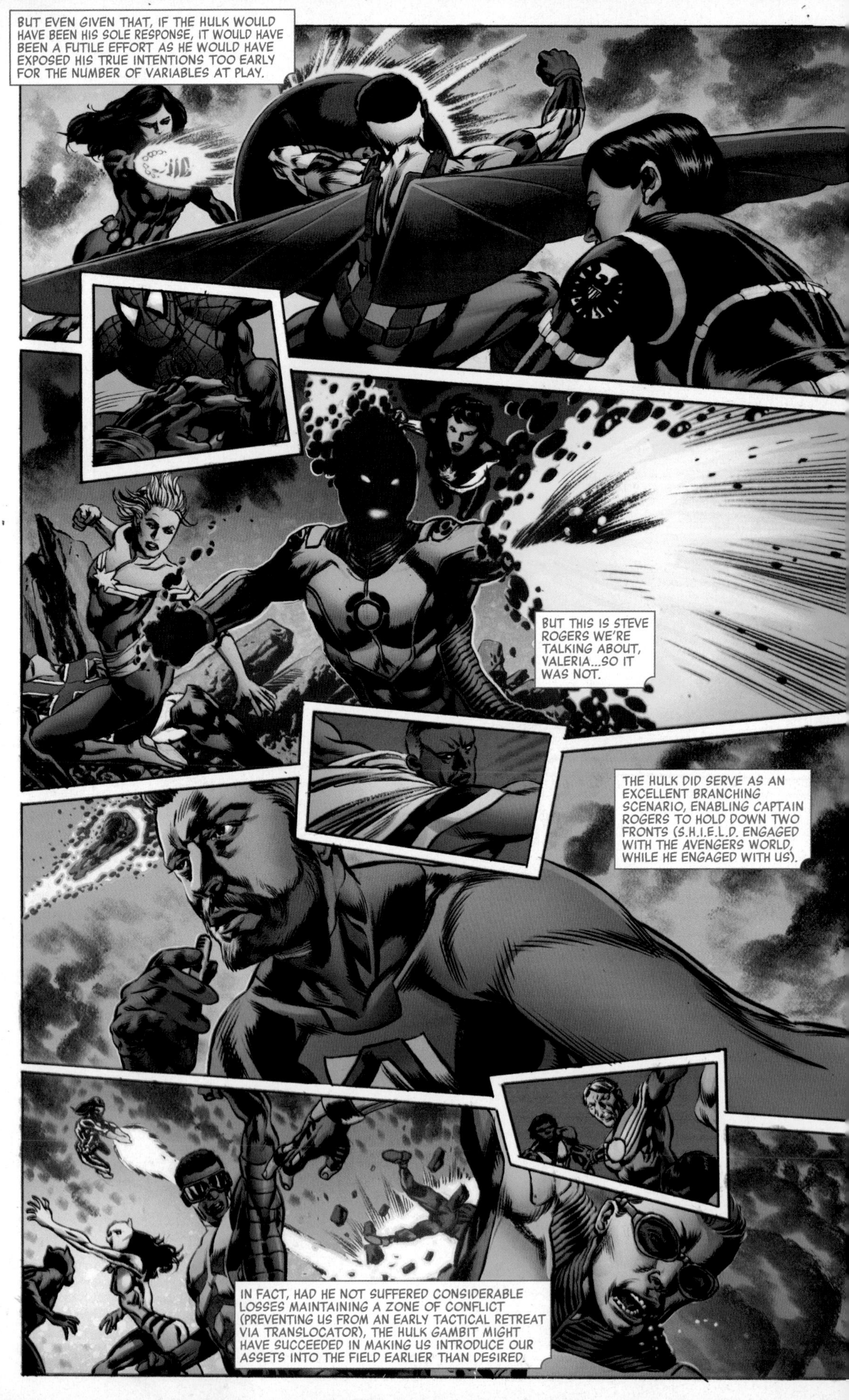
BUT EVEN GIVEN THAT, IF THE HULK WOULD HAVE BEEN HIS SOLE RESPONSE, IT WOULD HAVE BEEN A FUTILE EFFORT AS HE WOULD HAVE EXPOSED HIS TRUE INTENTIONS TOO EARLY FOR THE NUMBER OF VARIABLES AT PLAY.
BUT THIS IS STEVE ROGERS WE'RE TALKING ABOUT, VALERIA...SO IT WAS NOT.
THE HULK DID SERVE AS AN EXCELLENT BRANCHING SCENARIO, ENABLING CAPTAIN ROGERS TO HOLD DOWN TWO FRONTS (S.H.I.E.L.D. ENGAGED WITH THE AVENGERS WORLD, WHILE HE ENGAGED WITH US).
IN FACT, HAD HE NOT SUFFERED CONSIDERABLE LOSSES MAINTAINING A ZONE OF CONFLICT (PREVENTING US FROM AN EARLY TACTICAL RETREAT VIA TRANSLOCATOR), THE HULK GAMBIT MIGHT HAVE SUCCEEDED IN MAKING US INTRODUCE OUR ASSETS INTO THE FIELD EARLIER THAN DESIRED.

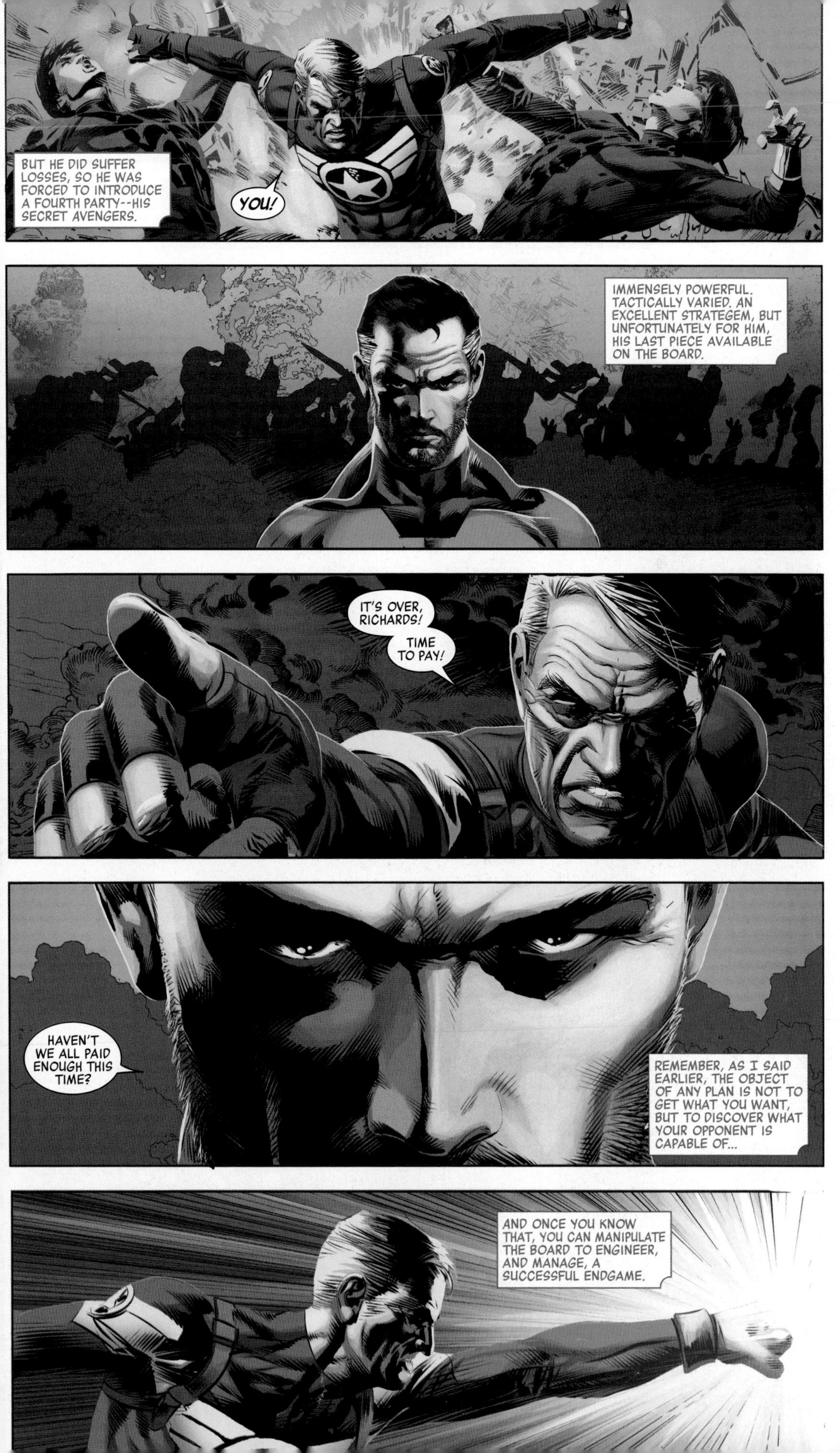
BUT HE DID SUFFER LOSSES, SO HE WAS FORCED TO INTRODUCE A FOURTH PARTY--HIS SECRET AVENGERS.
YOU!
IMMENSELY POWERFUL. TACTICALLY VARIED. AN EXCELLENT STRATEGEM, BUT UNFORTUNATELY FOR HIM, HIS LAST PIECE AVAILABLE ON THE BOARD.
IT'S OVER, RICHARDS!
TIME TO PAY!
HAVEN'T WE ALL PAID ENOUGH THIS TIME?
REMEMBER, AS I SAID EARLIER, THE OBJECT OF ANY PLAN IS NOT TO GET WHAT YOU WANT, BUT TO DISCOVER WHAT YOUR OPPONENT IS CAPABLE OF...
AND ONCE YOU KNOW THAT, YOU CAN MANIPULATE THE BOARD TO ENGINEER, AND MANAGE, A SUCCESSFUL ENDGAME.

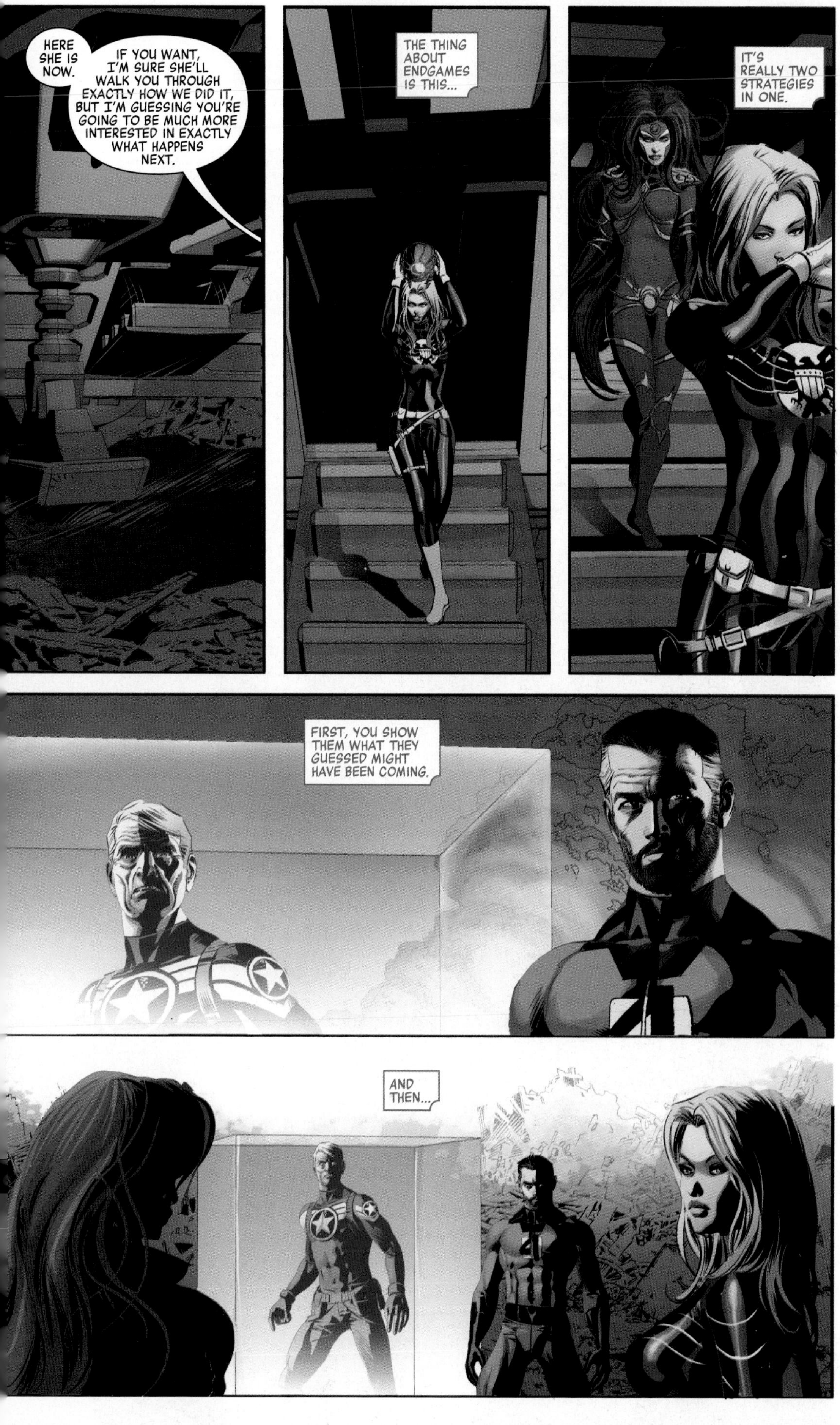
HERE SHE IS NOW.
IF YOU WANT, I'M SURE SHE'LL WALK YOU THROUGH EXACTLY HOW WE DID IT, BUT I'M GUESSING YOU'RE GOING TO BE MUCH MORE INTERESTED IN EXACTLY WHAT HAPPENS NEXT.
THE THING ABOUT ENDGAMES IS THIS...
IT'S REALLY TWO STRATEGIES IN ONE.
FIRST, YOU SHOW THEM WHAT THEY GUESSED MIGHT HAVE BEEN COMING.
AND THEN...

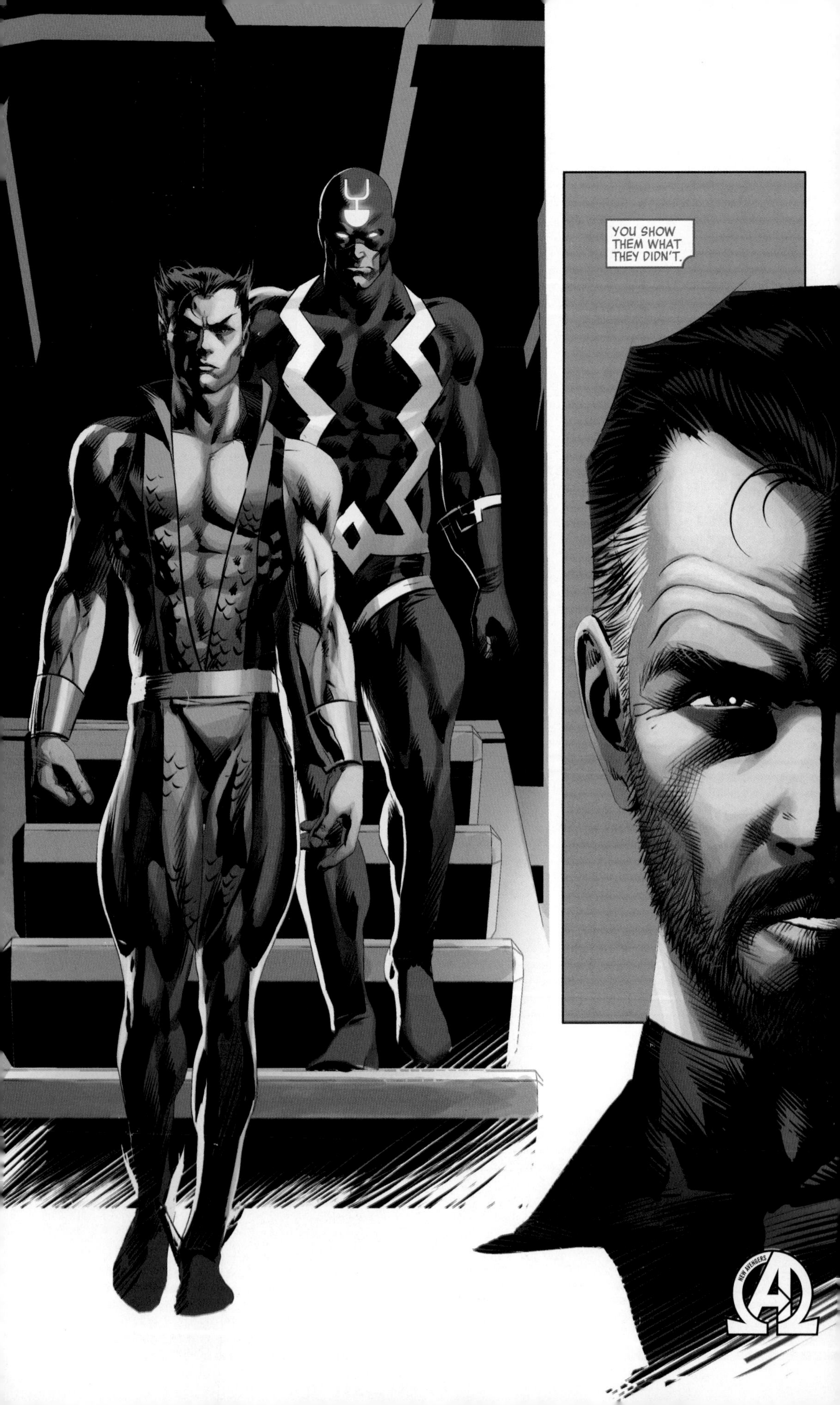
YOU SHOW THEM WHAT THEY DIDN'T.

COVER GALLERY

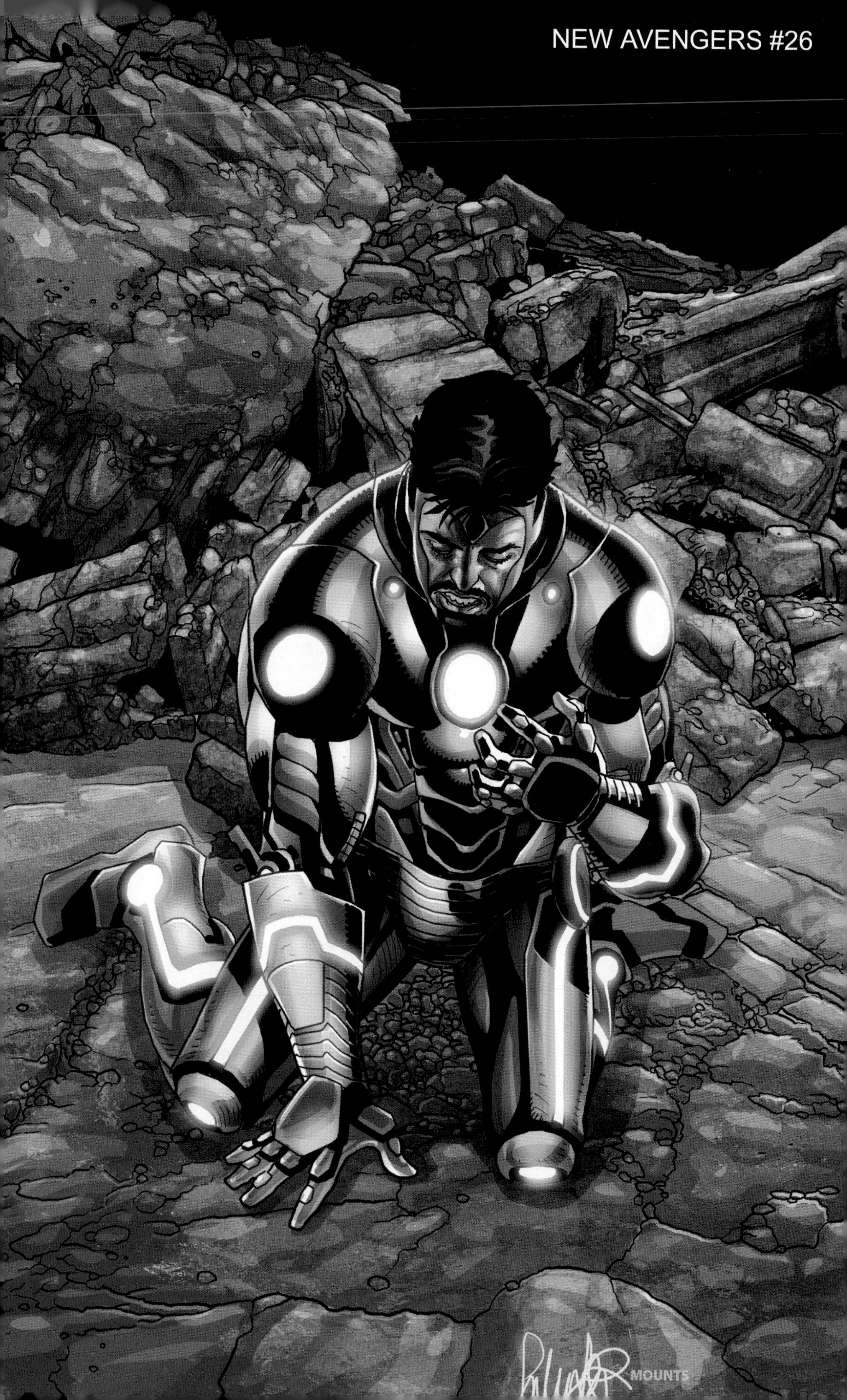
NEW AVENGERS #26
MOUNTS

AVENGERS #38

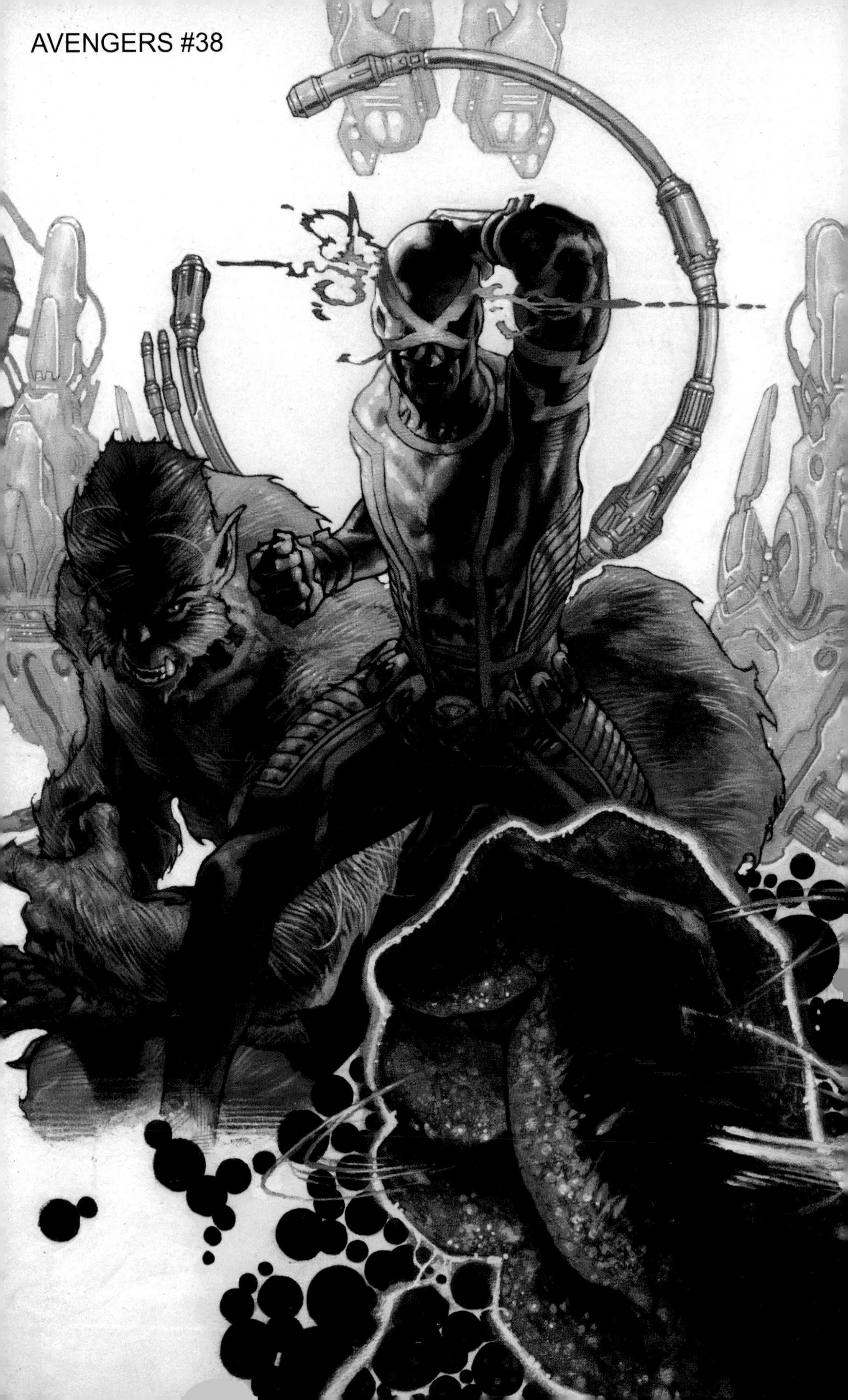

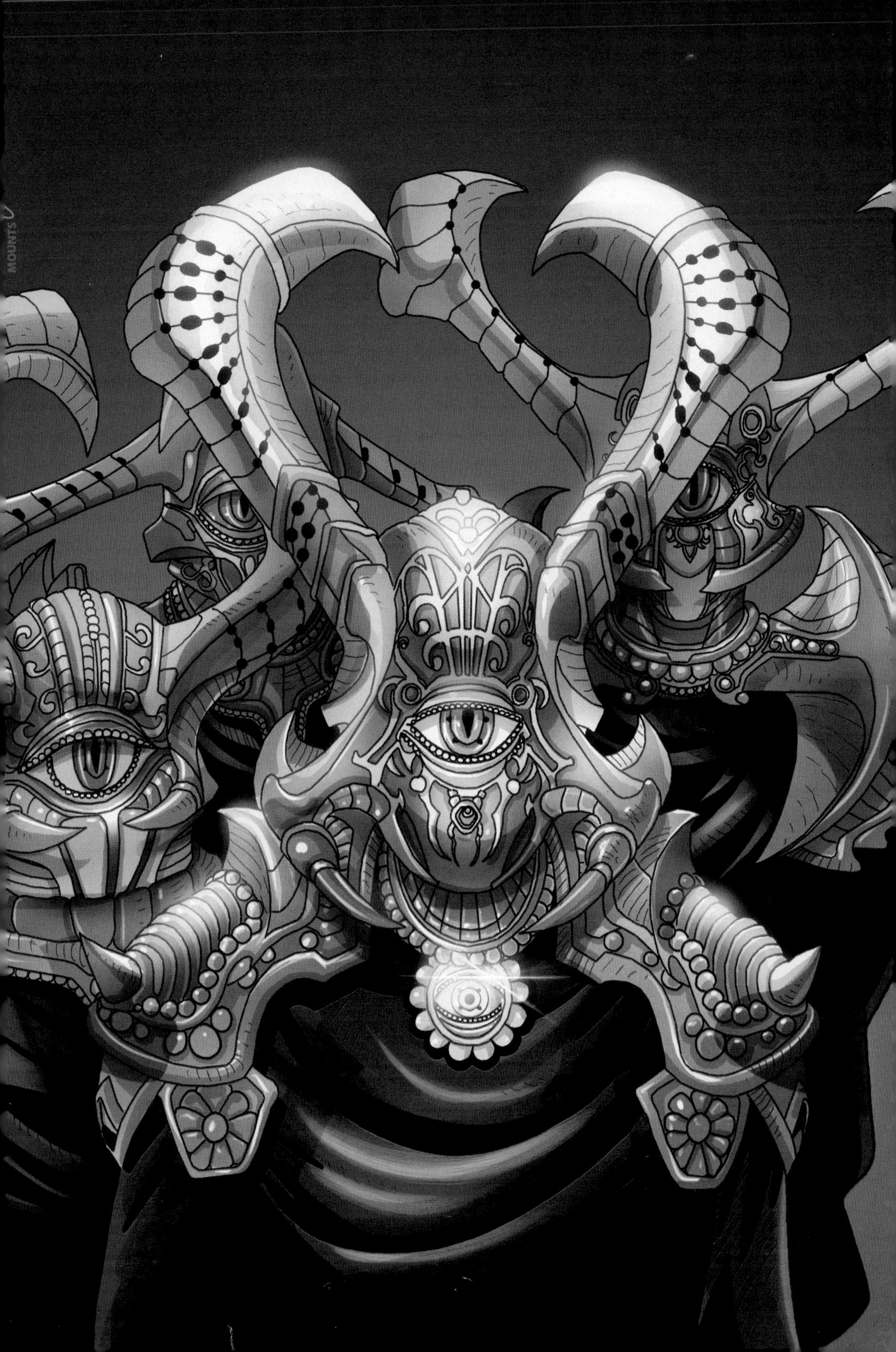

AVENGERS #39

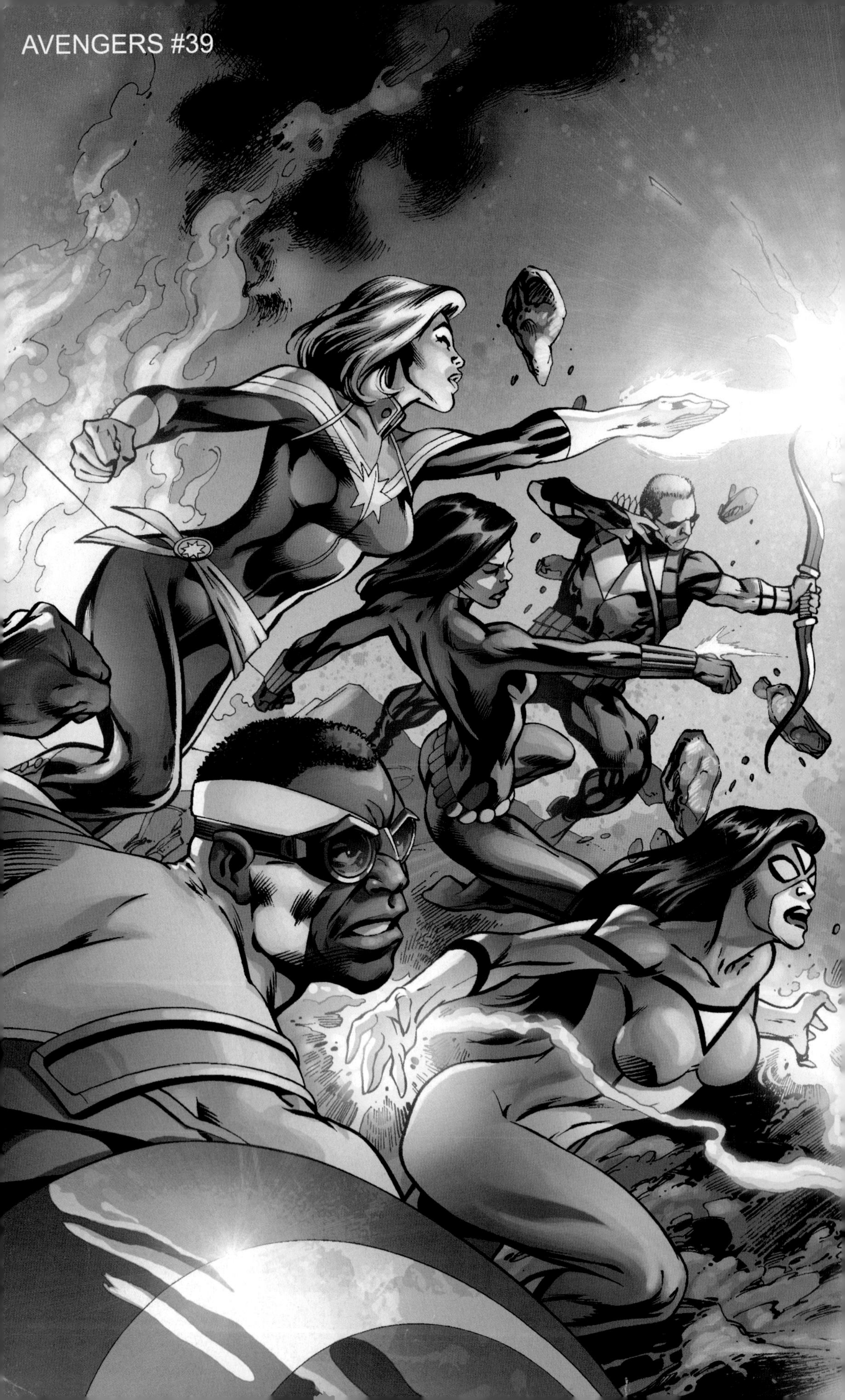

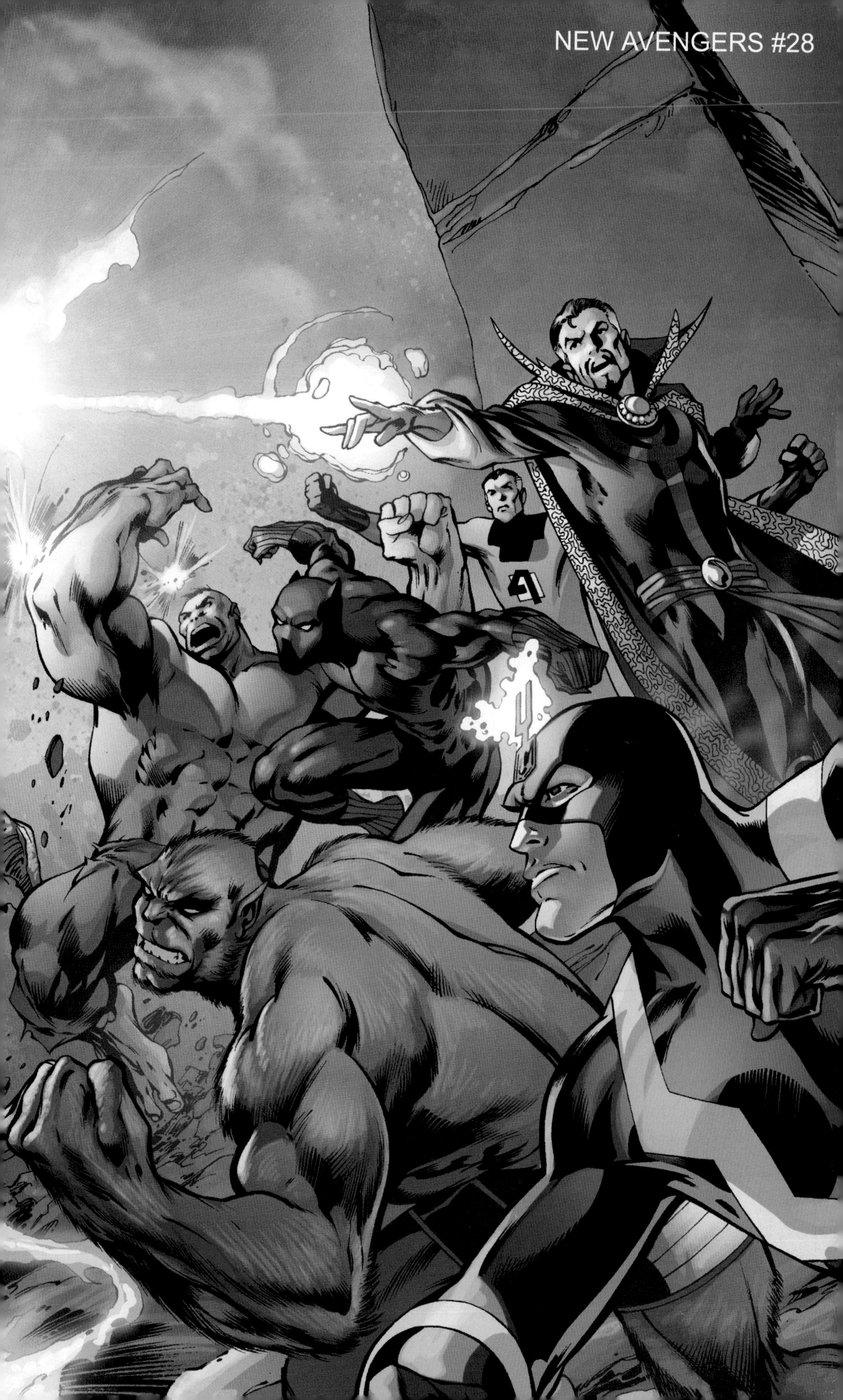
NEW AVENGERS #28

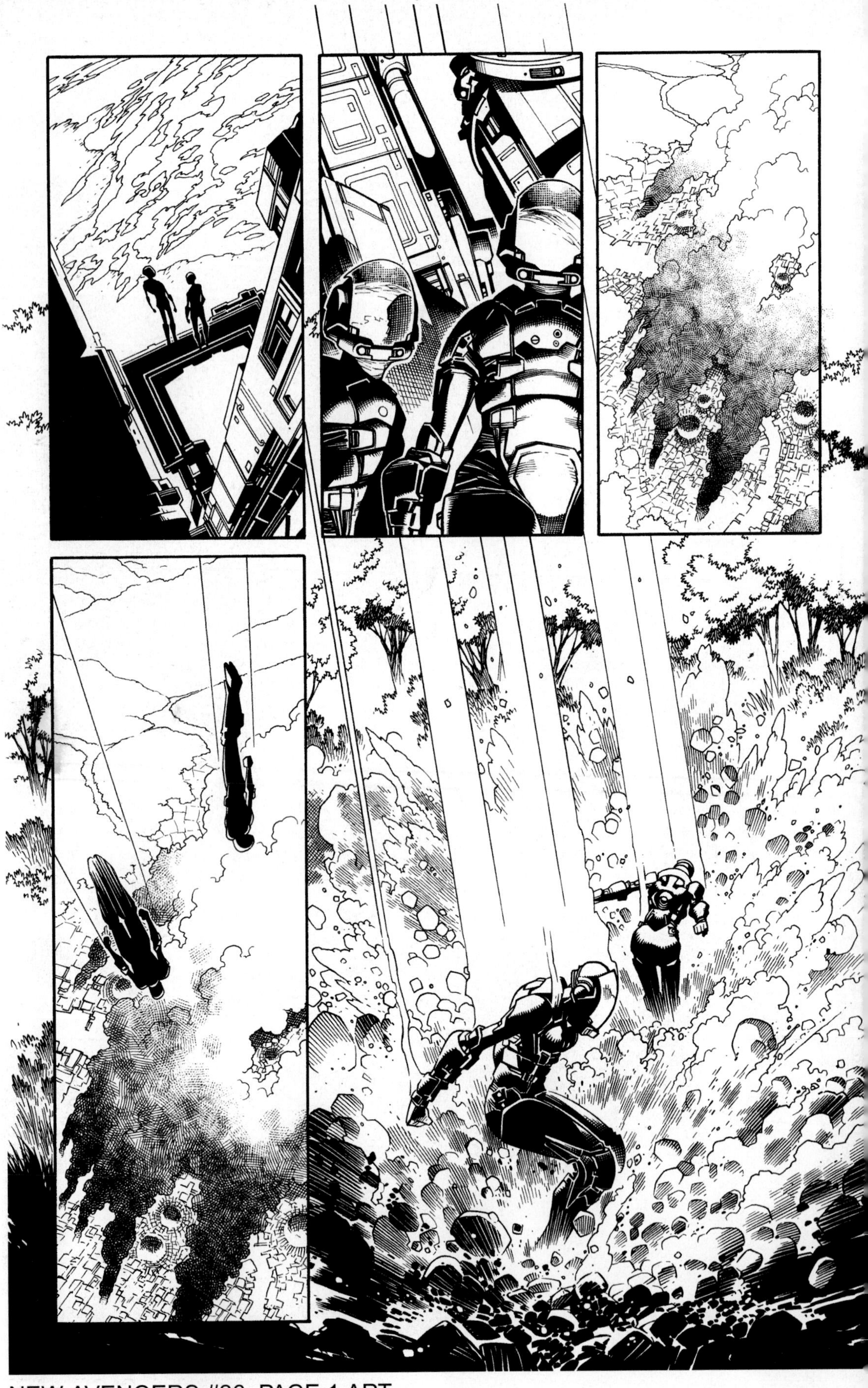

NEW AVENGERS #26, PAGE 1 ART
BY KEV WALKER

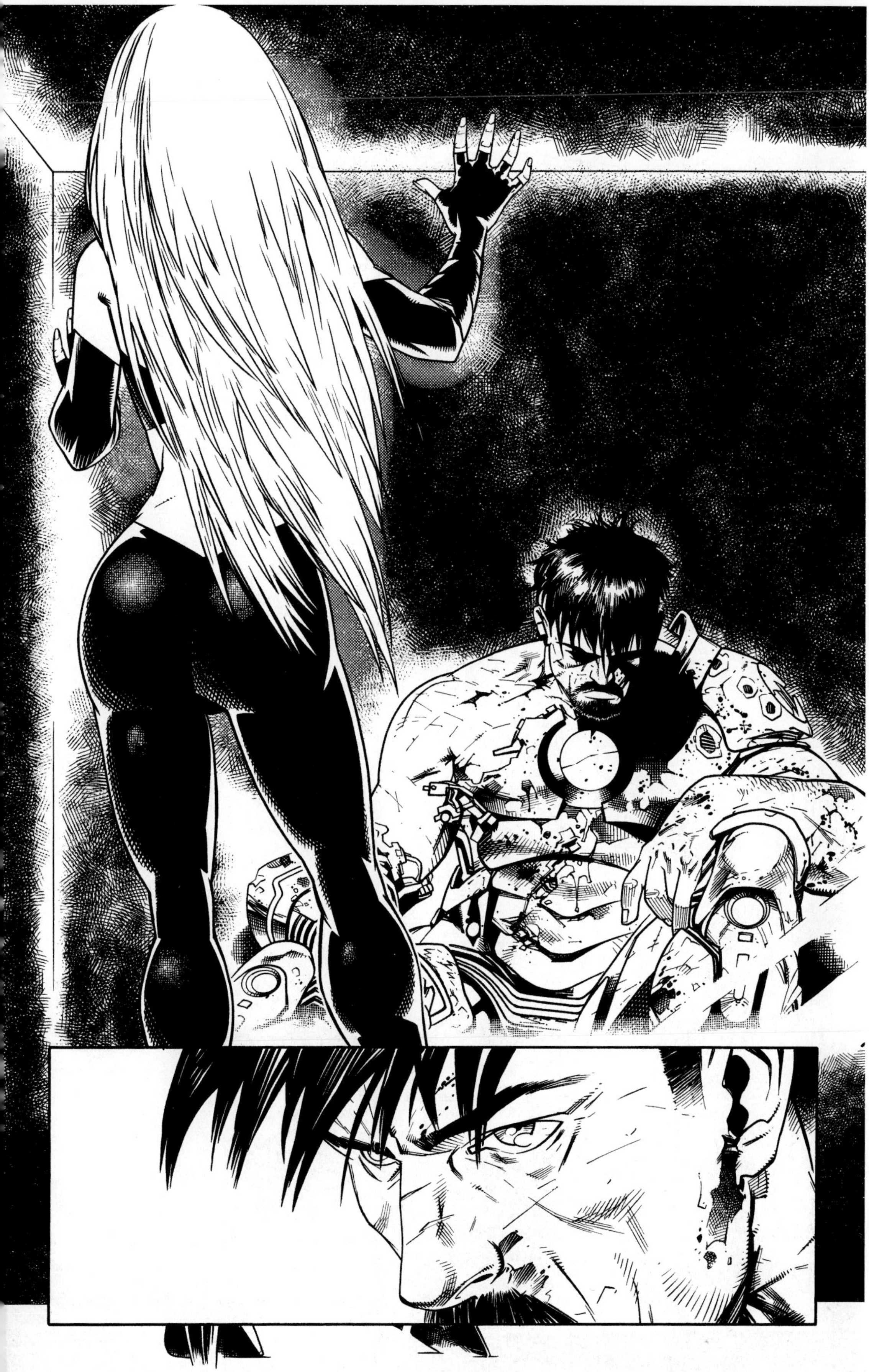

NEW AVENGERS #26, PAGE 3 ART
BY KEV WALKER

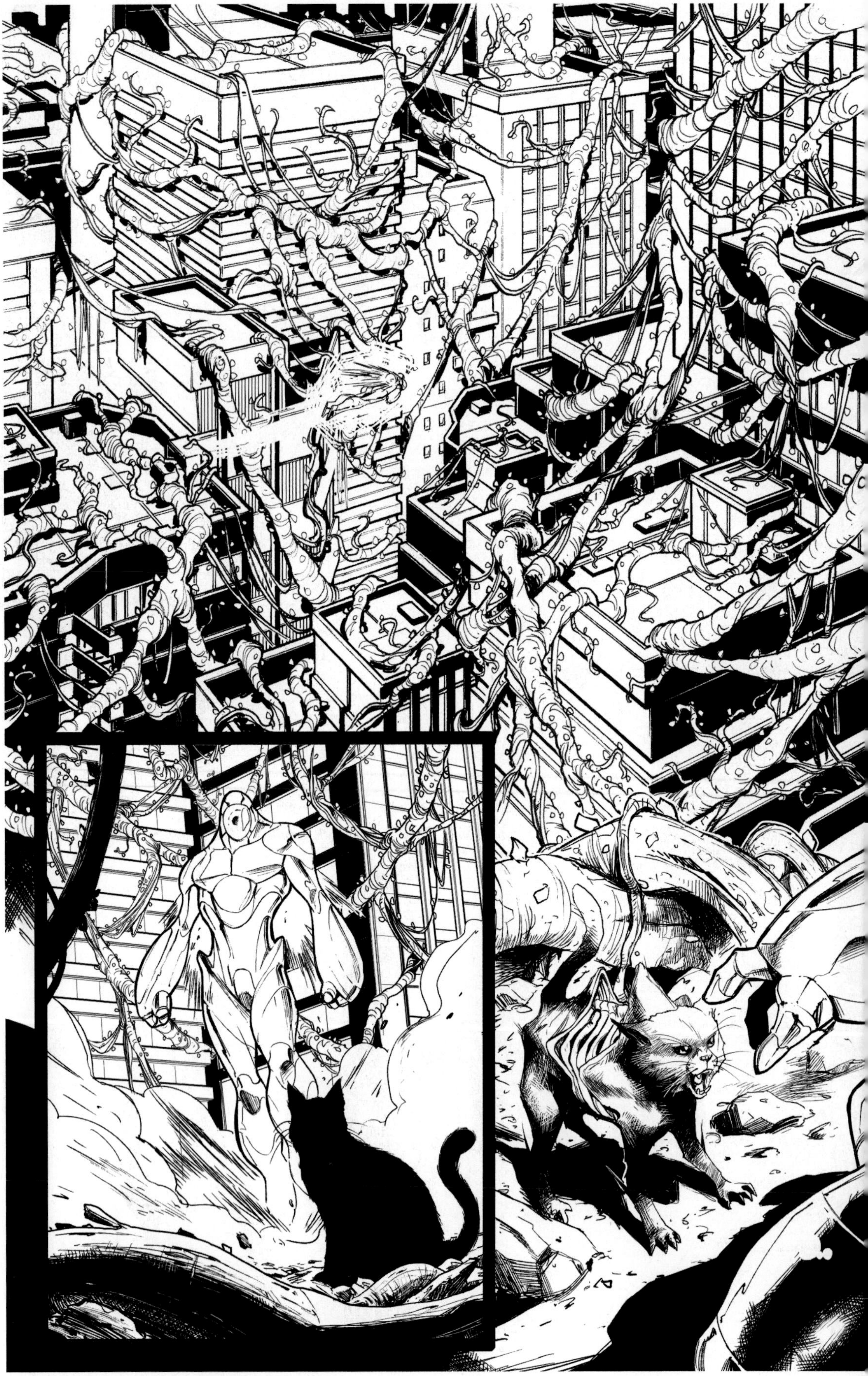

AVENGERS #38, PAGE 1 ART
BY STEFANO CASELLI

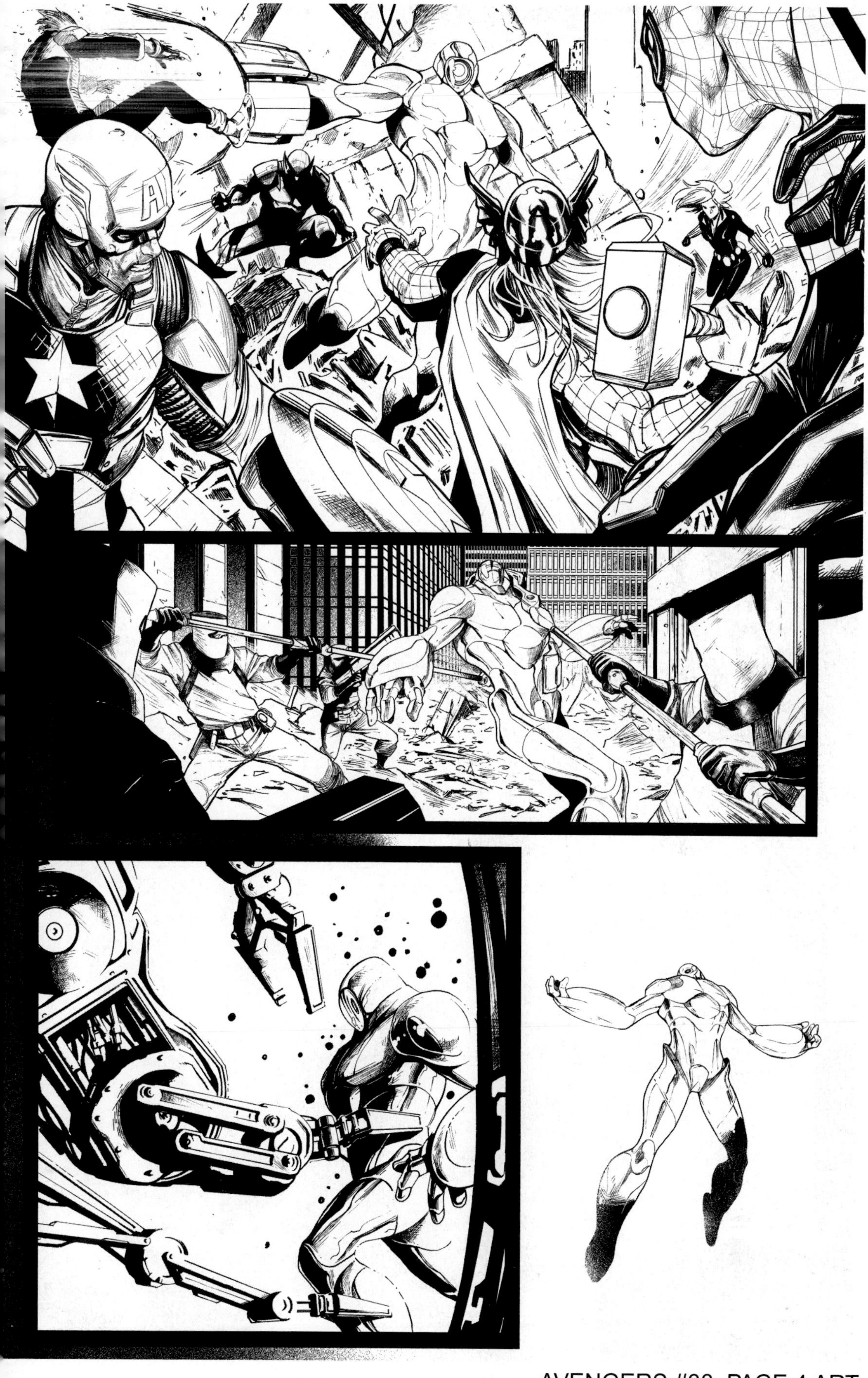

AVENGERS #38, PAGE 4 ART
BY STEFANO CASELLI

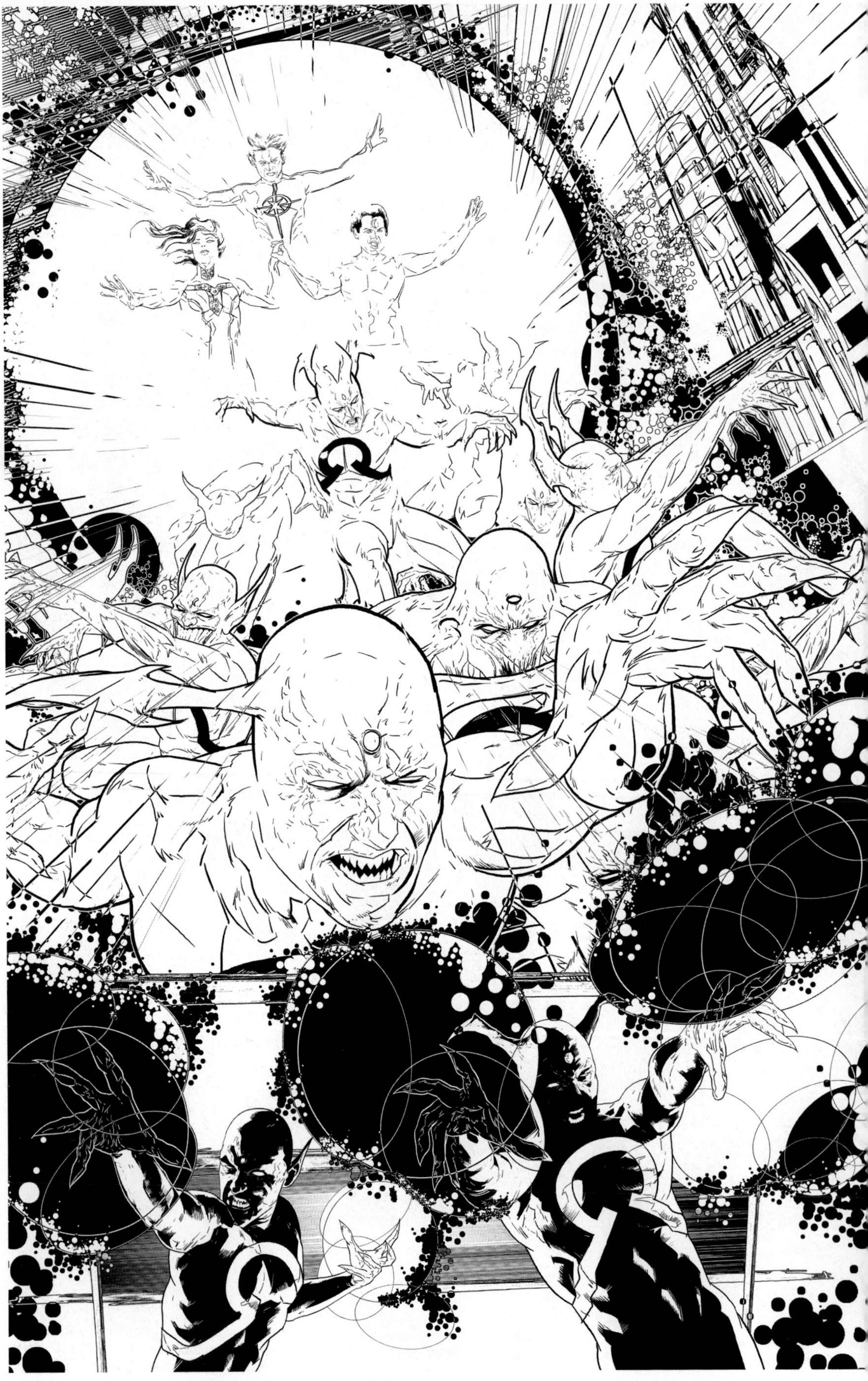

NEW AVENGERS #27, PAGE 2 ART
BY SZYMON KUDRANSKI

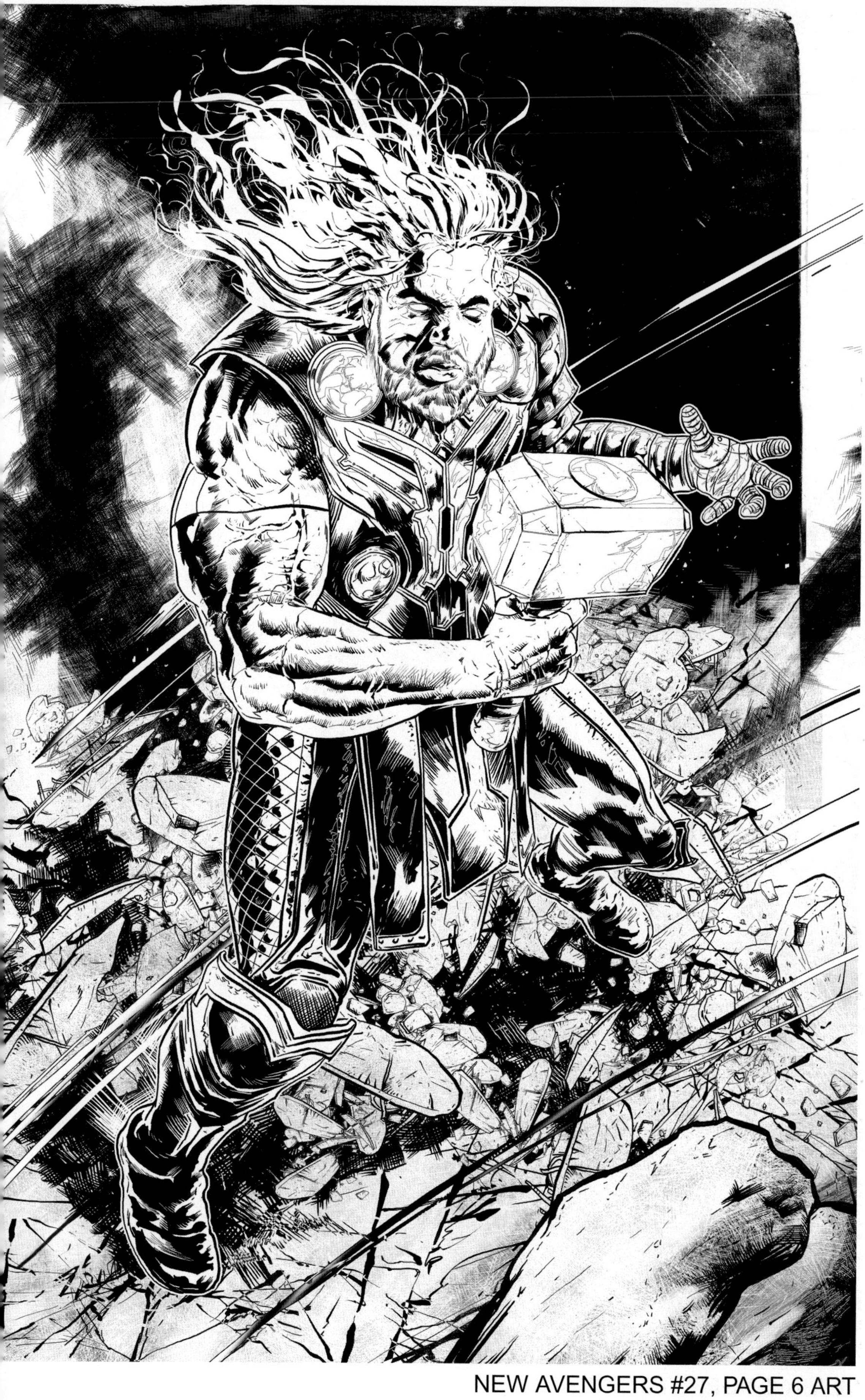

NEW AVENGERS #27, PAGE 6 ART
BY SZYMON KUDRANSKI

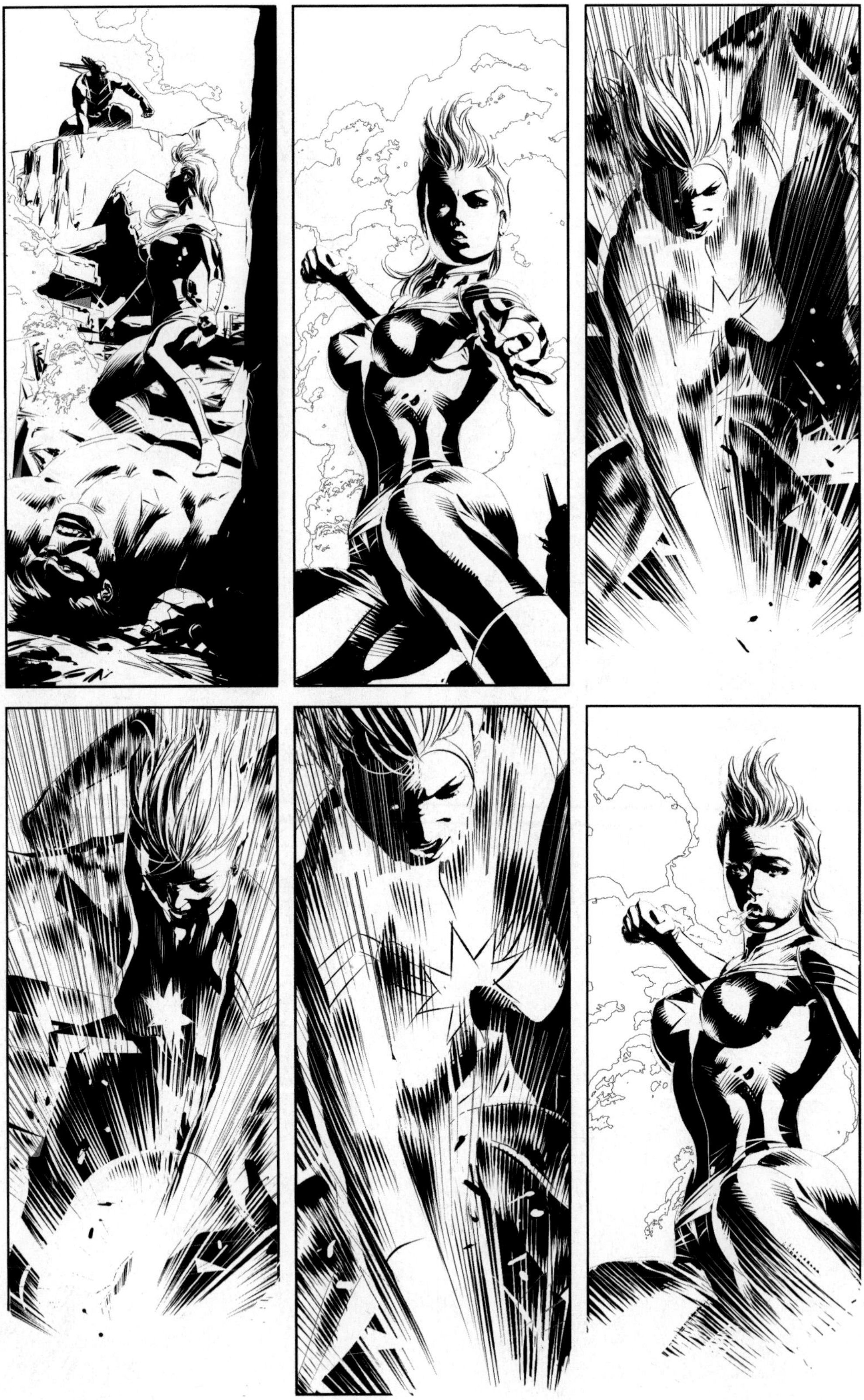

AVENGERS #39, PAGE 15 ART
BY MIKE DEODATO

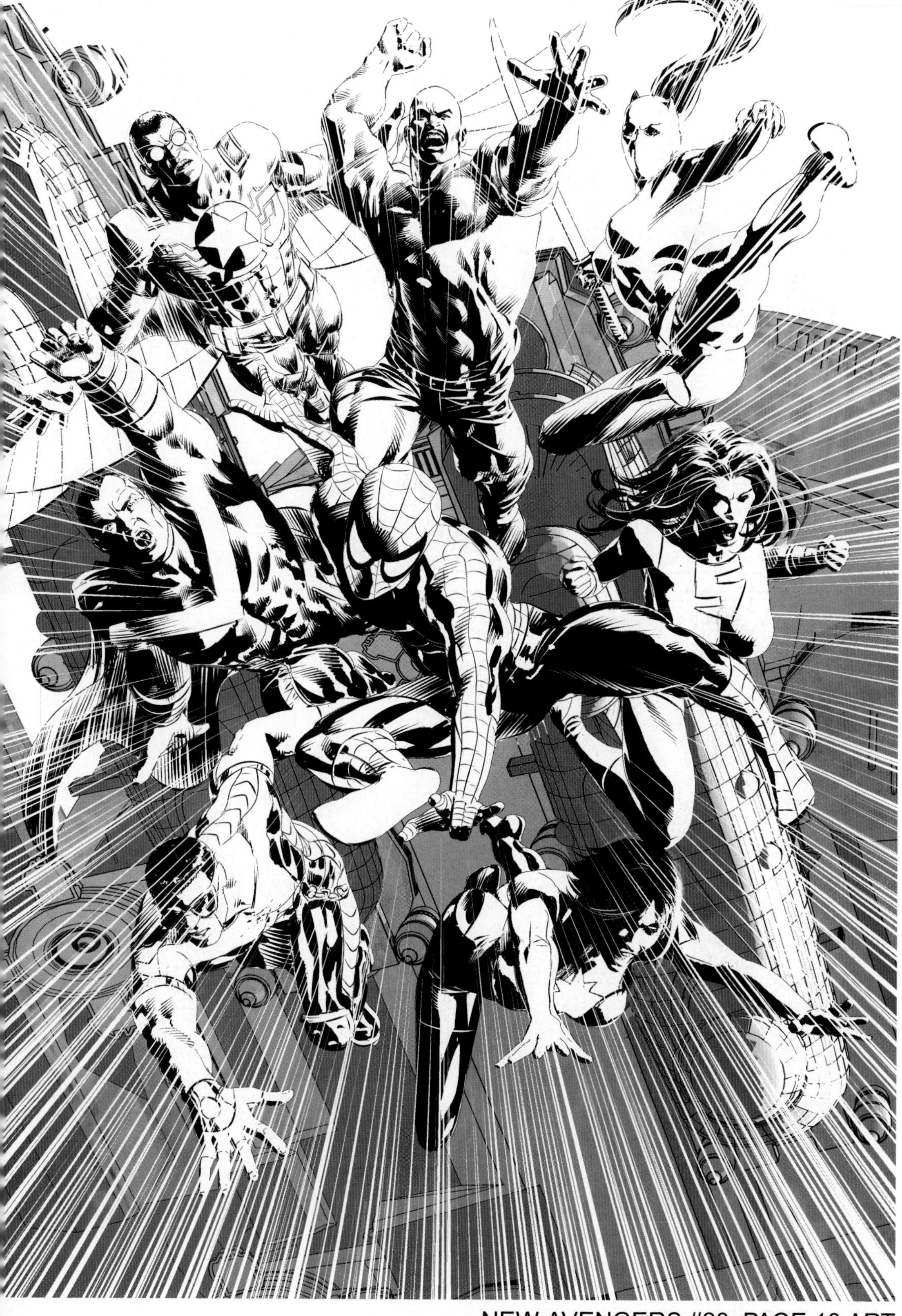

NEW AVENGERS #28, PAGE 13 ART
BY MIKE DEODATO

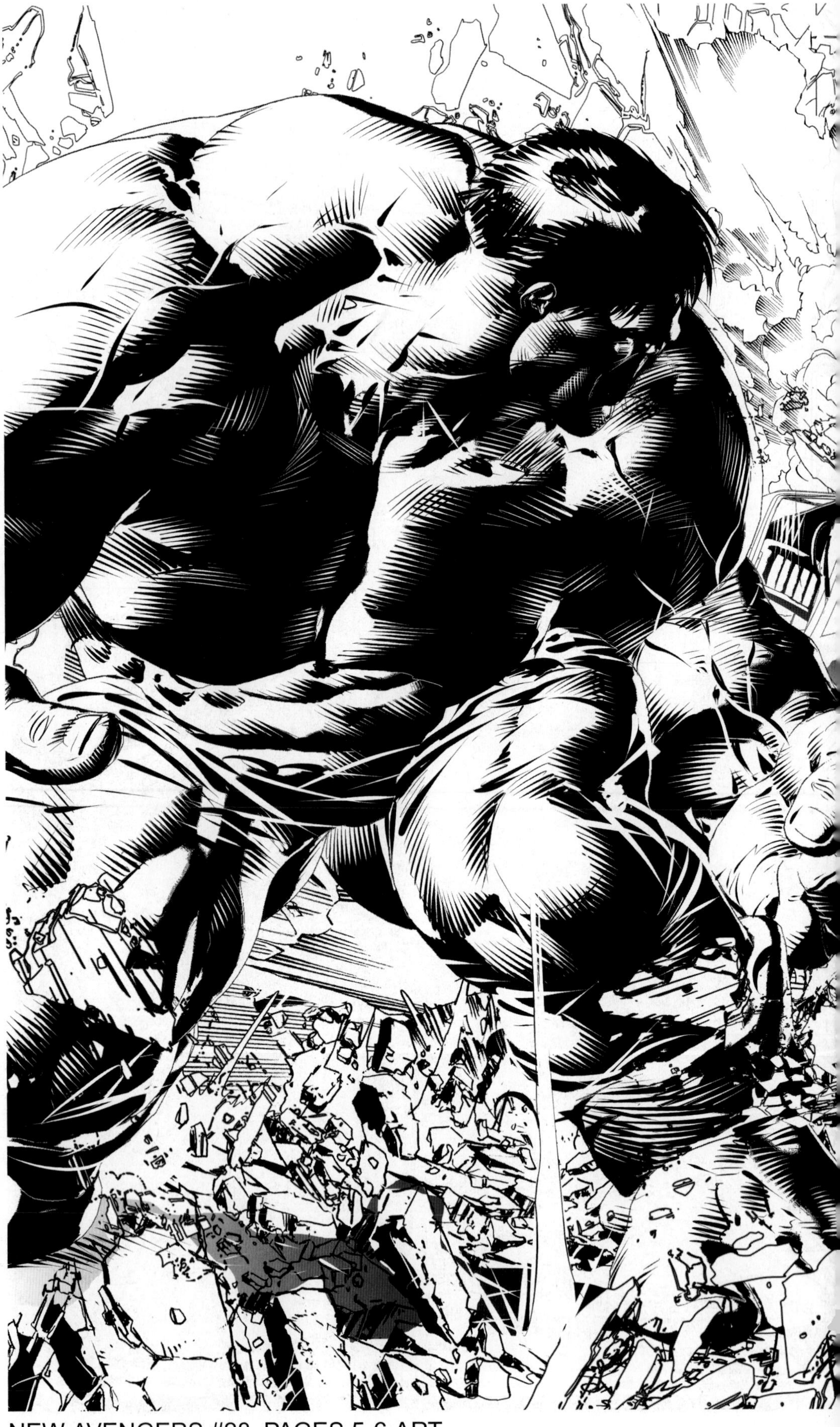

NEW AVENGERS #28, PAGES 5-6 ART
BY MIKE DEODATO

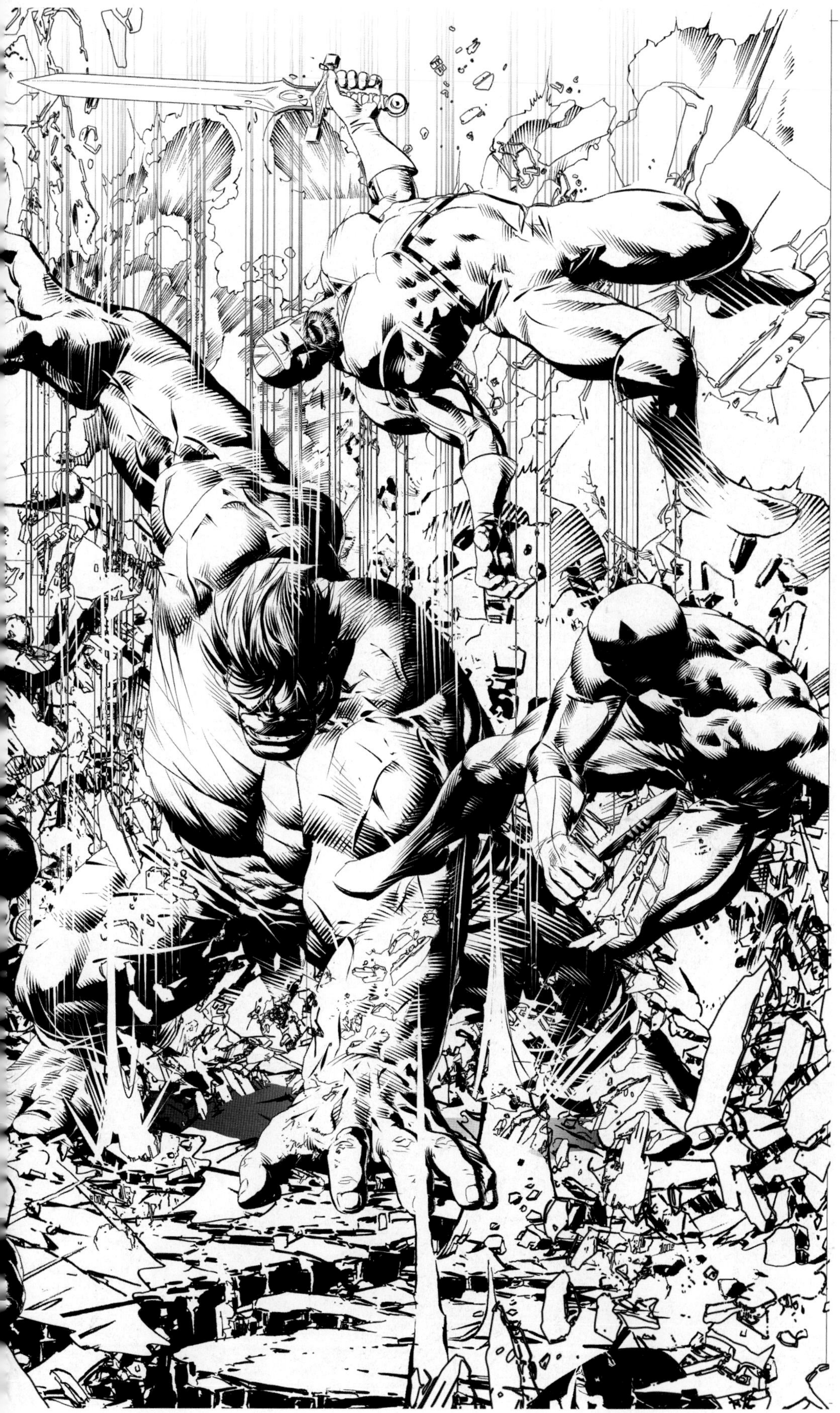

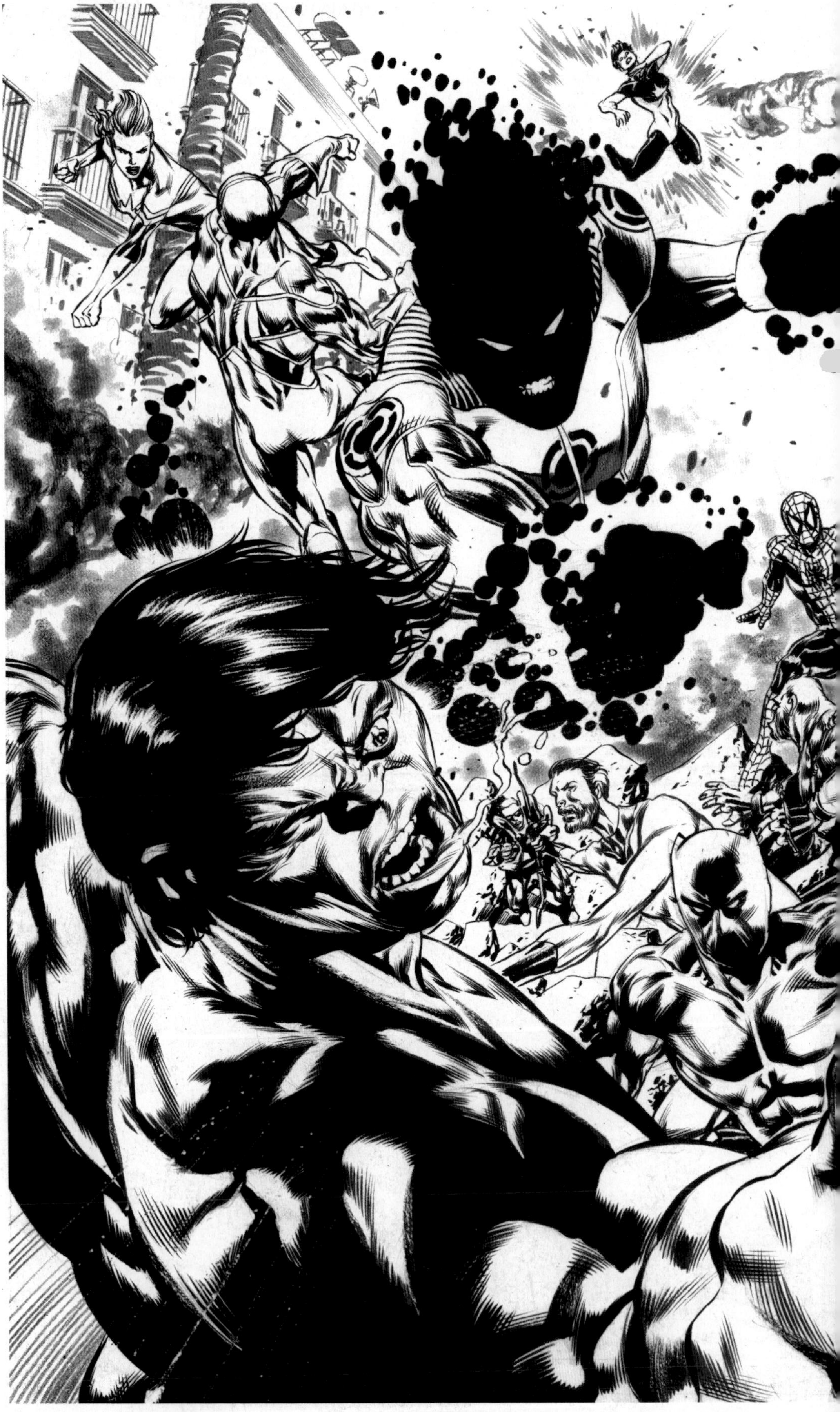

NEW AVENGERS #28, PAGES 14-15 ART
BY MIKE PERKINS

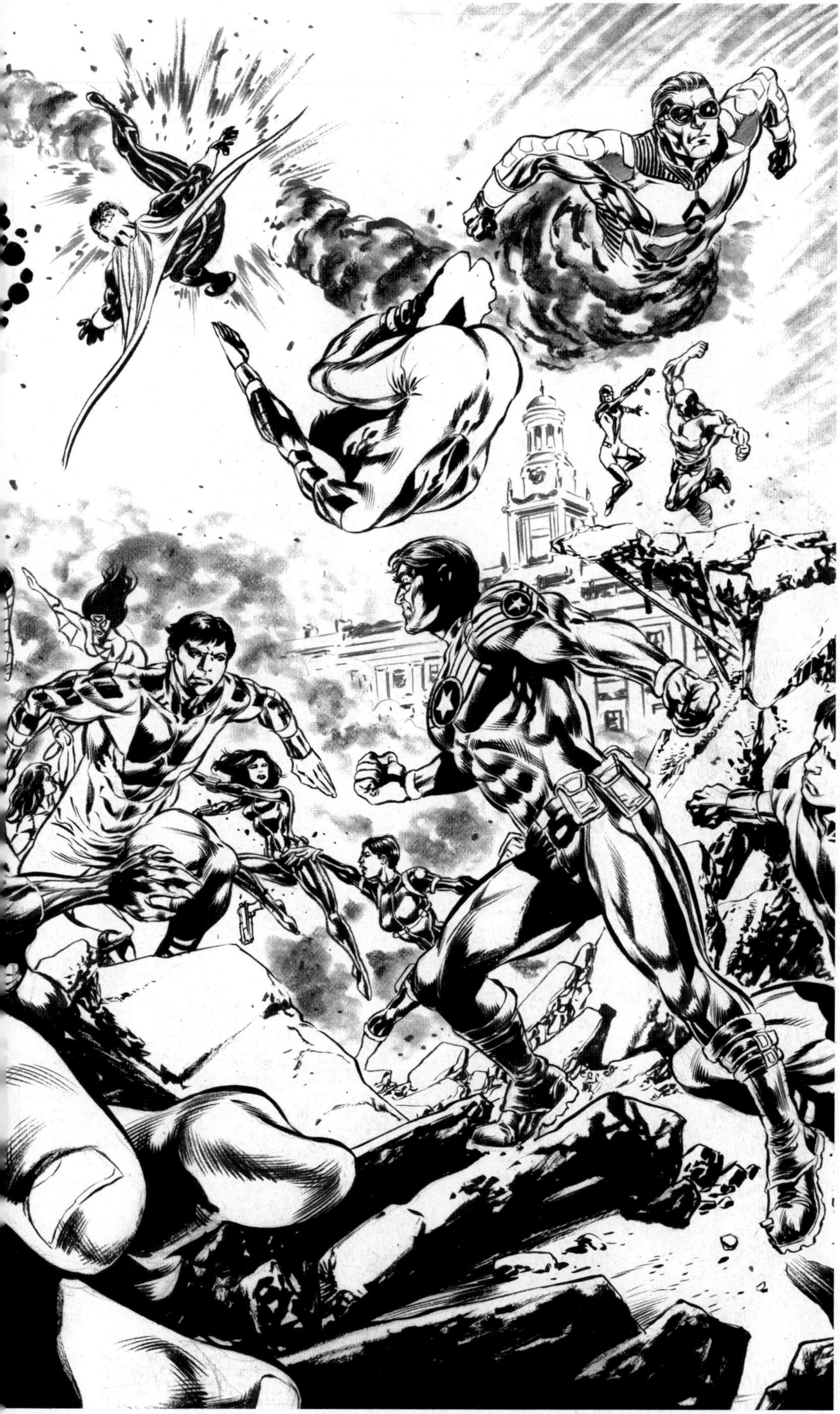

MARVEL AR AUGMENTED REALITY

MARVEL AUGMENTED REALITY (AR) ENHANCES AND CHANGES THE WAY YOU EXPERIENCE COMICS!

TO ACCESS THE FREE MARVEL AR CONTENT IN THIS BOOK*:

1. **Locate the AR logo within the comic.**
2. **Go to Marvel.com/AR in your web browser.**
3. **Search by series title to find the corresponding AR.**
4. **Enjoy Marvel AR!**

*All AR content that appears in this book has been archived and will be available only at Marvel.com/AR – no longer in the Marvel AR App. Content subject to change and availability.

AVENGERS

AR INDEX

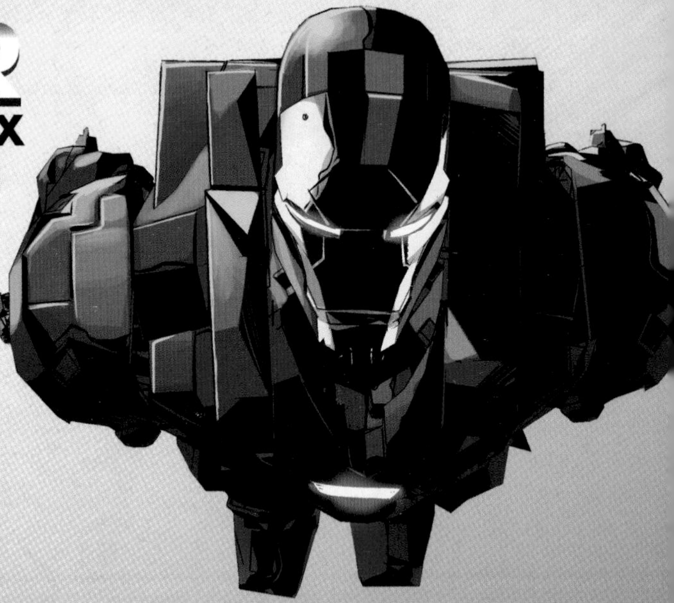